# Modeling Ethnomusicology

# Modeling Ethnomusicology

**TIMOTHY RICE**

OXFORD
UNIVERSITY PRESS

OXFORD
UNIVERSITY PRESS

Oxford University Press is a department of the University of Oxford. It furthers
the University's objective of excellence in research, scholarship, and education
by publishing worldwide. Oxford is a registered trade mark of Oxford University
Press in the UK and certain other countries.

Published in the United States of America by Oxford University Press
198 Madison Avenue, New York, NY 10016, United States of America.

Library of Congress Cataloging-in-Publication Data
Names: Rice, Timothy, 1945–
Title: Modeling ethnomusicology / Timothy Rice.
Description: New York, NY : Oxford University Press, [2016] |
    Includes bibliographical references and index.
Identifiers: LCCN 2016033655 (print) | LCCN 2016034734 (ebook) |
    ISBN 9780190616885 (hardcover : alk. paper) | ISBN 9780190616892 (pbk. : alk. paper) |
    ISBN 9780190616908 (updf) | ISBN 9780190616915 (epub)
Subjects: LCSH: Ethnomusicology.
Classification: LCC ML3798 .R55 2016 (print) | LCC ML3798 (ebook) |
    DDC 780.89—dc23
LC record available at https://lccn.loc.gov/2016033655

9 8 7 6 5 4 3 2 1

Paperback printed by Webcom Inc., Canada
Hardback printed by Bridgeport National Bindery, Inc., United States of America

# CONTENTS

## ACKNOWLEDGMENTS

Chapter 1 was originally published as "Toward the Remodeling of Ethno-musicology," *Ethnomusicology* 31(3): 469-488 (1987). Chapter 2, "Toward a Mediation of Field Methods and Field Experience in Ethnomusicology," first appeared as a chapter in *Shadows in the Field: New Perspectives for Field-work in Ethnomusicology*, edited by Gregory F. Barz and Timothy J. Cooley (Oxford University Press, 1996) and is reprinted here by permission of Oxford University Press. Chapter 3 was published as "Reflections on Music and Meaning: Metaphor, Signification, and Control in the Bulgarian Case," *British Journal of Ethnomusicology* 10 (1): 19–38 (2001). Chapter 4 appeared as "Time, Place, and Metaphor in Musical Experience and Ethnography," *Ethnomusicology* 47(2): 151–179 (2003). Chapter 5 began as "Reflections on Music and Identity in *Ethnomusicology*," *Muzikologija* (Musicology, Belgrade) 7: 17–38 (2007). Chapter 6 was published as "Ethnomusicological Theory," *Yearbook for Traditional Music* 42: 100–134 (2010). Chapter 7, "The Individual in Musical Ethnography," *Ethnomusicology* 56(2): 299–327 (2012), was coau-thored with Jesse D. Ruskin. Chapter 8 was published as "Ethnomusicology in Times of Trouble," *Yearbook for Traditional Music* 46: 191–209 (2014).

For permission to reprint the articles and chapters in this book, I am grateful to the Society for Ethnomusicology, publisher of *Ethnomusicology*; the British Forum for Ethnomusicology, publisher of the *British Journal of Ethnomusicology* (today, *Ethnomusicology Forum*); the International Council for Traditional Music, publisher of the *Yearbook for Traditional Music*; the Institute for Music of the Serbian Academy of Sciences, publisher of *Muzikologija*; and Oxford University Press.

I also would like to thank the staff at Oxford University Press: editor Suzanne Ryan for her enthusiastic support of this project and Julia Turner, Eden Piacitelli, Jamie Kim, and Danielle Michaely for the care they took shepherding the book through the production process.

Modeling Ethnomusicology

# Introduction

*Ethnomusicological Theorizing*

On the thirtieth anniversary of the publication in 1987 of "Toward the Remodeling of Ethnomusicology," I am pleased to present this story of my long encounter with ethnomusicology through the writings of others and my own research in the area of Bulgarian traditional music. At another level, this continues my long interest in the nature of ethnomusicology as a discipline among other disciplines and my advocacy for a stronger sense of the communal, social nature of our work revealed through the processes of ethnomusicological theorizing.[1] Each essay in this collection, which follows the course of my career and thinking on the larger subject, represents a particular type of theorizing, illustrated by a specific thematic focus, shown in Figure 0.1.

Why did I write these essays? I entered the field as a graduate student at the University of Washington in 1968 already committed to the study of Bulgarian traditional music. As a named field of study, ethnomusicology was a youthful teenager, and the literature we read suggested that, like a human teenager, it was, as we said in those days, "trying to find itself." I found the arguments between those trained in musicology and those trained in anthropology and the articles defining the field and its methods more intellectually engaging than many of the descriptive articles about particular music cultures. I loved the clangorous engagement with self-reflexive questions like who are we?, what are we doing?, how and why are we doing it?, and what should we be doing differently?, questions that still engage us today. I realize, in retrospect, that my interest in these questions was consonant with my interests in the study of history, my college major. I always found historiography, the study of the cultural, social, political, and personal conditions that produced histories, more

1. For another recent personal retrospective in the form of collected essays, see Koskoff 2014.

| Year | Title | Theorizing Type | Thematic Focus |
|------|-------|-----------------|----------------|
| 1987 | "Toward the Remodeling of Ethnomusicology" | Structuring the data | Ethnomusicology |
| 1996 | "Toward a Mediation of Field Methods and Field Experience in Ethnomusicology" | Explaining the data | Field research |
| 2001 | "Reflections on Music and Meaning: Metaphor, Signification, and Control in the Bulgarian Case" | Explaining the data | Musical meaning |
| 2003 | "Time, Place, and Metaphor in Musical Experience and Ethnography" | Structuring the data | Musical experience |
| 2007 | "Reflections on Music and Identity in *Ethnomusicology*" | Organizing the data | Identity and music |
| 2010 | "Ethnomusicological Theory" | Structuring the data | Ethnomusicology |
| 2012 | "The Individual in Musical Ethnography" | Organizing the data | Individual in music cultures |
| 2014 | "Ethnomusicology in Times of Trouble" | Organizing the data | Ethnomusicology |

**Figure 0.1** Rice essays that model ethnomusicology.

fascinating than the stuff of history itself. (That is no longer so true for me, as it happens.) These essays flowed in no small part from my early experiences as a university student.

Fast-forward through my years of dissertation research and writing on Bulgarian traditional music to 1980, when I received a call from Society for Ethnomusicology (SEM) president Gerard Béhague offering me the editorship of the society's journal, *Ethnomusicology*. I was pleased, of course, but also amazed. I had only received my PhD three years earlier, in 1977, and was just publishing my first two refereed journal articles that very year (Rice 1980a, 1980b). After accepting this honor, I wrote to family and friends that I was the only person on the editorial board I had never heard of. My appointment confirmed the famous advice that 80% of life is showing up. I had been attending SEM annual meetings for a decade at that point, and perhaps it seemed to others in those years, when the field was so young, that I was already an old hand. This kind of opportunity for a young scholar is almost impossible to imagine today.

From my perch as editor of *Ethnomusicology* from 1981 to 1984, I had a great view of our maturing, thirty-year-old field. Key to those observations was the refereeing process. I sent each submitted article to two referees, people whose research would allow them to provide an authoritative opinion on whether the submission represented original research and an important contribution to knowledge in our field. Referees' comments allowed me to see the sausage being made, as it were. They were advising the authors and me about what constituted good work in our field. Most telling were reports that suggested that the submission not be published because the work was "not ethnomusicology." At a time when I and many other ethnomusicologists were unclear about how to define what ethnomusicology was, some apparently did not find it difficult to say what it wasn't.

In those days the two qualities that placed a submission beyond the pale of ethnomusicology were ones that did not involve fieldwork and those that depended on value judgments about the relative quality, in aesthetic terms, of genres of music, especially submissions that valorized European or European-derived classical music in comparison to other types of music. I suppose that guardians of the frontiers of our disciplines, if there are any left, would still be on the lookout for these transgressions, and perhaps new ones. The field today clearly admits historical studies not dependent on fieldwork (see, e.g., Lam 1998), and a paper by Michael Tenzer (2015) evinces an interest in "objective aesthetics," although informed by an ethnomusicological sensibility far from the puerile, tendentious judgments of musicological aesthetics, which Canadian philosopher Francis E. Sparshott dismissed devastatingly in his article on aesthetics in the 1980 edition of *The New Grove Dictionary of Music and Musicians*.[2]

While most ethnomusicologists adopt a stance that advocates for the human value of all music and that brackets critical judgments, especially invidious comparisons of classical versus popular and disco versus rock favored by fans, a critical strain beyond such comparisons has underlain ethnomusicological writing since its beginnings. The first was Jaap Kunst's definition of the field, which excluded popular and European classical music from its purview (Kunst 1959).[3] Later John Blacking (1973) argued that judgments about the human, as

2. In the current Grove Music Online, Sparshott's article on the aesthetics of music and its critique of musicological aesthetics no longer appears in its original form. Rather, Lydia Goehr summarizes some of his ideas about aesthetics in an article on "Philosophy of Music I: Introduction" and joins him as coauthor of a section called "Philosophy of Music: Historical Survey, Antiquity-1750."

3. A few years after Kunst's original definition in 1950, Willard Rhodes (1956a: 460, 462) proposed a more capacious definition of ethnomusicology. Citing Charles Seeger, he wrote, "If the term ethnomusicology were to be interpreted in its broadest sense it would include as its domain the total music of man, without limitations of time or space. . . . Let us not become narrow in the pursuit of our special field." And in another article in the same year he specifically included popular music, writing, "To these fields of study ['Oriental art music and the folk music of the world'] we inherit from the past [of comparative musicology] should be added

opposed to the aesthetic, value of music may be a part of the ethnomusicologist's responsibility. Since then, Charles Keil, Jeff Todd Titon, Thomas Turino,
and others have suggested on occasion that they find participatory modes of
musicking of more human value than some music played by expert musicians
for a passive listening audience. So the strain of judgment has always been present in ethnomusicology even if attenuated by our professional stance, which
requires us to overcome aesthetic biases in the study of all the world's music.[4]

Choreographing the discussions between writers and referees over what
constituted acceptable research in ethnomusicology forced me to think more
intently than I otherwise might have about the nature of the field.[5] In those
days, the most influential model of the field was known as the Merriam model,
published two decades earlier in the book *The Anthropology of Music*. In it,
Alan Merriam (1964: 32), an anthropologist and one of the four founders of the
Society for Ethnomusicology, proposed what he called a "simple" model that
had three "analytical levels": "conceptualization about music, behavior in relation to music, and the music sound itself."

Merriam's model had at least three advantages, I thought. First, with only
three parts, it was easy to remember. In those days if people from outside the
field asked us what we did, some of us, after giving them Merriam's even shorter
answer, "the study of music in culture," could easily reel off Merriam's three levels. Second, it had the quality of completeness. As such, it was more than a list of
analytical levels; here, I am defining a list as incomplete or provisional—other
items can be added to it or it can be reconstituted in various ways. Merriam's
model is a typology, which I define as a complete list or structural representation of the qualities or features of a domain, in this case the domain of research
in ethnomusicology. Third, Merriam's model was also what the anthropologist Clifford Geertz called a "model for" reality, in Merriam's case a model

---

two categories which seem rightfully to belong within the framework of our discipline, popular
music and dance" (Rhodes 1956b: 3). Still, he could not refrain from a judgmental tone, continuing with, "In more complex civilizations this category would include jazz as well as most
of the commercial music that clogs our airwaves" (p. 4). I am grateful to Timothy Cooley for
directing me to this latter source.

4. See Berger (2009) for a detailed treatment of the notion of stance.

5. For this Introduction I choreographed another kind exchange about the field of ethnomusicology by inviting comments on an earlier draft of this Introduction from former students
(Michael Bakan, Dave Wilson, and Louise Wrazen); colleagues at my home institution, UCLA
(Daniel Neuman, Helen Rees, Roger Savage, Anthony Seeger, and Timothy Taylor); and scholars whose work I cite (Gregory Barz, Harris Berger, Timothy Cooley, Steven Feld, Ellen Koskoff,
Kay Kaufman Shelemay, Gabriel Solis, Martin Stokes, and J. Lawrence Witzleben). I am grateful to each of them for their perspicacious comments and suggestions and for directing me to
sources that illustrate some of my arguments.

for the way a "music culture" works. Geertz (1973) distinguished two kinds of models: models of reality and models for reality. Models "give meaning, that is, objective conceptual form, to social and psychological reality both by shaping themselves to it [models of] and by shaping it to themselves [models for]" (Geertz 1973: 93). This distinction can be applied to Merriam's model. Merriam's is a model of music culture that tells us what it consists of and gives its form a structure. Merriam's model also shaped a musical culture to it by suggesting that in a music culture, native concepts about music would drive social behaviors with respect to music, which would in turn affect the music sound itself. The model then predicted that if something new emerged in the musical sound, then concepts about music would change, creating a feedback loop that would explain musical change, a phenomenon Merriam and many ethnomusicologists were interested in at that time.

What interests me to this day about simple models like Merriam's is their heuristic function. By heuristic function I mean the ability of a model to help researchers think about and discover patterns in their data and explanations for the particular things they are studying. Had I employed Merriam's model heuristically for my own research on Bulgarian music, it would have suggested to me questions I might otherwise not have asked, and I might have tried, for example, to find an instance where a change in musical concepts changed musical behaviors. As it turns out, I am not sure whether anyone took the heuristic potential of Merriam's model seriously, but, if true, that says more about the field than about the value of his model. Many similar theoretical points have been made since 1964, but I have a feeling none could be understood as either enriching Merriam's model or requiring its remodeling.

In retrospect, I realize that I might have invoked it in one of the first articles I published in a scholarly journal (Rice 1980b). For my dissertation on Bulgarian polyphonic singing (Rice 1977), I was influenced by a theory about culture called cognitive anthropology, which claimed that culture was in the mind and that a researcher could access culture through carefully constructed interview protocols and the creation of taxonomies, typologies, and other conceptual structures that emerged from those conversations. During the course of my research I learned that Bulgarian villagers did not seem to have a cover term for the linguistic domain we label music in English. Rather, this unnamed domain had five subdomains in Bulgarian: (1) instrumental music (a "plaything") and its playing, (2) songs and singing, (3) laments and lamenting, (4) drums and drumming, and (5) dances and dancing. Had I used Merriam's model as a heuristic device, I might more quickly have realized the behavioral correlates that accompanied these conceptual distinctions: men were almost exclusively the instrumentalists, women the most important singers, minority Roma the drummers, and so on. Thinking with the model might have led me to ask about the relationship between concept and behavior and whether or not it could be plausibly argued that there was a causal relationship between concept and behavior in the Bulgarian case. I might also have broadened the theoretical claim for the mechanisms of change by demonstrating that each of the analytical levels was glued to its counterparts in culture such that changes in cultural concepts might cause changes in musical concepts, a common notion in ethnomusicology today. In one study (Rice 2003), I did just that, reporting on how new, modern concepts of behaviors appropriate to women led to a woman taking on the social behavior of a bagpiper, a role traditionally limited to men. But that explanation flowed less from the Merriam model than from fieldwork observations.

After my term as editor of *Ethnomusicology* ended, I decided to remodel ethnomusicology not because I was unhappy with the Merriam model's heuristic potential (I actually hadn't thought about that at the time) or because I didn't think it was satisfactory as a "model for" the way music cultures worked. Rather, I came to realize, based on my editorial experience, that in the early 1980s it didn't work very well as a Geertzian "model of" ethnomusicology. In those days, while twenty years had passed since Merriam had proposed his model, not everyone in the field had followed him down that path. Although studies along the lines he suggested were growing in number, an awful lot of work in the early 1980s had other foci. It was at that point that I encountered Clifford Geertz's (1973: 363–364) epigrammatic formulation about culture, that it was "historically constructed, socially maintained, and individually applied." I immediately recognized this simple three-part formula as a better "model of" ethnomusicological writing at that time than Merriam's model and as a potential "model for" the "formative processes" at work in music cultures. My model states that "music is historically constructed, socially maintained, and individually created and experienced."[6]

Chapter 1, "Toward the Remodeling of Ethnomusicology," was first presented as a paper at the 1986 SEM meeting and published in 1987 with responses from three ethnomusicologists, each representing one of the dimensions of the model, plus a fourth by a historical musicologist (Shelemay 1987 on historical construction; Koskoff 1987 on individual creativity and

---

6. Recently I learned that sociologist C. Wright Mills (1959) had created a similar model for "the sociological imagination," which involved history, biography, and social structure. That model, through biography, allowed him and those whom he studied to connect "personal troubles of milieu" to "the public issues of social structure" (p. 2), a move similar to my sense that individual experience and creativity are a formative process in music making and thus central to ethnomusicological research: "No study that does not come back to the problems of biography, of history and of their intersections within society has completed its intellectual journey" (p. 6).

experience; Seeger 1987 on social maintenance; and Crawford 1987, the music historian). Predictably, historians Kay Shelemay and Richard Crawford generally approved of the model, mainly because it is an accepting "model of" the field that includes historical studies within ethnomusicology and that connects us to our sister discipline, historical ethnomusicology. In other words, they could see themselves in it. They also understood its heuristic nature: Shelemay (1987: 489) called it "a useful guide for future inquiry," and Crawford (1987: 511) referred to it as a conceptual "Swiss Army knife." Ellen Koskoff and Anthony Seeger argued that Merriam's thinking about the field was more complex than suggested by what he called his simple model. This is, of course, true: ethnomusicology is endlessly complex and changing as rapidly as the musical world it purports to study. But a simple model doesn't mean that the thinking or the phenomena it represents are simple. Simple models are "what if" statements. What if we bracketed some of the complexity? Would simple patterns emerge? In physics, for example, what if we pretended that friction doesn't exist? Could we find a simple formula to explain the forces at work when a ball rolls down an inclined plane? Yes, as it turns out. Merriam's and my models ask, "what if" we thought about ethnomusicological research not in its full complexity but in a simple, three-dimensional way? Could we see patterns and forces at work that we might not have otherwise? The answer for both models is yes, I would argue.

Not all models have to be simple, of course, and A. Seeger, in his response, and Bell Yung, in the audience for my presentation in 1986, preferred the complexity of Charles Seeger's (1977) unitary field theory of ethnomusicology to Merriam's and my "simple" models (see Yung and Rees 1999 on the legacy of Charles Seeger). The C. Seeger model, in a way a remodeling of Guido Adler's 1885 taxonomy outlining the *Gesammtgebäude* (total structure) of *Musikwissenschaft* (Mugglestone and Adler 1981), goes in the opposite direction of simple models by trying to understand musicology in its full complexity rather than sifting through that complexity for simple patterns. C. Seeger's overview of musicology, a broader category than ethnomusicology traditionally understood, spreads across two pages with eight major divisions, each, in turn, with many subdivisions and further sub-subdivisions; it aspires to completeness or totality. He regards it as a "two-dimensional road map ... whose miraculous terrain the musicologist may drive at his pleasure" (p. 127):

Begin at the top and as you read down ... remember that you are tracing your own progress over the terrain. When you come to a fork, you must decide which path to follow first but not to stay on it so long that you forget to go back and follow the other fork; for it is the drawing of the two together that is essential to the reading of the table. (C. Seeger 1977: 125)

He is outlining how to use his "total structure" as a heuristic device to ask as many questions as possible about music, the same goal that I find so attractive about Merriam's and my simpler models.[7] I prefer the latter, however, because they make easier-to-remember claims about the nature of music than his model does: I can keep them in my head and repeat them from memory on demand, whereas, like a real road map or GPS app, I would have to keep his open beside me to remember its features and figure out where I was going. My preference in this regard is partly a matter of style (simplicity versus complexity) and partly a matter of substance (the goals of the project). Both clearly share an important heuristic, question-asking value as researchers approach their particular case studies.

But how well did my model account for the current literature in *Ethnomusicology*? Looking over articles in issues from 1978 to 1986, I classified them using this model (Figure 0.2). Publications at that time addressed these three formative processes in a pretty balanced way, although, to provide an inductive model of ethnomusicology at that time, I had to add three other categories: (4) musical analysis (Merriam's "the music sound itself"), (5) surveys of musical cultures, and (6) general theoretical reflections. As it turned out, my model provided a pretty good basis for a model of ethnomusicology in those days, though even at that, it only accounted for 73% of the articles in the issues I surveyed.

What would a similar survey of articles published in *Ethnomusicology* in the last ten years (2006 to 2015) reveal?[8] As Figure 0.3 shows, my model accounts for 81% of the articles, a little better than the 73% in Figure 0.2 for the period nearly thirty years earlier. The relative weight of the three parts of the model remains close to the same as well, with the percentages of articles on history and society growing slightly and those on individuals being lower than before. I continue to find it a useful model of research in ethnomusicology, and I used it as the basis for three chapters of my recently published "very short introduction" to ethnomusicology (Rice 2014).

Satisfied that this was a good model of ethnomusicology, I also recognized that its simplicity made it a useful heuristic model for thinking about processes in music cultures. Each of the three elements of the model is connected to the other two elements in a bidirectional fashion, as in Figure 0.4 reproduced here

---

7. Anthony Seeger (1992: 94) elaborated on his view of the utility of his grandfather's model, pointing out, among other things, that its totality allows us to see where on the road map we have been and where we have not been and to trace the history of the way "the questions musicologists have asked about music have waxed and waned." Later, after worrying about "some missing continents yet to be discovered," he remodeled one part of the C. Seeger road map: V. The Audiocommunicatory Event (A. Seeger 2006: 229, 231).

8. Jesse Ruskin, a recent PhD graduate from UCLA, compiled the data for me in Figure 0.3.

| 13% | General theory and method |
|---|---|
| 4% | Surveys |
| 10% | Music analysis |
| 22% | History/change |
| 34% | Social processes |
| 17% | Individual processes |
| 100% | TOTAL |

**Figure 0.2** A classification and count of articles in *Ethnomusicology* from 1978 to 1986 (Rice 1987: 476).

| 11% | General theory and method |
|---|---|
| 2% | Surveys |
| 6% | Music analysis |
| 29% | History/change |
| 44% | Social processes |
| 8% | Individual processes |
| 100% | TOTAL |

**Figure 0.3** A classification and count of articles in *Ethnomusicology* from 2006 to 2015.

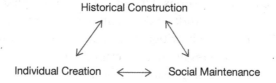

Historical Construction

Individual Creation ⟷ Social Maintenance

**Figure 0.4** A model for reciprocal relations between formative processes in music.

from the original article. I suppose one measure of the success of this or any model for research might be how often it is credited with being used. Though I have no way of reliably measuring that, I regularly hear from students around the world who have applied it to their case studies. On the other hand, I don't find much evidence that ethnomusicologists regularly engage with heuristic models, whether by Merriam, C. Seeger, or me, as an aid in their research. I am left to wonder whether ethnomusicology would be more fun if there were more play with these kinds of models. I still think so all these years after this article was originally published.

My next foray into thinking about larger issues in the field of ethnomusicology, presented here as Chapter 2, "Toward a Mediation of Field Methods and Field Experience in Ethnomusicology," and published in 1996, had to wait until I had finished a book-length musical ethnography on Bulgarian traditional and neotraditional music entitled *May It Fill Your Soul: Experiencing Bulgarian Music* (Rice 1994). During the course of writing that book, Roger Savage, a colleague and philosopher of music at UCLA, introduced me to the German philosophical tradition of hermeneutics and to the phenomenological hermeneutics of French philosopher Paul Ricoeur. This line of argument, it seemed to me at the time, provided a strong foundation for a version of the social sciences that recognized the impossibility of a positivist, scientific approach to truth. As Paul Ricoeur (1981: 193) memorably wrote, "Between hermeneutics and absolute truth one has to choose." Whereas the starting point for good science is to erase biases and prejudices and to start afresh in some intellectually neutral position, hermeneutic philosophers take as their starting point the notion that human beings are "thrown" into an existing world that enculturates them in ways of being in the world and of understanding the world. What hermeneutics asks of us is not the truth of science but better understandings and better interpretations of the way the social world, as opposed to the physical world, works. Ricoeur labels the path to those understandings a "hermeneutic arc" from "preunderstandings" of the world as experienced and known before the investigation begins, through "explanation" based on disciplined observation and empirical research techniques, to "new understandings" of the social world and its workings. This philosophical tradition appealed to me for three reasons. First, it put on a solid philosophical footing the kind of qualitative work we do in ethnomusicology. Kenneth Gourlay, in the late 1970s, had already critiqued the field for its scientific pretensions, arguing that our research results and our claims to truth about music cultures depend in no small part on researchers' social and historical positions and the kinds of conversations they have with other socially and historically positioned individuals during fieldwork (Gourlay 1978). Gourlay and the hermeneutic philosophers were pointing out that in this kind of social-scientific and humanistic research, the scientific injunction to eliminate prejudice and bias (preunderstandings) was not going to be possible. And yet I was suspicious. Before majoring in history, I had trained in the physical and biological sciences and hoped to become a medical researcher. Although I was sympathetic to Gourlay's critique, I was loath to give up scientific research principles as the intellectual foundation of our discipline in favor of vague relativistic claims, as attractive and even obvious as those claims were. The hermeneutic tradition provided me with the philosophically grounded foundation that I needed to be able to choose hermeneutics, with its attention to situated interpretations and multiple truths, over science, with its "absolute truth."

The second reason I was attracted to phenomenological hermeneutics was that its notion of being thrown into a world that one cannot at first understand and can never completely master and explain seemed an apt description of field research. Ethnomusicologists who set out to understand a foreign music culture, as so many of us do, have little to carry into the field but our preunderstandings of the formal structures and "elements" of music and of the social order and human values given to us by our culture and its music. With these preunderstandings we set about to explain to ourselves and our readers how this other culture works musically, culturally, socially, politically, and economically. My own fieldwork process, which I describe in hermeneutic terms in this chapter, provided continuous challenges to my musical and social preunderstandings. Although my encounters with music and people in the field did not erase the concepts and values I brought with me, the data I was collecting and the experiences I was having could be characterized as new understandings that I could explain.

The third reason I found the phenomenological aspect of this tradition attractive was that it provided the philosophical basis for writing self-reflexively about the self-knowledge generated during fieldwork and the hermeneutical arc that all fieldworkers travel along. Self-reflexivity in the form of first-person accounts for research processes and insights have figured prominently in book-length musical ethnographies since the efflorescence of the genre in the late 1970s (Berliner 1978, Chernoff 1979, Keil 1979, and Feld 1982 are well-known examples from this period). In my own book in this genre, self-reflexivity took two forms: juxtapositions of my interpretations with those of the people I worked with, and introspective self-understandings of playing music when my teachers couldn't explain something to me. For example, I wanted to interpret the meanings of some song lyrics differently from the woman who sang them for me. She interpreted them as literally true reports of events that actually had happened, while I preferred to interpret them metaphorically within a genre that, after long experience, I came to understand had been composed by, as the singer told me, "some sharp-witted woman" to express women's often troubled relationships with men. Her interpretation and mine stand side by side in my book. Readers may prefer one interpretation over the other, but I felt free to report them both and not to choose one as "true." Perhaps they both are, a position that hermeneutics allows.

The other intellectual problem where hermeneutic self-reflexivity was at work in the book concerned my attempt to learn to play the Bulgarian bagpipe. I have written about this extensively elsewhere (Rice 1985, 1994, 1995) but also in Chapter 2. When I threw myself into the project of learning to play this instrument, my teacher could not "explain" to me the ornamentation in a way that I could understand. I had to explain it to myself through introspection and trial and error. After a long and frustrating struggle, I finally acquired what my teacher told me I would have to: "bagpiper's fingers." Once I could play with these fingers, which by the way often seemed to be driven not by me but magically by something beyond myself (perhaps by my "new understanding" while "I" was still the I of my preunderstandings), my musical interpretations were confirmed by Bulgarians' verbal and nonverbal behavior: they danced to my playing, they called me a bagpiper, and they noticed that my fingers moved like my teacher's fingers. Their comments and actions were the confirmation I needed that I had acquired bagpiper's fingers. But I was left to wonder whether my new understanding, located in my head and hands and which I could report in words, corresponded to understandings in the heads of "real" Bulgarian bag-pipers, understandings that my teacher could not express in words. To answer this question, which remains open in Chapter 2, today I would turn to phenomenology, which eschews the psychology inherent in my question to argue that the confirmations I received of my playing were indicative of shared intersubjective understandings; they were signs that I had entered the horizons of understanding of the Bulgarian musical world into which I had been thrown.

Chapter 3, "Reflections on Music and Meaning: Metaphor, Signification, and Control in the Bulgarian Case," published in 2001, resulted from an invitation to contribute to a special issue of the *British Forum for Ethnomusicology* (today *Ethnomusicology Forum*) devoted to music and meaning. As I point out in the opening paragraphs, the question of whether and how music references ideas and emotions beyond itself and the way it resembles or differs from the referential, semantic, discursive features of language has been an inveterate question in (ethno) musicology and one still open for discussion. Volume editor Martin Clayton (2001) distinguished between two senses of the concept of musical meaning: a narrow sense involving its structural properties and semiotic potential for referencing ideas and emotions within and beyond itself, perhaps reducible to the term *signification*, and a broad sense involving musical experience and its *significance* for individuals and groups. Clayton's and my consideration at some length of the "meaning of meaning" is not simply a pedant's errand. Naming and defining concepts is fundamental to descriptive and theoretical work in ethnomusicology and indeed any academic field. For example, in Chapter 5 of this book, I examine a subset of the literature on the theme of music and identity and find it wanting precisely because authors leave the term *identity* undefined. By taking its meaning for granted, these authors deny themselves the possibility of contributing to general understandings of music's role in creating and reflecting individual and social identities. In ethnomusicology, one master of this definitional tactic is Thomas Turino. In all his publications, he can be counted on to define carefully the terms and concepts he is using. To give just one example, his monograph *Nationalists, Cosmopolitans, and Popular Music in Zimbabwe* (Turino 2000) is frequently cited not least because of his careful definitions of cosmopolitanism, nationalism, and national sentiment.

In the section of Chapter 3 called "Metaphors and the Nature of Music," for the first time I make a claim that will resonate through a couple of other publications, namely, that ethnomusicologists' metaphorical claims about the nature of music are among its most important contributions to music studies. A metaphor is a verbal (is) or analogical (as) structure that by some accounts guides all human thinking (Lakoff and Johnson 1980). This is/as structure links one domain of human experience to another in a way that attributes qualities of the predicate domain to those of the subject domain. "Time is money" is a classic one in English; its "truth" leads us to spend, save, invest, and waste time just as we do money. Some metaphors are fleeting and literary, but I argue here that some take on a life that infuses the way our research subjects act and the way we design and conduct research. I conclude with an example of the way four metaphors (music as art, as social behavior, as text, and as commodity) interact in a study of Bulgarian musical experience. I continue to think that analyzing particular music cultures through the lens of their subjects' metaphorical claims about the nature of music and sound is a fruitful heuristic tool. This section on metaphor corresponds roughly to Clayton's broad notion of meaning, that is, its significance.

The next section of Chapter 3, on musical signification, matches his narrow notion of meaning and employs Peircean semiotic theory as outlined for music by Thomas Turino (1999, 2008, 2014). Here I employ semiotics to answer questions about the way Bulgarian musical signs and sign-types (icons, indexes, symbols) are interpreted. The chapter does not deal as thoroughly as it might have with one of Turino's most important claims about musical semiotics, namely, that the iconic and indexical properties of musical signs explain the affective power of music. I have come to believe that, particularly as Turino has elaborated it, it is one of the most important theories (music as sign) we have about the nature of music and the way it works for individuals and in music cultures. Theories such as this function as effective heuristic tools for thinking analytically about particular ethnographic cases.

In the last section of Chapter 3, I look at "the control of meaning," inspired partly by Michel Foucault's skepticism about the freedom of free will and partly by my ethnographic experience in Bulgaria's totalitarian political regime.[9] Here I argue that, while everyone has their own deeply personal musical experiences, some of us work in areas where state government, other organs of power, and powerful groups and individuals try to determine and control those experiences. Sometimes they are successful and sometimes not. If their attempts at control are not successful, that may be explained by music's semiotic fluidity and force, which enable musicians to evade control and bend musical practice to their own political and expressive ends.

In Chapter 4, "Time, Place, and Metaphor in Musical Experience and Ethnography," published in 2003, I use metaphorical understandings of the nature of music as one of three building blocks of a model of musical experience. I do so because I believe that, beyond the hundreds of music cultures ethnomusicologists have documented and described, our most important contributions to the general study of music are our claims about the nature of music, expressed most cogently and powerfully in metaphors. In this article musical metaphors are placed along one axis of a three-dimensional space I label "the space of musical experience and ethnography." In other words, musical experience and ethnography are structurally similar. The other two axes are time and place. As a theoretical model, it does a number of things. First, it argues that the studiers and the studied experience and understand the musical world within a common abstract experiential framework. It makes more precise my claim in Chapter 2 that ethnomusicologists' interpretations are never objectively true but always begin with preunderstandings that are modified into new understandings during fieldwork. (By the way, in hermeneutic terms, these new understandings, because they are confirmed intersubjectively in the field, fall outside the common subjective-objective dichotomy of science.) In Chapter 4 I suggest that the hermeneutic arc of Chapter 2 can be rendered analytically and visually as travel through this three-dimensional space of time, place, and metaphor. In this chapter I do not give an example of my own self-reflexive ethnographic travels through this space, but Figure 0.5 is a model of musical ethnography, that is, of the way imaginary ethnographers navigate this space in their trajectories from preunderstandings through explanation to new understandings. A similarly structured abstract three-dimensional space also functions as a "model for" musical experience, in other words as a way to think about and explain particular musical ethnographic projects. In Chapter 4 I give

9. "I believe the great fantasy is the idea of a social body constituted by the universality of wills. Now the phenomenon of the social body is the effect not of a consensus but of the materiality of power operating on the very bodies of individuals.... The individual, with his identity and characteristics, is the product of a relationship of power exercised over bodies" (Foucault 1980: 55, 74).

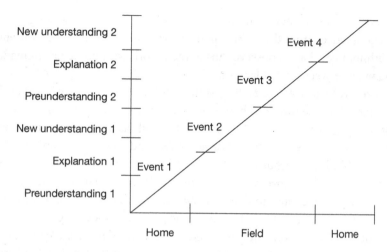

**Figure 0.5** A three-dimensional model of musical ethnography.

examples from my fieldwork in Bulgaria to illustrate the way it can be used to explain changes in individual musical experience and conflicts between individuals and groups who hold different views on the nature of music, conflicts that create what I label "experiential tension."

Why am I interested in individual musical experience and conflicts among individuals when the name *ethno*musicology and much of its history are based on the study of groups of people in societies, communities, subcultures, microcultures, scenes, ethnicities, tribes, nations, or races? There are two reasons. First, ethnomusicologists have long reported on individual differences in musical taste, values, and behaviors within particular music cultures. This model of a conceptual space for thinking about musical experience offers an explanation for those observed differences: they appear when individuals occupy different positions within the shared space of musical experience and when they have traveled along different trajectories through it. Second, in the modern world, a large and growing number of individuals are wandering the globe in search of new homes. To account for this new world, ethnomusicologists have added a consideration of the complexity of modern societies to older ideas of musical styles as coherent expressions of homogeneous cultures. This complexity includes societies that are still holding together and those that are breaking up (see Slobin 1993). In such modern circumstances, I suggest that researchers might engage in what I call "subject-centered music ethnography," and in Chapter 4 I create a model for such work. Using that model, ethnomusicologists can observe and analyze the way their subjects view their own musical practices and those of others from three different perspectives: their place in society understood geographically and socially, the time periods they have lived through, and the metaphors they use to express their understandings of the nature of music. Analyzing modern musical practices from these three perspectives helps to explain the variability that ethnomusicologists observe during their work with particular individuals living in or between particular cultures.

Andrew Killick (2003: 182) did just that, taking my model for a "road test" by "steer[ing] a course through the history of three related musical narrative and theatrical genres from Korea." He found it useful "as a conceptual framework for charting a course of historical development and changing meanings within a culture" (ibid.). He argues that this model, and I dare say similar models by others, "help[s] us achieve more ambitious goals than the description of single cultures or practices, and to that end, should lead us to a comparative stance," (ibid.) just what I have always hoped for the process of modeling.

Chapter 5, "Reflections on Music and Identity in *Ethnomusicology*," resulted from an invitation from the Institute for Musicology of the Serbian Academy of Sciences to contribute to the 2007 issue of their journal, *Muzikologiya*, on the theme of music and identity. I suppose they expected me to write something on Bulgarian music, but I decided to take the opportunity their invitation afforded me to write more generally on this theme. In this chapter I argue for the first time that one "model of" ethnomusicology consists of a list of "themes" around which ethnomusicologists organize their research. I list a few of them here, including, for example, native concepts about music (Merriam 1964); music and gender, which became common in the 1980s; and music in relation to war, violence, and conflict, a more recent theme since the late 1990s. Among the most ubiquitous of these themes has been music and identity, which entered the field in the 1980s after I completed my doctoral dissertation in 1977. The concept figured not at all in my graduate education, but, given its prominence today, it is hard to imagine a time when it did not even register as a theme ethnomusicologists explored.

For reasons of time, I limited my survey of this theme for this article to the journal *Ethnomusicology* (hence the italics in the title).[10] I began the study curious to know when the theme entered the field. I also assumed that two questions animated this theme: how do people use music to construct an identity? and how does music making give people their sense of identity? I learned that ethnomusicologists began to write about this theme early in the 1980s, and my survey demonstrated that ethnomusicologists' writing on this theme had developed more fine-grained ways of treating this theme than I had anticipated. Unfortunately, from my point of view, I had to classify those ways because the authors did not seem to understand themselves as writing within a tradition of studies on this

---

10. In the wake of this article, Nolan Warden (2016) has surveyed this theme in reference to a much broader swath of the literature.

theme: none defined identity and, with one exception, none cited the work of any of the others. Each article was an idiographic account of a music culture; they effectively created what I called, uncharitably I know, an "arid desert" of ethnographic "grains of sand." This chapter argues that a serious discipline cannot be built on such infertile soil, and that ethnomusicologists must read each other's work on the themes that interest them and generate questions, issues, and problems within that theme if we hope to place our discipline on a solid foundation and make important contributions to knowledge of humankind.

One way to think about the way our particular studies might relate to a common ethnomusicological theme would be to list its subthemes and theories and the issues, questions, and problems they suggest. In the case of identity, for example, there appear to be two broad subthemes: individual identity and social identity. A theory is a claim or explanation about what music is or does or how it is structured. Questions arise from fieldwork or from previous literature in or outside of ethnomusicology. An issue is a disagreement that flows either from inconsistencies in the fieldwork data or from conflicting theoretical positions that previous writers have taken. Problems are persistent questions and issues that have resisted analysis, explanation, and understanding. Answers are explanations that writers provide to the questions, issues, and problems they encounter in their work on the theme. In Chapter 5 I presented my analysis of the music-and-identity theme and its subthemes narratively, but, to make my assessment clearer, I provide in Figure 0.6 an outlined list of the way the theme of music and identity was subdivided in this corpus of work. Similar lists for the large and growing number of themes that are engaging ethnomusicologists today would surely generate the kind of theorizing (question answering if you will) that I argue in Chapter 5 would strengthen the intellectual vitality of our field.

After publishing the essay in Chapter 5 in an important national journal, I decided to register my concerns about the field in a "call to action" on the part of readers of and contributors to the journal on which the article is based, *Ethnomusicology* (Rice 2010). The editor invited seven responses. Those responses, with one exception, seemed to be in the category of "yes, but. . . ." That is, most agreed that I had identified a real problem, but they wanted to register caveats or propose alternate solutions. For example, one wrote, "We really ought to have an ethnomusicology keyword website . . . that could serve as a gauge of keyword elasticity" (Slobin 2010: 338). One concern of some was that perhaps journal articles are not the place to engage in lengthy disquisitions on theoretical matters and literature reviews, that those are better left to book-length musical ethnographies and edited collections on particular themes. There is no question that both of these writing genres are rich sources of ethnomusicological theorizing on music and identity, and had I looked there I might have found the "theoretical moisture" I couldn't find in the *Ethnomusicology* articles. But as

---

**Music and Identity**

---

  I. Subtheme: Individual Self-Identity
    A. Theory: Musical allegiance is an alternative to given identities based on gender, class, occupation, age, and so on.
    B. Theory: Musical taste and practice are a way to "suture" the self to a social group.
    C. Issue: Do individuals act freely as individuals to create their own identity, or are our musical and identity choices given to us by hegemonic social and commercial "regimes" and "techniques"?
 II. Subtheme: Group Identity (Collective Self-Understanding)
    A. Theory: Music is an index or icon of group identity.
        1. Issue: Is the group identity to which music is associated already there, or do musical signs help to create the group identity?
        2. Question: How many group identities do we possess, and how does music express and support them?
        3. Questions: Who or what institutions have the power to institutionalize social identities? Everyone or only the powerful? When there is a conflict between the weak and the powerful, who wins, and why?
    B. Question: What does music, as opposed to other expressive and symbolic forms, contribute to group identity?
       Answer 1: The feel or affect of identity.
       Answer 2: The temporal iconicity of music and identity.
       Answer 3: The iconicity of music's many "elements" with identity's many types.
       Answer 4: The ability to perform a group's identity in public to itself and others.
       Answer 5: The positive valence associated with music reverses the negative valence associated with some identities, such as those of minorities and the subaltern.

---

**Figure 0.6** Music and identity: its subthemes, theories, questions, issues, problems, and answers.

my title indicates, I was writing about *Ethnomusicology*, not ethnomusicology. I don't agree that journal articles, because of their brevity, are not the place for the sort of thematic comparisons I call for in Chapter 5. They just have to take a form appropriate to the genre and to the ethnographic case under discussion. It does not have to take the form of a lengthy review of the literature, although where questions, issues, and problems relevant to the case study suffuse the literature, such a review might be more extensive and the article might try to answer the questions, resolve the issues, or solve the problems. If such considerations are not the point of the article, if it is mainly ethnographic, and if a concept like identity is at the core of an article, as is the case for the articles reviewed in Chapter 5, I still would expect something like the following: "I take identity to mean. ...." I wouldn't even insist on a footnote, but one could explain telegraphically the subset of the literature that the author has examined. It might go something like this: "I arrived at this definition after reviewing Smith (1998) . . ." and then, if relevant, continuing to summarize in a condensed form the range of definitions or the sources of the definitions or the issues created by differing definitions, none of which, presumably, are at stake in this article.

One reason some scholars refuse this kind of contextualization of their case study is that the culture of *Ethnomusicology* sanctions this sort of descriptive, ethnographic, noncomparative writing. As Ellen Koskoff (2010: 332) pointed out, the articles in *Ethnomusicology* are "indices to future contributors of what they should be publishing." That model "militates against intertextuality," not because of the brevity of the form itself but because of the culture of the journal. In my call to action I argued for changing the culture of *Ethnomusicology*, and Jane Sugarman (2010: 343) provides a concise characterization of the form that new culture, those new indices, might take:

> I have always admired the way that the advancement of theory is built into the practices of cultural anthropology. First, anthropologists generally begin individual articles with a substantial introduction that situates their thesis and argument within recent literature on a given theoretical topic, often identifying a specific "problem" that their article seeks to address. Adopting such a convention in ethnomusicology would encourage us not only to cite our fellow researchers more often, but also to be more self-conscious and explicit about the approach that we are taking and the underlying premises on which it is based.

Neither Sugarman nor I am advocating for what some of the respondents seemed to fear will come, apparently by the nature of the thing, with calls to theorize: the unhappy specter of "grand theory" and a move toward intellectual hegemony.[11] I am not, in this chapter, trying to build a general or "grand" theory or "centralized theoretical generalization" (Stokes 2010: 339) of music and identity but rather to list the subthemes, theories, questions, issues, and problems that ethnomusicologists writing in *Ethnomusicology* have treated in their idiographic studies, but which they do not identify in a manner approaching Sugarman's elegant description of what anthropologists do and what, I contend, we should do.

The list of music-and-identity subthemes I identified after reading the literature is, like all lists, incomplete, especially if one continues to read on the topic. Martin Stokes (2010: 340) responded helpfully with yet more questions and

---

11. The capitalized term *Grand Theory* was a pejorative label the sociologist C. Wright Mills applied in his 1959 book *The Sociological Imagination* to highly abstract "general theories" (p. 22) like structural functionalism or structural Marxism, which claim universal application but which are, in Wright's view, disconnected from the concerns of everyday people and their problems. He devoted an entire chapter to it, claiming that "the work of Talcott Parsons is the leading contemporary example in American sociology" (p. 23).

subthemes, believing that the questions arising around this theme, and probably all the many other ethnomusicological themes that define our discipline, are "diverse and highly mobile." What, for example, would the literature on identity look like in theoretical terms if we examined the writings on this theme by a more diverse set of authors?

Based on my critique of the literature on the theme of music and identity in *Ethnomusicology*, I can now offer a model for the contents of musical ethnographies, whether books, dissertations, journal articles, or conference presentations. I call it "Tim's Four Ts" and present it as a pseudo-mathematical equation:

$$\text{Topic} = \text{Tradition} + \text{Theme} + \text{Theory}$$

Good writing in ethnomusicology should position the particular musical ethnography within scholarship on the musical tradition under discussion; the principal theme or themes being addressed and one or more of the subthemes, theories, issues, questions, and problems associated with that theme; and any large-scale social, musical, or biological theories, with their associated issues, theories, questions, and problems, that are at stake in the ethnography. If more of us used this formula, I believe the writing in our field would be more engaging and productive.

Chapter 6, "Ethnomusicological Theory," published in 2010, is the culmination, until this Introduction, of my attempts to model ethnomusicology. My frustration with the absence of intradisciplinary conversations on the music-and-identity theme led me to wonder about what ethnomusicological theory looks like. After having been so critical, I thought it would only be fair if I proposed something productive. For the identity article in Chapter 5, I only demanded two pretty low-level kinds of theory (and certainly not "grand theory"): first, that discussions of music be linked to extradisciplinary discussions of identity, so that we could benefit from general theories about identity in psychology, sociology, and other social sciences, and second, that we position our particular work in relation to previous work on music and identity in the very journal we were publishing in. But I knew that even these modest demands hardly exhausted the theoretical work other ethnomusicologists were doing (for one compilation, see Stone 2008).

I began my own attempt to theorize about ethnomusicological theory by trying to invent another three-dimensional space like those I had created in Chapter 1 on remodeling ethnomusicology and Chapter 4 on the space of musical experience and ethnography. But little by little the thing grew in unexpected ways, and the result, almost C. Seegeresque in its multiplicity, is what you find in Chapter 6.

I am perhaps not being fair, but on the basis of the music-and-identity survey, I concluded that some ethnomusicologists had a vexed relationship with theory. Ruth Stone confirmed this feeling of mine when she wrote in her *Theory for Ethnomusicology* (2008) that a lot of prestige accrues to ethnomusicologists who do theory, but that not all do it. Turino (2015: 379) reports colleagues telling him that "I don't do theory." But as Turino, Stone, and I (and many others starting at least with Alan Merriam) would maintain, theory in the form of attempting to understand and explain things in our world of experience is necessary and unavoidable. We do it all the time in our professional and personal lives. But if we are right about the unavoidability of theory, then what is going on? How could theory be necessary and yet only some of us seem to do it? Nothing could be more diagnostic of a malaise in our field than the space between necessity and absence.

I don't know for certain the root causes of this gap, but I suppose it has a few sources. First, many ethnomusicologists enter the field with training, not like mine in history and science, but in the arts and humanities. Perhaps they are so blown away by the beauty and stupefying complexity of individual instances that the thought of comparing them and, worse, simplifying them for the sake of modeling and theory is distasteful. Second, some imagine that going into the field with a theory, especially one borrowed from the social sciences, will overdetermine the results of their investigation, that they will observe only those things that support the theory. This worry is completely without merit and at odds with both scientific empiricism and hermeneutical interpretation. Minimally, theory in the form of preunderstandings is inescapable. The objective of both scientific research and hermeneutics is to push beyond the horizons of the known into the unknown through observation, explanation, and revision of theories and preunderstandings. Third, some seem to be leery of theory imported from beyond the culture under study. This is a more pointed version of the second reason, but, although there is some reason for it, it too misses the point in something like the same way. In ethnomusicology, the goal has long been to understand the musical and social world in the way that the people we work with understand it. Hence, there is some worry that an imported way of seeing the world, a theory from the social sciences or a concept from European music theory, might distort our reports on the musical lives of others. But the test of the effectiveness of such imported theories is not whether they come from inside or outside the culture but whether they provide a convincing explanation or an eye-opening insight into the workings of the local music culture we are studying. From a hermeneutic perspective, it is predictable that some of these interpretations will match those of the people with whom we work and some will not. But when they don't match, we or some local observer will point that out. That's the way scholarship is supposed to work.

Because of my assessment, correct or incorrect, of the odd position of theory in our field, in Chapter 6 I took the most inclusive approach to theory that

I could think of. Sometimes in ethnomusicology, theory refers to social theory imported from the social sciences; this is what Stone is getting at in her "theory *for* ethnomusicology" and what Turino (2015), citing a conversation with Gabriel Solis, calls theory with a capital "T," that is, Theory. In Chapter 6 I reoriented the question away from the theories (or Theories) that ethnomusicologists borrow from other fields to the question of the way ethnomusicologists theorize, that is, the theorizing *of* and *by* ethnomusicologists, which Gabriel Solis, in a response to this chapter, labels "autochthonous modes of theorizing" (Solis 2012: 530). My notion of ethnomusicological theory, or what I have taken to calling "ethnomusicological theorizing," extends from the social Theory we use to make large-scale claims about the way humans work together culturally, socially, politically, and economically to our own "autochthonous" general claims about the way humans think and act musically. At the conclusion of this Introduction, I revisit ethnomusicological theory as "ethnomusicological theorizing" to make as clear as possible the difference between what I propose in Chapter 5, *theorizing in* ethnomusicology, and what Ruth Stone reviews and explains, *theory for* ethnomusicology.

Chapter 6 inspired an article-length response from Gabriel Solis (2012) and initiated just the sort of conversation we need more of in ethnomusicology. He was concerned that, although I "engage[] with musical sound deeply" in my own ethnographic work and in some passages in the chapter, I "marginalize[] it meta-discursively" in my modeling of ethnomusicological theory (p. 546). This was certainly not my intent, but the difference between my intent and Solis's interpretation is something for which I take responsibility. My aim was to register, in as even-handed and accepting way as I could, all the ways ethnomusicologists are theoretical, including (1) claims about music sound as a domain of aesthetic practice and reflection that says something about the nature of musical thinking in a particular culture and by human beings in general and (2) claims about musicking as a deeply social practice. I do think it is fair to say that ethnomusicology of the last thirty years has moved in the second direction, something that Solis seems to agree with, but, that said, both he and I cite the work of Michael Tenzer as an example, among others, of the first kind of claim (see, e.g., Tenzer 2006, 2015). Solis usefully fleshes out one aspect of my model of ethnomusicological theory by reviewing current and historical trends in theorizing about music as sound and the connection between musicking and social practice. At the end of the day there is no space between his conclusion that "many of our most valuable contributions to creating a discipline and to the larger worlds of music study and the humanities at large have come from the investigation of musical sound and musical process as part of integrative, synthetic studies" (Solis 2012: 549) and my own views on ethnomusicological theory.

Chapter 7, "The Individual in Musical Ethnography," published in 2012, flows from two sources. First, it dives in some detail into one of the three

formative processes I proposed in Chapter 1, that music is "individually created and experienced." My surveys of articles published in *Ethnomusicology*
showed that this process is the least well represented of my three formative
processes, but Chapter 7, cowritten with then–graduate student Jesse Ruskin,
documents the extent to which this process is very well represented in book-
length musical ethnographies. Second, in the 1990s I began to read and hold
seminars on these book-length musical ethnographies with the idea of writing a book about them, my "book of books" I called it. I noted, among other
things, the formative processes and themes and issues they treated. I was interested in these books not only for their content but also for what they represented about a major change in the field in the late 1970s. This was the period
when scholars trained in music began to integrate ideas from anthropology,
such as those in Merriam's *The Anthropology of Music*, into their publications.
Before the late 1970s, books by musicologically trained ethnomusicologists
focused on analyses and transcriptions of musical style (e.g., Nettl 1954, Hood
1971, Garfias 1975), while anthropologists examined music's role and function in society, the social behavior of musicians, native concepts about music,
and homologies between music and social structure (e.g., McAllester 1954,
Merriam 1967, Blacking 1965).

In the late 1970s, however, ethnomusicologists trained in ethnomusicology
programs began to write musical ethnographies that inscribed the twenty-five-
year-long hope for a union of the field's anthropological and musicological
roots. *Music in the Culture of Northern Afghanistan* (1976) by Mark Slobin, who
had studied at the School of Music of the University of Michigan but whose
research was supported by a grant from the Wenner-Gren Foundation, and *The
Soul of Mbira* (1978) by Paul Berliner, who had studied ethnomusicology at
Wesleyan with anthropologist David McAllester, began the trend. From that
time on, one or two book-length musical ethnographies appeared each year,
growing to eight or nine per year by 2002. I prepared a detailed questionnaire
and recorded my and my student's observations about them. Before I could fin-
ish the project, the rapidly growing number of them (today often more than
twenty are published in a single year and the total number has risen to over
300) overwhelmed my ability to keep up, and I abandoned the project. But one
aspect of its legacy is Chapter 7. It examines why and how these books include
individuals. As my model in Chapter 1 predicted, ethnomusicologists had, from
the 1970s to 2002 and beyond, paid significant attention to "individual creativity and experience" in their book-length musical ethnographies, and Chapter 7
outlines the ways and the reasons for doing so.

Ruskin and I make a gross distinction between the individual as a single
human biological unit and societies as sets of socially interacting individuals.
We left unexamined other terms that ethnomusicologists have used with reference to individuals, including agent, subject, and person. Oversimplifying

somewhat, the notion of agent flows from Pierre Bourdieu's (1977) practice theory and Anthony Giddens's (1979) theory of social action; Michel Foucault raised questions about the free will of subjects and their subjectivity, arguing for the power of institutions to form the subject; and person comes from legal concepts about an individual's rights and responsibilities. Ethnomusicologists have used the notion of agent and subject productively, but we left the review of the literature on those perspectives to the reader.

The final chapter, Chapter 8, "Ethnomusicology in Times of Trouble," published in 2014, returns to my interest in themes as one way to model ethnomusicology. This interest grew out of my reading of musical ethnographies. As I tracked the themes found in these ethnographies, I began watching for the themes discussed ever so briefly in this chapter, themes like music, violence and conflict, music and climate change, and music and the HIV/AIDS pandemic. My interest in these themes was sparked in 1992, when I was invited to present a paper on musical aesthetics at the annual meeting of the American Anthropological Society (AAA). At the meeting I was, quite frankly, stunned by how few papers were reporting the details of traditional cultural and social phenomena and how many were about modernity's deleterious effects on traditional societies, whether caused by intrusive government policies, civil wars, missionaries, or mining and agribusiness. They were painting a rather depressing picture of the world I inhabited as an ethnomusicologist listening to happy reports of "people making music" (Titon 2009: xviii). I wondered when papers and journal articles like those I heard at the AAA meeting would enter our field. I didn't have to wait too long. In 1998, Svanibor Pettan published an edited book about music and war during the breakup of Yugoslavia in the early 1990s, and in 1999, Adelaida Reyes published a book about the music of Vietnamese refugees displaced by the Vietnam War. Since that time some ethnomusicologists, including a remarkable number of students from UCLA, have moved resolutely toward documenting music's relationship to society and culture in some of the most troubled areas of the world.[12] Chapter 8

12. During this period, students at UCLA, my home institution, were an inspiration, writing dissertations on many of these themes: Alviso (2002) on music, crime, and poverty; Mijatovic (2003) on music and war; Van Buren (2006) on music and the HIV/AIDS epidemic; Ritter (2006) on music and violence; Hogan (2011) on music and disability; Silvers (2012) on music and the environment; Dirksen (2012) on music in the wake of a particular tragedy; and Hernandez (2014) on music and forced migration. Former students were also turning to these topics during this period, including Ritter and Daughtry (2007) on the effects of terrorism on music; Daughtry (2012) on music and war; O'Connell and El-Shawan Castelo-Branco (2010) on violence and conflict; and Bakan (2009) on music and autism. Many of these authors have also contributed important journal articles to these themes and a recent book on the sounds of war (Daughtry 2015).

summarizes that move in the form of a list of ethnomusicological themes that seemed new to me (and many others) since the late 1990s. I conclude with how writing on these themes might affect ethnomusicologists' theorizing about the nature of music.

As a form of theorizing, a list of themes is a relatively low-level "model of" ethnomusicology, and lists are always incomplete and capable of being reformulated by other writers. After reading all those musical ethnographies, in 2008 I created my first list of forty-three ethnomusicology themes ordered chronologically for an outline for a book I called "Ethnomusicology: A Conceptual Sketch," which became, in even sketchier form, *Ethnomusicology: A Very Short Introduction* (Rice 2014). The list began with the twelve themes Merriam outlined in 1964 for an anthropology of music. On that list were three items I included in Chapter 8: (1) music, war, violence, and conflict; (2) medical ethnomusicology; music and HIV/AIDS; and (3) migration and minority studies. Chapter 8 adds three more: (4) music in particular tragedies; (5) music, violence, and poverty; and (6) music, climate change, and the environment. Figure 0.7 contains a revised version of that original chronological list of themes as one sort of "model of" ethnomusicology; it paints a picture of the history of ethnomusicology since 1964 and the development since the late 1990s of new themes engaged with the realities of modern life. Like all such lists, it does not promise completeness; others would add other themes or reorder the ones I include. Every year a dozen small conferences pop up around the world suggesting yet more themes around which our research might crystalize. On its website, the Society for Ethnomusicology calls these themes "topics" and lists ninety-two of them!

To conclude this introduction, I would like to make one more foray into modeling ethnomusicology by reconsidering ethnomusicological theory and modeling not as a series of products, that is, theories and models, but as a process I call "theorizing by ethnomusicologists" or "ethnomusicological theorizing."[13] My questions are these: how do ethnomusicologists theorize, and what constitutes ethnomusicological theorizing? Given some of the discomfort my previous efforts have generated, I should reiterate that my purpose in thinking this way about the field is not to impose on it a particular "grand theory" or any particular set of theories or to create a hegemony of theoretical thinking in the field. Nor am I more interested in theorizing about music as a social process than about music as a musical process. Both have their place in the

---

13. Thinking about theory as a process rather than a product was inspired in no small part by sociologist Richard Swedburg's delightful book, *The Art of Social Theory* (2014a). It is divided into two main parts: "how to theorize" and "preparing to theorize." Along the way he discusses various ways of theorizing, including some mentioned later in this section: naming, concept, and typology. He also has a useful chapter on heuristics. See also Swedburg (2014b).

A. Themes in ethnomusicology listed by Alan Merriam in *The Anthropology of Music* (1964)
    1. Native concepts about music
    2. Synesthesia and intersense modalities (experience of music)
    3. Physical behavior with respect to music
    4. Social behavior of musicians
    5. Music learning
    6. Creativity and the process of composition
    7. Song texts
    8. Uses and functions of music
    9. Music as symbolic behavior (meaning of music)
    10. Aesthetics and the interrelationship of the arts
    11. Musical study in the service of culture history studies
    12. Music change and cultural change
B. New themes between 1964 and 1983
    13. Musical encounters with and adaptation to modernity
    14. Performance and event analysis
    15. Religion, ritual, and music (but see, e.g., McAllester 1954)
    16. Emotion, euphoria, and trance as responses to music
    17. Patronage and economics of music
    18. Iconicity of musical and cultural style
    19. Homology of musical and social structures
    20. Genre
    21. Individual musicians
    22. Urban and popular music
C. Emerging themes in book-length musical ethnographies between 1983 and 2000
    23. 1983 Gender
    24. 1985 History
    25. 1985 Ethnicity/race
    26. 1987 Individual agency
    27. 1988 Media
    28. 1990 Politics and power
    29. 1993 Institutions
    30. 1993 Migration
    31. 1993 Identity
    32. 1996 Diaspora
    33. 1997 Authenticity and tradition
    34. 1997 Minorities
    35. 1998 Globalization/transnationalism/cosmopolitanism
    36. 2000 Nationalism
    37. 2000 Tourism
D. Emerging themes and questions in books since 2001
    38. Music in relation to war, violence, and conflict
    39. Medical ethnomusicology; music and HIV/AIDS
    40. Unmarked and unremarkable music
    41. Music of affinity groups (rather than ethnic or national groups)
    42. Music of virtual communities on the Internet
    43. Memory/nostalgia
    44. Music in particular tragedies
    45. Music and poverty
    46. Music, climate change, and the environment (ecomusicology)
    47. Sound studies
    48. Embodied musical experience
    49. Musical analysis revived
    50. Applied ethnomusicology revived[1]

[1]See, in 2015 and 2016 alone, Bakan (2015), Howe et al. (2016), and Pettan and Titon (2015). I am grateful to Michael Bakan for pointing these out to me.

**Figure 0.7** A history of ethnomusicology as a list of themes.

"interdiscipline" called ethnomusicology (Solis 2012). I am interested in arguing that all the thinking ethnomusicologists do about music is theoretical in one way or another, and I hope that through my writing about it, theorizing in ethnomusicology can more richly suffuse our work.

I imagine ethnomusicological theorizing beginning in one of two places: either with explicit capital "T" Theory or with implicit preunderstandings.[14] Theorizing based on one (and in some cases both) of these types always precedes empirical research in the field, but theorizing can start from either position.

Some will start with a Theory, which will then guide their fieldwork. By Theory I mean a range of general claims about the nature of music or about the social world. An example of a Theory might be the phenomenologist's claim that intersubjectivity allows us to understand our own and others' musical experience in a way that is neither subjective nor objective. That Theory then suggests certain kinds of interviewing protocols, and it affects the way we conduct our fieldwork, the kinds of data we gather, and the way we interpret and explain the data we have collected. Ruth Stone (1982) advocated for a version of social phenomenology indebted to Alfred Schütz and conducted "feedback interviews" during which she asked Kpelle people to comment on her recordings of music and dance events. Harris Berger (1999) used other strains of phenomenology to study the microlevel musical experience of jazz and rock musicians in Ohio. The data collected during fieldwork using this Theory and its associated methods provide a basis for ethnomusicological theorizing, but the Theory in these two cases preceded the data collecting and later theorizing.

Some might worry that entering the field with such a Theory and its associated methods would prejudice the research and blind the researcher to what is really going on, or at least to something else that is going on. Although Theories focus the researcher's attention, they are not blindingly bright. They may direct the gaze intently in one direction, but the researcher is not a horse with blinders on; peripheral vision is still possible. Let's imagine a couple of scenarios. In one the researcher applies his phenomenological interview methods only to discover that people have, for whatever reason, no ability or desire to talk about musical experience. The researcher may want to ask why not, but that question doesn't arise from the Theory per se. Surely the sensible researcher will either find another fieldwork site where the Theory can be applied or turn his attention to another topic, either applying another Theory or collecting fieldwork

---

14. The distinction between implicit preunderstandings and explicit Theories is very abstract, but it suits my purposes for this discussion. Other, more practical places where theorizing might start include curiosity about something one doesn't understand, a concern for the sustainability of a musical tradition, and fieldwork experiences.

data based on various personal or disciplinary preunderstandings, without Theory. In a second scenario the researcher is happily collecting data through interviews on musical experience while the musicians she is talking to are suffering in poverty. The Theory has not blinded the researcher to what is going on in her subject's world, but now the fieldworker has a choice. Does she give up her Theory and her project to work on a topic that is of more pressing interest to those whom she is consulting, or does she continue her research, not blinded to what is going on but believing that it is an important Theory and an important topic of research? Different researchers and different specific situations will suggest different solutions to this ethical dilemma.

Now let's imagine a researcher who, like so many of us, loves some music he has heard and wants to go into the field to study it. He arrives in the field with a burning interest but no commitment to Theory; maybe he "doesn't do theory" or has never even heard of theory. But does he really arrive with no theory? Perhaps he doesn't bring along a Theory like phenomenology, semiotics, Marxian economics, Weberian sociology, Ricoerian hermeneutics, or the like, but he does bring implicit theories, or what I call preunderstandings, about the way music and musicking work even if he hasn't reflected on them. He may think, for example, that music is pleasant humanly organized sonic entertainment; that it is made up of elements like melody, harmony, and rhythm; that some people are better at it than others; and that these people, called musicians, are the people he wants to talk to and hang out with. These statements are theory-like because they generate a whole set of associated fieldwork methods: learning to play the music, attending musical events, making recordings, transcribing and analyzing the music, and living with musicians. These preunderstandings constitute, in scientific parlance, theories about the nature of music, but perhaps they are so commonplace that they are neither grand nor capitalized. They are, however, the starting point for data collection in the field, just as Theory is.

So if these are the two starting positions for ethnomusicological theorizing, what does theorizing itself consist of? Theorizing starts with selecting, from observations in the field, data made meaningful by either our preunderstandings or our Theory. That is, not all observations are registered as data during fieldwork. Some examples of ethnomusicological data are given in Figure 0.8. "Data point" is a cold, telegraphic way of referring to the sorts of deeply moving experiences we have in the field of songs, musical instruments, musicians, performance events, interviews, music lessons, and so on.

From this figure one can easily imagine the way different preunderstandings and Theories might affect data collection. The phenomenologist or the discourse analyst might worry only about interview data and perhaps fail to record and describe in detail an actual event from beginning to end. After a

| |
|---|
| Data point 1 = song 1 = instrument 1 = musician 1 = event 1 = interview 1 = lesson 1 |
| Data point 2 = song 2 = instrument 2 = musician 2 = event 2 = interview 2 = lesson 2 |
| Data point 3 = song 3 = instrument 3 = musician 3 = event 3 = interview 3 = lesson 3 |
| Data point 4 = song 4 = instrument 4 = musician 4 = event 4 = interview 4 = lesson 4 |
| Data point 5 = song 5 = instrument 5 = musician 5 = event 5 = interview 5 = lesson 5 |

**Figure 0.8** Data points in ethnomusicology.

while the researcher might notice that instrumental music was played only for dancing and add a line "data point 6 = dance 1 . . ." to the chart in Figure 0.8. Anthropologists Anthony Seeger and Steven Feld have argued that the object of study needs to be the larger domain of sound, and so they would add other lines for natural sounds, noise, speech, weeping, and so on. There was a time in the past when ethnomusicologists borrowed a "holistic" imperative from anthropology, and they might have insisted on collecting all this data. Today the field seems more oriented toward problems, questions, issues, and themes, which can have the effect of limiting data collection to those relevant to the researcher's particular theme, problem, issue, question, or Theory.

Is data collection the first step in theorizing, or does it precede theorizing? I want to cast a very wide net over the domain of theorizing, but I wonder about this. If we answer that it is, we would be saying that what we collect is not any old data but data that has been made meaningful in some way either by the Theory, the preunderstanding, or some new experience in the field. The fact that researchers always already attach meaning to the data they collect is a move perhaps worthy of the label theorizing. It would also be not unreasonable to argue that data collecting is a practical action and a method, even if driven by a preunderstanding or Theory, and that theorizing is what you do with the data once you collect it. I will leave it to the reader to choose between these alternatives.

If we, however, take the second position, that collecting data is not theorizing, then, I would argue, we arrive at theorizing immediately after that. Theorizing is, in broadest terms, what we do with our data. Theorizing consists of many activities, and Figure 0.9 contains a list of fifteen of them organized into four categories: (1) organizing the data, (2) structuring the data, (3) explaining the data, and (4) synthesizing the data. These categories proceed from low-level, indispensable, everyday types of theorizing (organizing the data) to higher level types (synthesizing the data), which I believe are necessary for the continued vitality of our field. In between are two categories (structuring the data and

A. Organizing data
  1. Analyzing and describing the data
  2. Classifying and categorizing the data
  3. Labeling categories and classes
  4. Listing categories
B. Structuring the data
  5. Creating typologies
  6. Creating taxonomies
  7. Modeling
C. Explaining the data
  8. Asking questions and answering them
  9. Naming a new concept
  10. Interpreting the meaning of the data
  11. Positing relationships among the data
D. Synthesizing the data
  12. Comparing findings with previous studies
  13. Revising preunderstandings and creating new understandings
  14. Interrogating and testing Theory with the data
  15. Creating new Theories based on the data

Figure 0.9  List of types of theorizing.

explaining the data) that probably account for the bulk of ethnomusicological theorizing today. All these categories will be obvious to most ethnomusicologists, but I hope that listing them in this way and discussing them here will clarify the process of ethnomusicological theorizing and its potential for invigorating our field.

The first large category, which I call "organizing the data," consists of four closely related subcategories: (1) analyzing and describing the data, (2) classifying and categorizing the data, (3) labeling categories and classes, and (4) listing categories in some order.

1. Analyzing and describing the data. Analyzing the data is what we routinely do when we describe data points like songs 1, 2, and 3 and performances 1, 2, and 3 and interviews 1, 2, and 3. In the first case we typically apply categories such as mode, scale, and rhythm from our preunderstandings or a Theory of music to the musical material we have collected (see, for a Theory, Rahn 1983). In the second case, we analyze data from behavior during performances, and that too may be driven by preunderstandings of musical and social behavior or by a Theory of the social order that we think is on display in performances. In the third case, we may look inductively for themes that appear in the interviews or for data that confirm hypotheses derived from some Theory we are intent on employing.

2. Classifying and categorizing our data (I take these two words as synonyms). We could, for example, categorize local musical instruments using the Hornbostel-Sachs system (Hornbostel and Sachs 1961) or some native system that we uncover during interviews (Zemp 1978 is a locus classicus).

3. Labeling categories and classes. This is another form of theorizing closely linked to categorizing. The Hornbostel-Sachs musical instrument classification is full of new labels (e.g., fretted, long-necked plucked lute) demanded by their system.

4. Listing of categories in some order. This is another form of theorizing associated with categorizing. It is important, however, to distinguish a list of categories from a list of data points; the former involves theorizing; the latter does not, unless we agree that the collecting of data involves theorizing. One of the important features of listing categories is that lists are, by their nature, incomplete and provisional; this list of categories of theorizing is one example. Another category is always possible, and further theorizing may illustrate connections between these categories.

The second large category of theorizing I call "structuring the data." It consists of three subcategories: (1) creating typologies, (2) creating taxonomies, and (3) modeling.[15] Structuring data in one or more of these ways can be an interesting and important research result with important theoretical implications.

5. Creating typologies. Typologies are classification systems that claim to be complete in a way lists do not. Often they consist of two or a very few mutually exclusive categories: up or down; in or out; fast, medium, or slow. Recently Helen Rees (2016) reported that a young Chinese scholar named Wu Jing created a typology of a rural, working-class phenomenon that middle-class, urban Chinese have dubbed "original ecology folksong." Its four categories are defined by two features, each with two classes: song performances in their original environment or outside their original environment and that are changed or unchanged from their original, rural style (Figure 0.10). A typology like this invites further theorizing in the form of questions. Does the typology account

15. My definitions of the terms *typology, taxonomy,* and *model* are my own. A search of the literature will reveal other definitions, some of which may be useful in further theorizing. In ethnomusicology Kartomi (1990) discusses the enormous variety of instrument classification systems in the world and distinguishes and defines four types of classification "schemes": taxonomies, keys, paradigms, and typologies.

| Original environment, unchanged | Original environment, changed |
|---|---|
| New environment, unchanged | New environment, changed |

**Figure 0.10** A typology of Chinese original ecology folksong performance (after Wu Jing, cited by Rees 2016: 62).

for every instance of the phenomenon, and does every instance fit neatly into its four boxes or do they land on its lines? If some examples land on its lines, between types, is that reason to find the typology wanting and to discard it, or is there a reason to continue to use it?

6. Creating taxonomies. Taxonomies are categorizations in which every category is defined by two positions: it contrasts with some other categories and it is included in some other category. The result is often called a "tree." The Hornbostel-Sachs and Zemp musical instrument classifications are taxonomies. In a more recent example Michael Tenzer (2011) theorizes by providing numerous taxonomies and other "categorization schemes" (p. 380) as "generalized representations of musical time and periodic structures." He concludes with an interesting discussion of the epistemological gap between "the rigors of classification and the truths of experience" (p. 383).

7. Modeling. Modeling is an act of structuring the data in a way that allows patterns in the data to be seen clearly. That some models are simple and not complex is their advantage, not their flaw. Models theorize in at least three ways. First, they predict what will or might happen. Mathematical models are the archetype here, but so are architects' models. Their simple three-dimensional renderings of their two-dimensional drawings allow them and their clients to see the project in miniature before it is built. Second, models suggest relations among the data that have the character of explanations, as, for example, in Merriam's model, which argues that musical change is the result of the interplay among concepts about music, behavior with respect to music, and the music sound itself. Third, models are heuristic tools for asking questions about particular research projects. For example, a researcher could play with my (re)model in Chapter 1 to ask numerous questions of his or her particular study. Was the musical change observed in the last decade the result of shifts in social practices or the intervention of an individual or both in combination? How is individual musical experience affected by the individual's history of involvement with music, and how does his or her position in the social order affect his or her musical experience? When people disagree over

whether or not to preserve or maintain a particular musical practice, what kinds of arguments are adduced by proponents and opponents? Do they harken back to history, memory, and tradition or do they talk about their right or need to be creative in the present or both?

The third large category of theorizing I call "explaining the data." It consists of four subcategories: (1) asking questions and answering them, (2) naming a new concept, (3) interpreting the meaning of the data, and (4) positing relationships among the data. This is probably the most common form of theorizing ethnomusicologists engage in today.

8. Asking questions and answering them. This act of theorizing has the potential to transform our research from the mundane to the exciting, and Anthony Seeger (1987), in his response to my proposed remodeling in Chapter 1, was wise to emphasize it. Sociologist Richard Swedburg (2014a) assigns asking questions of your data a central place in his account of "the art of social theory." He even wryly suggests that if, early in your research during what he calls the prestudy, you have not been able to come up with some interesting questions, you would be well advised to abandon your project and try to find some topic that is interesting. Many articles begin in this fashion, but I will cite a recent one. Leslie Tilley (2014: 482) was surprised to discover, after carefully studying and transcribing examples of the "constantly shifting art of improvised [drumming] patterns" in Bali, that "over-half-century-old patterns [of one musician were] still extant—in an unaltered form—in . . . a faraway and relatively unconnected village." To answer the how and why questions raised by this observation, she turned to ideas from sociolinguistics including "models of language contact and remnant dialectology . . . code-switching, and . . . weak/strong ties to linguistic communities" (pp. 500–501).[16] Whether a study is interesting or not is a subtle, arguable, and little-talked-about point in our field, but when we read the work of others, we often decide whether it is interesting or not and on that basis whether to put it on class reading lists and whether to give the researcher a job or not.

9. Naming a new concept. Naming a new concept is a theorizing gesture that brings into relief an entire constellation of phenomena, perhaps by drawing a boundary around them or by linking them to other domains. For example, naming the buying and selling of recorded and

---

16. I am grateful to Michael Tenzer for referring me to this source.

live music a "musical commodity" links musical practice to commonly
sold products and services that circulate within market economies,
and it directs our attention to different aspects of musicking than
the name "musical artistry" does. Kay Shelemay has done this sort
of theorizing on a number of occasions, naming such phenomena
as "historical ethnomusicology" (Shelemay 1980) and "musical
communities" (Shelemay 2011).

10. Positing relationships among the data. This is perhaps the single most
common form of theorizing in ethnomusicology in recent years,
especially claims about the relationships between musical practices
and social, cultural, political, and economic practices. Some work
also explains the inner workings of musical forms and elements
using transcriptions as a tool. Richard Widdess (1994) involved
his research subjects in this process, and Tara Browner (2009)
transcribed into a score the melody, the drumming, and the dance
steps of Native American pow-wow performances to understand and
illustrate relationships among three simultaneous strands of sonic
and motor experience and to "pay[] respects to Native traditions
and conceptualizations as well" (p. xxvii).[17] Such careful attention to
musical detail can lead to better understandings of the relationship
between musical practice and broader historical and cultural forces.

11. Interpreting the meaning of the data. Interpreting the meaning of the
data typically derives from any number of Theories about music. If the
researcher posits the Theory that music is social behavior, then he or
she will "read" its meanings in terms of its relationship to other social
behaviors. If the researcher holds the Theory that music is a cultural
practice, then he or she will try to find the ways it is similar to or different
from other cultural practices, such as the plastic arts, dance, religion and
ritual, costuming, house architecture, and marriage customs.

The fourth category of theorizing I call "synthesizing the data." It has four
subcategories: (1) comparing findings with previous studies, (2) revising preunderstandings and creating new understandings, (3) interrogating and testing
the Theory with the data, and (4) creating new Theories based on the data. This
is the highest level of theorizing, and one I find too rarely in ethnomusicology.

12. Comparing findings. Comparing findings in the current study with
previous findings on similar themes and traditions in other studies

17. I am grateful to Helen Rees for reminding me of the latter source, which includes transcriptions of thirteen song performances at a single pow-wow and whose introduction on transcription and its relationship to "the work of ethnography" is illuminating.

is the form of theorizing I called for more of in Chapter 5 on the theme of music and identity. In the context of this list of categories of theorizing, it should be clear that it is only one kind of theorizing in ethnomusicology, not the only one or even the best one. In fact, it may be much more common than my partial review of the literature on identity in Chapter 5 would suggest.

13. Revising preunderstandings and creating new understandings. For those not working from Theory, their theorizing should at least result in new understandings. For example, I learned that my preunderstandings of the difference between melody and ornamentation blocked me from understanding how to play the Bulgarian bagpipe. I needed to conceptualize the music in a new way: as hand movements that integrated those concepts into a sonic whole. This way of theorizing may be among the most common that ethnomusicologists report. Timothy Cooley, for example, recently wrote to me, "In Poland, my preunderstanding was that the Tatras were the way they were because of mountain isolation (the story most often told about the Górale of the Tatras). As I worked with my experiences and data, I found that Górale performance cultures and the concept of Górale as an ethnic group itself were instead created and constantly recreated through contact with diverse peoples—from contact, not isolation" (see Cooley 2005). These new understandings might then become the starting point for another round of theorizing.

14. Interrogating and testing Theory with data. If we base our study on a Theory, theorizing about what the data tells us about the Theory is a high-level theorizing move. If the Theory is new and with little empirical grounding, then studies confirming the Theory will be important. If the Theory has, through repeated testing, become a fact (e.g., some people use music to construct a sense of identity), then yet another study confirming the Theory will not be interesting.[18] Of course, in rare instances when our data allows us to refute a Theory, then that would be interesting. In between these extremes lies a huge space for using the results of our particular studies to modify and complicate the Theory.

18. It may come as a surprise that I invoke here the notion of "fact," having given up on absolute truth. Even within a hermeneutic frame, I think it is a useful concept. I once asked a colleague of mine in the physical sciences what he would call a Theory that had been proven over and over, and he answered, "a fact." A good example of this is "evolution," which scientists today take as a fact even though it is often called "the theory of evolution." All the studies in a growing number of sciences have confirmed the basic outlines of evolution, and scientists regard it as a fact of nature, no longer a theory in need of verification, though their studies keep verifying it—until they don't, of course.

15. Creating new Theories. Our research on particular music cultures might result in theorizing that propounds a new Theory, especially if the data do not fit well into existing Theories. The Theory could be about the nature of music, whether as a social, mental, or physical practice or about something local or regional. Such Theories have broad applicability beyond the particular case that generated them and could become a new starting point for research. I find the prospect of such theorizing exciting and admit to a bit of dismay when I read that some ethnomusicologists seem to fear this kind of theorizing. Their fear must come in part from our own experience of being victimized by the grand theory (well, ideology) that European classical music is, as my local radio station puts it, "the best music of all time." Scholars with strong local attachments may fear that claims to generality will erase or distort the richness of local specificity. But scholarship cannot run on fear. Proposing new Theories has to be a part of the game, along with the expectation that they will be critiqued from a variety of local perspectives.

This list of the categories of ethnomusicological theorizing is, by definition, incomplete; it awaits modification and revision. It would be my fondest hope that ethnomusicologists all over the world will join the project of ethnomusicological theorizing and modeling outlined here.[19] I think it is an inclusive, not an exclusive, project. In fact, I would argue that we all already have joined the project, that theorizing is an inherent, inescapable part of everyday life and of ethnomusicological research. We all theorize; it is unavoidable. We are all engaged in one or more of these categories of theorizing. Which ones we choose to engage in is up to us. Our choices have to make sense to us individually, to the music culture we are studying, and to our sense of the field of ethnomusicology. My sense is that our ethnomusicological theorizing must get better and better if our discipline is to enjoy a bright future.

## REFERENCES

Alviso, Ric. 2002. "Musical Aspects of the Corrido, the War on Drugs and Their Convergence in a Federal Prison." PhD dissertation, University of California, Los Angeles.

19. Witzleben (1997, 2010) puts Western and East Asian versions of ethnomusicology into interesting conversations.

Bakan, Michael. 2009. "Measuring Happiness in the Twenty-First Century: Ethnomusicology, Evidence-Based Research, and the New Science of Autism." *Ethnomusicology* 53(3): 510–518.

———. 2015. "'Don't Go Changing to Try and Please Me': Combating Essentialism through Ethnography in the Ethnomusicology of Autism." *Ethnomusicology* 59(1): 116–144.

Berger, Harris M. 1999. *Metal, Rock, and Jazz: Perception and Phenomenology of Musical Experience.* Hanover, NH: University Press of New England.

———. 2009. *Stance: Ideas about Emotion, Style, and Meaning for the Study of Expressive Culture.* Middletown, CT: Wesleyan University Press.

Berliner, Paul. 1978. *The Soul of Mbira: Music and Traditions of the Shona People of Zimbabwe.* Berkeley: University of California Press.

Blacking, John. 1965. *Venda Children's Song: A Study in Ethnomusicological Analysis.* Johannesburg: Witwatersrand University Press.

———. 1973. *How Musical Is Man?* Seattle: University of Washington Press.

Bourdieu, Pierre. 1977. *Outline of a Theory of Practice.* New York: Cambridge University Press.

Browner, Tara. 2009. "The Role of Musical Transcription in the Work of Musical Ethnography." In *Songs from 'A New Circle of Voices': The Sixteenth Annual Pow-Wow at UCLA.* Middleton, WS: A-R Editions, pp. xiii–xxvii.

Chernoff, John Miller. 1979. *African Rhythm and African Sensibility: Aesthetics and Social Action in African Musical Idioms.* Chicago: University of Chicago Press.

Clayton, Martin. 2001. "Introduction: Towards a Theory of Musical Meaning (in India and Elsewhere)." *British Journal of Ethnomusicology* 10(1): 1–17.

Cooley, Timothy J. 2005. *Making Music in the Polish Tatras: Tourists, Ethnographers, and Mountain Musicians.* Bloomington: Indiana University Press.

Crawford, Richard. 1987. "Response to Tim Rice." *Ethnomusicology* 31(3): 511–513.

Daughtry, J. Martin. 2012. "Belliphonic Sounds and Indoctrinated Ears: The Dynamics of Military Listening in Wartime Iraq." In Eric Weisbard, ed., *Pop When the World Falls Apart: Music and Troubled Times.* Durham, NC: Duke University Press, pp. 111–144.

———. 2015. *Listening to War: Sound, Music, Trauma, and Survival in Wartime Iraq.* New York: Oxford University Press.

Dirksen, Rebecca. 2012. "Power and Potential in Contemporary Haitian Music: *Mizik Angaje*, Cultural Action and Community-Led Development in Pre- and Post-Quake Port-au-Prince." PhD dissertation, University of California, Los Angeles.

Feld, Steven. 1982. *Sound and Sentiment: Birds, Weeping, Poetics, and Song in Kaluli Expression.* Philadelphia: University of Pennsylvania Press.

Foucault, Michel. 1980. *Power/Knowledge: Selected Interviews and Other Writings, 1972–1977*, edited by Colin Gordon. New York: Vintage Books.

Garfias, Robert. 1975. *Music of a Thousand Autumns: The Togaku Style of Japanese Court Music.* Berkeley: University of California Press.

Geertz, Clifford. 1973. "Religion as a Cultural System." In *The Interpretation of Cultures: Selected Essays.* New York: Basic Books, pp. 87–125.

Giddens, Anthony. 1979. *Central Problems in Social Theory.* Berkeley: University of California Press.

Gourlay, Kenneth. 1978. "Towards a Reassessment of the Ethnomusicologist's Role in Research." *Ethnomusicology* 22(3): 1–35.

Hernandez, Alejandro. 2014. "The *Son Jarocho* and *Fandango* amidst Struggle and Social Movements: Migratory Transformation and Reinterpretation of the *Son Jarocho* in La Nueva España, México, and the United States." PhD dissertation, University of California, Los Angeles.

Hogan, Brian. 2011. "Enemy Music: Blind Birifor Xylophonists of Northwest Ghana." PhD dissertation, University of California, Los Angeles.

Hood, Mantle. 1971. *The Ethnomusicologist*. New York: McGraw-Hill.

Hornbostel, Erich von, and Curt Sachs. 1961. "Classification of Musical Instruments: Translated from the Original German by Anthony Baines and Klaus P. Wachsmann." *Galpin Society Journal* 14: 3–29.

Howe, Blake, Stephanie Jensen-Moulton, Neil Lerner, and Joseph Straus, eds. 2016. *The Oxford Handbook of Music and Disability Studies*. New York: Oxford University Press.

Kartomi, Margaret. 1990. *On Concepts and Classifications of Musical Instruments*. Chicago: University of Chicago Press.

Keil, Charles. 1979. *Tiv Song*. Chicago: University of Chicago Press.

Killick, Andrew. 2003. "Road Test for a New Model: Korean Musical Narrative and Theater in Comparative Context." *Ethnomusicology* 47(2): 180–204.

Koskoff, Ellen. 1987. "Response to Rice." *Ethnomusicology* 31(3): 497–502.

———. 2010. "Response to Rice: A Re-Call to Arms." *Ethnomusicology* 54(2): 329–331.

———. 2014. *A Feminist Ethnomusicology: Writings on Music and Gender*. Urbana: University of Illinois Press.

Kunst, Jaap. 1959. *Ethnomusicology*, 3rd ed. The Hague: M. Nijhoff.

Lakoff, George, and Mark Johnson. 1980. *Metaphors We Live By*. Chicago: University of Chicago Press.

Lam, Joseph S. C. 1998. *State Sacrifices and Music in Ming China: Orthodoxy, Creativity, and Expressiveness*. Albany: State University of New York Press.

McAllester, David P. 1954. *Enemy Way Music: A Study of Social and Esthetic Values as Seen in Navajo Music*. Cambridge, MA: Peabody Museum.

Merriam, Alan P. 1964. *The Anthropology of Music*. Evanston, IL: Northwestern University Press.

———. 1967. *Music of the Flathead Indians*. Chicago: Aldine.

Mijatovic, Brana. 2003. "Music and Politics in Serbia (1989-2000)." PhD dissertation, University of California, Los Angeles.

Mills, C. Wright. 1959. *The Sociological Imagination*. New York: Oxford University Press.

Mugglestone, Erica, and Guido Adler. 1981. "Guido Adler's 'The Scope, Method, and Aim of Musicology' (1885): An English Translation with an Historico-Analytical Commentary." *Yearbook for Traditional Music* 13: 1–21.

Nettl, Bruno. 1954. *North American Indian Musical Style*. Philadelphia: American Folklore Society.

O'Connell, John Morgan, and Salwa El-Shawan Castelo-Branco, eds. 2010. *Music and Conflict*. Urbana: University of Illinois Press.

Pettan, Svanibor, ed. 1998. *Music, Politics, and War: Views from Croatia*. Zagreb: Institute of Ethnology and Folklore Research.

Pettan, Svanibor, and Jeff Todd Titon, eds. 2015. *The Oxford Handbook of Applied Ethnomusicology*. New York: Oxford University Press.

Rahn, Jay. 1983. *A Theory for All Music: Problems and Solutions in the Analysis of Non-Western Forms*. Toronto: University of Toronto Press.

Rees, Helen. 2016. "Environmental Crisis, Culture Loss, and a New Musical Aesthetic: China's 'Original Ecology Folksongs' in Theory and Practice." *Ethnomusicology* 60(1): 53–88.

Reyes, Adelaida. 1999. *Songs of the Caged, Songs of the Free: Music and the Vietnamese Refugee Experience*. Philadelphia: Temple University Press.

Rhodes, Willard. 1956a. "Toward a Definition of Ethnomusicology." *American Anthropologist* 58(3): 457–463.

——. 1956b. "On the Subject of Ethno-Musicology." *Ethnomusicology* 1(7): 1–9.

Rice, Timothy. 1977. "Polyphony in Bulgarian Folk Music." PhD dissertation, University of Washington, Seattle.

——. 1980a. "A Macedonian *Sobor*: Anatomy of a Celebration." *Journal of American Folklore* 93(368): 113–128.

——. 1980b. "Aspects of Bulgarian Musical Thought." *Yearbook of the International Folk Music Council* 12: 43–67.

——. 1985. "Music That Is Learned but Not Taught: The Bulgarian Case." In *Becoming Human Through Music: The Wesleyan Symposium on the Perspectives of Social Anthropology on the Teaching and Learning of Music*. Reston, VA: Music Educators National Conference, pp. 115–122.

——. 1987. "Toward the Remodeling of Ethnomusicology." *Ethnomusicology* 31(3): 469–488.

——. 1994. *May It Fill Your Soul: Experiencing Bulgarian Music*. Chicago: University of Chicago Press.

——. 1995. "Understanding and Producing the Variability of Oral Tradition: Learning From a Bulgarian Bagpiper." *Journal of American Folklore* 108 (429): 266–276.

——. 2003. "Time, Place, and Metaphor in Musical Experience and Ethnography." *Ethnomusicology* 47(2): 151–179.

——. 2010. "Disciplining *Ethnomusicology*: A Call for a New Approach." *Ethnomusicology* 54(2): 318–325.

——. 2014. *Ethnomusicology: A Very Short Introduction*. New York: Oxford University Press.

Ricoeur, Paul. 1981. *Hermeneutics and the Human Sciences*, edited and translated by John B. Thompson. Evanston, IL: Northwestern University Press.

Ritter, Jonathan. 2006. "A River of Blood: Music, Memory, and Violence in Ayacucho, Peru." PhD dissertation, University of California, Los Angeles.

Ritter, Jonathan, and J. Martin Daughtry, eds. 2007. *Music in the Post-9/11 World*. New York: Routledge.

Seeger, Anthony. 1987. "Do We Need to Remodel Ethnomusicology?" *Ethnomusicology* 31(3): 491–495.

——. 1992. "Ethnography of Music." In Helen Myers, ed., *Ethnomusicology: An Introduction*. London: Macmillan, pp. 88–109.

——. 2006. "Lost Lineages and Neglected Peers: Ethnomusicologists Outside Academia." *Ethnomusicology* 50(2): 214–235.

Seeger, Charles. 1977. "Toward a Unitary Field Theory for Musicology." In *Studies in Musicology, 1935-1975*. Berkeley: University of California Press, pp. 102–138. Originally published in 1970 in *Selected Reports in Ethnomusicology* 1(3): 171–210.

Shelemay, Kay Kaufman. 1980. "'Historical Ethnomusicology': Reconstructing Falasha Liturgical History." *Ethnomusicology* 24(2): 233–258.

———. 1987. "Response to Rice." *Ethnomusicology* 31(3): 489–490.

———. 2011. "Musical Communities: Rethinking the Collective in Music." *Journal of the American Musicological Society* 64(2): 349–390.

Silvers, Michael. 2012. "Sounding Ceará: Music and the Environment in Northeastern Brazil." PhD dissertation, University of California, Los Angeles.

Slobin, Mark. 1976. *Music in the Culture of Northern Afghanistan*. Tucson: University of Arizona Press.

———. 1993. *Subcultural Sounds: Micromusics of the West*. Middletown, CT: Wesleyan University Press.

———. 2010. "Rice's 'Crisis.'" *Ethnomusicology* 54(2): 337–338.

Solis, Gabriel. 2012. "Thoughts on an Interdiscipline: Music Theory, Analysis, and Social Theory in Ethnomusicology." *Ethnomusicology* 56(3): 530–554.

Sparshott, Francis E. 1980. "Aesthetics." In Stanley Sadie, ed., *The New Grove Dictionary of Music and Musicians*. Vol. 1. London: Macmillan, 120–134

Stokes, Martin. 2010. "Response to Rice." *Ethnomusicology* 54(2): 339–341.

Stone, Ruth M. 1982. *Let the Inside Be Sweet: The Interpretation of Music Event among the Kpelle of Liberia*. Bloomington: Indiana University Press.

———. 2008. *Theory for Ethnomusicology*. Upper Saddle River, NJ: Pearson Prentice-Hall.

Sugarman, Jane. 2010. "Building and Teaching Theory in Ethnomusicology." *Ethnomusicology* 54(2): 341–344.

Swedburg, Richard. 2014a. *The Art of Social Theory*. Princeton, NJ: Princeton University Press.

———, ed. 2014b. *Theorizing in Social Science: The Context of Discovery*. Stanford, CA: Stanford University Press.

Tenzer, Michael, ed. 2006. *Analytical Studies in World Music*. New York: Oxford University Press.

———. 2011. "Generalized Representations of Musical Time and Periodic Structures." *Ethnomusicology* 55(3): 369–386.

———. 2015. "Meditations on Objective Aesthetics in World Music." *Ethnomusicology* 59(1): 369–386.

Tilley, Leslie. 2014. "Dialect, Diffusion, and Balinese Drumming: Using Sociolinguistic Models for the Analysis of Regional Variation in Kendang Arja." *Ethnomusicology* 58(3): 481–505.

Titon, Jeff Todd, ed. 2009. *Worlds of Music: An Introduction to the Music of the World's Peoples*. Shorter Version, 3rd ed. New York: Schirmer.

Turino, Thomas. 1999. "Signs of Imagination, Identity, and Experience: A Peircian Semiotic Theory for Music." *Ethnomusicology* 43(2): 221–255.

———. 2000. *Nationalists, Cosmopolitans, and Popular Music in Zimbabwe*. Chicago: University of Chicago Press.

———. 2008. *Music as Social Life: The Politics of Participation*. Chicago: University of Chicago Press.

———. 2014. "Peircean Thought as Core Theory for a Phenomenological Ethnomusicology." *Ethnomusicology* 58(2): 185–221.

———. 2015. "On Theory and Models: How to Make Our Ideas Clear." In Victoria Lindsay Levine and Philip V. Bohlman, eds., *This Thing Called Music: Essays in Honor of Bruno Nettl*. Lanham, MD: Rowman & Littlefield, pp. 378–390.

Van Buren, Kathleen. 2006. "Stealing Elephants, Creature Futures: Exploring Uses of Music and Other Arts for Community Education in Nairobi, Kenya." PhD dissertation, University of California, Los Angeles.

Warden, Nolan. 2016. "Ethnomusicology's 'Identity' Problem: The History and Definitions of a Troubled Term in Music Research." *El oído pensante* 4(2). http://ppct. caicytgov.ar/index.php/oidopensante [Accessed 9/12/216].

Widdess, Richard. 1994. "Involving the Performers in Transcription and Analysis: A Collaborative Approach to *Dhrupad*." *Ethnomusicology* 38(1): 59–80.

Witzleben, J. Lawrence. 1997. "Whose Ethnomusicology?: Western Ethnomusicology and the Study of Asian Music." *Ethnomusicology* 41(2): 220–242.

———. 2010. "Performing in the Shadows: Learning and Making Music as Ethnomusicological Practice and Theory." *Yearbook for Traditional Music* 42: 135–166.

Yung, Bell, and Helen Rees, eds. 1999. *Understanding Charles Seeger, Pioneer in American Musicology*. Urbana: University of Illinois Press.

Zemp, Hugo. 1978. "'Are'are Classification of Musical Types and Instruments." *Ethnomusicology* 22(1): 37–67.

# Toward the Remodeling
# of Ethnomusicology

Ethnomusicology, like any academic field, is constantly being created and recreated through the research, writing, and teaching of its practitioners. Direct
action in the form of new data, interpretations, theories, and methods effectively
defines the field. Modeling a discipline, on the other hand, requires a step back
from direct engagement in research to ask the descriptive question, what are we
doing?, and the prescriptive question, what ought we be doing? The answer will
surely depend on the intellectual and social matrix of the modeler (Blum 1975;
C. Seeger 1977), and the effectiveness of the model will depend on the extent
to which it either captures simply and elegantly the current work being done in
the field or provides a kind of "moral imperative" for future action.

Probably the best example of an effective model in the recent history of ethnomusicology is Merriam's model proposed in 1964 in the *The Anthropology of
Music.* His "simple model . . . involves study on three analytic levels—conceptualization about music, behavior in relation to music, and music sound itself"
(Merriam 1964: 32). The model is essentially circular in form (Figure 1.1), with
concept affecting behavior, which produces the sound product. And, Merriam
continues, "there is a constant feedback from the product to the concepts about
music, and this is what accounts both for change and stability in a music system" (p. 33). This model was seminal in the history of ethnomusicology and to
that date was the most forceful and cogent statement of anthropological concerns with respect to music. The model defined ethnomusicology as "the study
of music in culture" and that view—even as modified to "music as culture" and
"the relationship between music and culture"—has remained one of the core
concepts in the discipline ever since.

We can of course argue about the extent of its influence during the last
twenty years, but there can be no doubt that it continues to be influential. It is

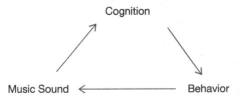

**Figure 1.1** The Merriam model.

still frequently cited to contextualize particular research problems (e.g., Yung 1984; Sawa 1983); Bruno Nettl (1983) called it "definitive," not just of the study of music but apparently of music itself; and it provided the basic model for the collaborative textbook *Worlds of Music* (Titon 1984). If that book's authors, coming from a very wide range of backgrounds, could agree on this model, then the continuing extent of its influence is clear—at least as an overall image or model of the field.

In addition to defining the field and being influential, Merriam's model has three other attractive properties that make it a useful foil for the "remodeling" proposed here. First, it is a simple model with three analytic levels. Part of the reason it has been influential is that it is easy to remember. Second, its levels seem to be relatively complete and inclusive. They cover a broad range of concerns. Third, it is a cogent model in the sense that its analytic levels are supposed to interrelate. In spite of these attractive properties, I acknowledge that not everyone has agreed with this model, and we have certainly wrestled with it as much as we have embraced it. But because it is simple, inclusive, cogent, definitive, and influential, I am going to refer to it frequently in the "remodeling" that follows, partly because I hope the model proposed here has many of these same qualities.[1]

The first and most immediate effect of the Merriam model was to increase the amount and prestige of work done on social, physical, and verbal behaviors associated with music. Its second effect was to set in motion a search for ways to relate these behaviors to the "music sound itself." Much of the subsequent work in "the anthropological study of music" (Blacking 1979) can be interpreted as attempts to find the points of intersection, causation, or homologies between Merriam's analytic levels.

In the search for those connections, a number of social science paradigms have been borrowed and invoked over the last twenty years, including biological approaches (Blacking 1977), semiotics (Nattiez 1983), ethnoscience (Zemp 1978), ethnography of performance (Herndon and McLeod 1980) and

1. For a recent list of "research models" in ethnomusicology, see Modir (1986).

communications (Feld 1984), structuralism (A. Seeger 1980), symbolic inter-
actionism (Stone 1982), Marxism (Shepherd 1982), hermeneutics (Becker
and Becker 1984), and an eclectic mix of numerous approaches (Feld 1982).
Although these paradigms and methods are often seen as conflicting or mutually exclusive within anthropology and sociology, and certainly differ from the
structural functionalism behind Merriam's *The Anthropology of Music,* their
application within ethnomusicology can be interpreted as an attempt to solve
the central problem created by Merriam's model: how can we convincingly
speak about the relationship between music and other human behaviors?

Although much of the "theory" developed in ethnomusicology over the last
twenty years has addressed this question, there are obvious signs of resistance
to the sought-after perfect union between so-called musicological and anthropological approaches. An incident from 1985's annual meeting in Vancouver
can serve to illustrate the divergence of opinion in the field and some of the
continued resistance to anthropological approaches. During the discussion following Stephen Blum's paper, "The Ethnomusicologist vis-à-vis the Fallacies
of Contemporary Musical Life," someone commented that in the paper and
response and discussion to that point, he had not heard much reference to contemporary social theory, particularly coming out of anthropology, and worried
that ethnomusicologists were perhaps twenty years out of date in their view
of society and culture. The responses by prominent ethnomusicologists to this
observation covered an astonishing range. Someone responded that she and
probably others did keep up; someone else said she wished she could keep up
but was so busy as a teacher covering "the whole earth" that she couldn't keep
up; and two people responded essentially with, "Who cares if we keep up?" If
anyone were laboring under the impression that ethnomusicology was a unified discipline or even that there was widespread agreement that it represented
a union of anthropological and musicological approaches, this interchange
would have been illuminating and perhaps discouraging.

In addition to this lack of agreement about the methods and disciplinary
roots of our field, there is evidence of pessimism about what we have achieved
in the way of a union between anthropological and musicological approaches
even by those deeply committed to such a union.[2] Gerard Béhague (1984:
7) recently wrote that "our analytical tools for establishing that relationship
[between "social context" and "music sound structure"] unequivocally lack in
sophistication." Herndon and McLeod (1979: iii), in the late 1970s, still complained that "the wholeness ... which gives equal consideration to the music,

2. Carol Robertson (1984: 450) complained of the "dozens of dissertations" that comment on
"ecology, geography and history without tying these introductory chapters into subsequent
chapters on musical sounds."

itself, and the behavior surrounding its origin, production, and evaluation still eludes us." Ruth Stone (1982: 127), whose innovative approach to event analysis was designed to solve this problem, admits that "it is not yet possible to achieve the ideal unitary analysis."

Thus, ethnomusicology seems to be in a rather odd position. On the one hand, we have an old model that continues to exert a fair bit of influence and to define the core problem for the field. On the other hand, there is pessimism about the extent of our achievements in solving the problem, continued open resistance to anthropological models,[3] and competition among a host of social science paradigms that have been rushed into the breach in an attempt to solve all or some of our problems. In this context, I think it is time to rethink the relationship between ethnomusicology and its cognate disciplines and perhaps, like an old house, remodel it along lines that describe and prescribe what we actually do rather than what particular scholarly traditions tell us we ought to do.

Some might argue that modeling a discipline is not necessary. Obviously research will continue largely along lines dictated by personal interest, intellectual training, traditions of scholarship, and social and institutional demands. Yet disciplinary models are attractive for a number of reasons.[4] They provide a kind of intellectual framework that helps us contextualize, interpret, classify, and evaluate our work, and they can provide some sense of direction or purpose. Lewis Thomas (1974), the well-known essayist on biological topics, characterizes the scientific enterprise as analogous to the building of an anthill. He guesses that individual ants, like most scientists, have no idea of the shape of the anthill they are building. The combined intelligence of masses of ants and scientists achieves spectacular results even though individual ants and scientists cannot imagine exactly to what purpose their work is directed. Modeling is an

3. Larry Shumway (1986) criticizes *Worlds of Music* for a "social science orientation" with not enough emphasis on aesthetics and the personal experience of music, a sign that he and others still resist the emphases of much recent research and writing.

4. While the best writers in any field probably have no need for simple models, it strikes me that models may be particularly helpful to students and others trying to find a context for their work. I did a casual survey of dissertations completed in the last seven years at US schools of ethnomusicology and was surprised, perhaps naively, to find that few contextualized their work even perfunctorily within a general theoretical framework in ethnomusicology—they simply considered a particular musical tradition and previous scholarship on it. (The exceptions tended to be work on ethnicity and identity, for which there is a clear and identifiable body of literature.) In effect, ethnomusicology does not exist as a discipline in these dissertations. If they can be taken as an indicator of the field, then ethnomusicology is, as Blacking (1971: 94) has lamented, "little more than a meeting ground for those interested in the anthropology of music and in music of different cultures." A model, particularly an inclusive one of the sort being suggested here, might allow a higher percentage of students and scholars than at present to imagine the general shape of the field and the place of their work in it.

attempt to imagine the shape—however hazy—of the metaphorical anthill that we are building.

## THE MODEL

There are two immediate, personal sources for the model presented here. One comes from my teaching experience, the other from reading in the secondary literature. First, I teach an introductory course to all first-year students in a large conservatory-style music program at the University of Toronto. The course treats all kinds of music (Western and non-Western, classical, folk, popular, and so on) as a prelude to a more detailed study of Western classical music. The course description, generated in committee, reads, "Formative processes in music cultures of the world." Thus, I have been forced to wonder in a very practical, pedagogical context just what the formative processes in music are. Are they melody, harmony, and rhythm, as some of my colleagues in the faculty of music seem to imagine? Or are they the relationship between music and politics, economics, social structure, music events, and language, as ethnomusicologists have claimed in the last twenty years? Was there a way to pull some semblance of order out of the long lists one could make? Was there a way of reconciling the music structural concerns of many music history courses with the anthropological concerns of many ethnomusicology courses?[5]

I developed various ways to deal with this problem, and then about four years ago, while rereading Clifford Geertz's *The Interpretation of Cultures,* I was struck by his claim that "symbolic systems ... are historically constructed, socially maintained and individually applied" (1973: 363–364). Instantly I recognized these as the "formative processes" that I had been searching for. Here was a three-part model, analogous to Merriam's, that was easy to remember and that seemed to balance social, historical, and individual processes and forces in ways that seemed immediately and intuitively satisfying. The Merriam model, or at least its working out over the last twenty years, has tended to lead to an emphasis on social processes and, as a consequence, alienated ethnomusicology from the concerns of historical musicology. How could one teach about all music when the perspectives brought to bear on different musics seemed so different?

---

5. While the perspectives brought to bear on Western and non-Western music often seem different, that does not imply, as Kerman (1985: 174) has suggested, that "Western music is just too different from other musics, and its cultural contexts too different from other cultural contexts" to allow ethnomusicological research to "impinge directly on the study of Western music." It is not the music and contexts that are so different as to preclude comparative study so much as it is the mainstream approaches and values in the two areas that often seem to be at odds.

I would like to examine the implications of a slightly modified form of this statement by Geertz as a "model for ethnomusicology." Simply put, I now believe that ethnomusicologists should study the formative processes in music, that they should ask and attempt to answer this deceptively simple question: how do people make music, or, in its more elaborate form, how do people historically construct, socially maintain, and individually create and experience music?[6]

It is hard to capture the overlapping strands of theory and practice as they currently operate in our field, but if this statement by Geertz struck a responsive chord in me, then it probably is because this sort of thinking is in the air. When I looked more closely at recent literature with this model in mind, I indeed found pre-echoes of it in the writing of a number of our colleagues.[7] For example, Herndon and McLeod ask this same question (i.e., how does man make music?), in their book, *Music as Culture,* but do not then go on to make the coherent series of claims that this model does. John Blacking has argued perhaps most persuasively for the emphasis on process, as opposed to product, that is modeled here.

6. Another slightly more cumbersome way to articulate the question might be:

$$\text{how do people} \left\{ \begin{array}{l} \text{historically} \\ \text{socially} \\ \text{individually} \end{array} \right\} \left\{ \begin{array}{l} \text{create/construct} \\ \text{maintain} \\ \text{experience} \end{array} \right\} \text{music?}$$

The question might also be phrased, how and why do people make music?, but the answer to the "why" question may follow rather naturally from a consideration of "how." In any case, Herndon and McLeod (1979) and Erdman (1982), among others, have all retreated from asking why to asking how. Blacking (1976b: 4) has pointed out that there are important senses in which music makes man, but while this is an engaging aphorism, I prefer the notion that man is always the active agent in the creation, experience, and maintenance of music.

7. J. H. Kwabena Nketia (1981, 1985) has struggled with the problem of defining the field in two interesting articles. Among other things, he is critical of a shift of emphasis from musical experience to the behavior that surrounds music and the assumption "that there is a one-to-one correspondence and a relationship of causality between aspects of music and aspects of culture and society.... The assumption is not easily demonstrated even for individual cultures" (1981: 24–25). In his 1985 study he complains that "current approaches in ethnomusicology tend to be monistic or characterised by one dimension of music" (p. 12). He then goes on to call for "the development of an integrative technique that enables the scholar to group and regroup his data" (p. 15) and for "developing methods of synthesis that bring together the different aspects of music and music making in a meaningful and coherent manner" (p. 18)—precisely the kind of approach being modeled here. He goes on to construct a categorization of the field based on "three cognitive dimensions of music" (p. 14), which really are more like three methodological stances vis-à-vis music: as culture, as the object of aesthetic interest, and as language. He claims that his cognitive dimensions provide scope for this integrative approach but, without demonstrating how this might happen, leaves it as a "challenge" for ethnomusicology. In fact, it may be precisely this sort of methodological classification, which seems to separate rather than unite us, that may have to be overcome or altered.

Probably the place where the general emphases of this model are currently being worked on most clearly is in the area of performance practice or ethnography of performance and communications. Steven Feld (1984: 6), for example, argues for a focus on listeners "as socially and historically implicated beings"—a statement that captures the three poles of this model. Bonnie Wade (1984: 47) points out that "creativity in the performance practice of Indian art music ... involves ... the role of the individual performer, how he sees his own creativity in relationship to his musical tradition, to his fellow performers, and to his audience." Creativity as individual experience, history as tradition, and social processes involving musicians and audience represent one of many ways that the three parts of this model can be interrelated to tell an interesting story. That story gets at fundamental musical processes without belaboring points about homologies between musical and cultural forms, and yet it manages to integrate the study of music into the study of history, society, and cognition.

Kenneth Gourlay (1982: 413) came very close to modeling the field along these lines. Gourlay's A.B.C. calls for "a humanizing ethnomusicology with three distinct, if related, fields of inquiry." "A," for Armstrong's affecting presence, involves the study of "how musical symbols operate to produce their effect or meaning, and what effects they produce." "B" stands for Blacking's model of change, and "C" stands for condition, context, and conceptualization. He does not go on to show, however, how the three fields can be related.[8]

Thus, the general outline of the model proposed here is clearly in the wind. But this relatively recent atmosphere in the field has yet to be developed into a simple, cogent, and inclusive model, and to have its implications for the field examined.

## THE PARTS OF THE MODEL

First, the model needs to be explained in terms of how it organizes the welter of "issues and concepts," to use Nettl's (1983) phrase, generated by ethnomusicologists.

---

8. The thrust of this model may, at first glance, appear to be insular and academic, in comparison to Gourlay's simultaneously pessimistic and activist "humanizing ethnomusicology." In fact, the model has as an important component of its social matrix the teaching enterprise. What are the important lessons about music that we want to convey in the course of a pedagogical process that, at its best and most optimistic, ought to be "humanizing"? I see a great potential for a model like this at least to humanize the environments in which we work and the students and colleagues whom we teach.

"Historical construction" comprises two important processes: the process of change with the passage of time and the process of re-encountering and recreating the forms and legacy of the past in each moment of the present.[9] In synchronic, "in time" studies of music in a particular place at a particular time, the study of historically constructed forms as a legacy of the past finds a place here. Jean-Jacques Nattiez (1983: 472) has deplored what he calls the synchronic "culturalism" of much current ethnomusicology and argues for a greater emphasis on diachronic approaches to musical form. However, he concludes that "music generates music." I prefer this model's claim that people generate music while at the same time acknowledging the formative power of previously constructed musical forms. Individuals operating in society must come to grips with, learn, and choose among a host of previously constructed musical forms. Although this process is normally acted out in specific instances of learning, listening, and playing using the medium of music itself, analogous behavior in the speech domain requires musicologists to describe the intricacies of forms in words. Both operations—musician/performers making music for musician/listeners and musicologists writing or speaking to their readers or audience—require a sophisticated encounter with historically constructed forms.[10]

Historical construction can also be interpreted as the diachronic, "out of time" study of musical change or the history of music. In spite of the notorious difficulty of constructing music histories in many of the cultures we typically consider, ethnomusicologists have been fascinated by the issue of change. It

9. A third approach to historical issues is Kay Shelemay's (1980: 233) notion of "historical ethnomusicology," which involves "the potential that a synchronic study holds for illuminating the historical continuum from which it emerged," a remarkable reversal of the usual claims about the ability of history to illuminate the present. (For another recent reversal of the usual approach to history, see Yung's [1987] notion of "historical interdependency" as a process by which the new affects the perception, construction, and revision of the past.) Shelemay thinks that "the lack of emphasis on historical studies is the result of the break with historical musicology." The lack of emphasis, however, may be more in theory than in practice. Although our methods rest heavily on fieldwork and an implicitly synchronic approach to the "ethnographic present," a large percentage of our published work focuses on processes of change, either directly observed or reconstructed from previously available data. We have, in practice, identified change and historical processes not just as one of many processes, but as a fundamental one. Probably historical processes and interpretations have been resorted to as convenient interpretive gestures when social and cultural processes and interpretations were not observed or were more problematic.

10. Gourlay (1982: 142) objects that analysis is not an approach "to understanding what happens when men and women make music," but it may be a key to understanding what happened when people made music, to reconstructing past experience, and to understanding musical creativity (e.g., Cavanagh 1982).

would be descriptively accurate and therefore useful to have a model of our field that reflects the central importance of change, of historical processes. For us, history or "historical ethnomusicology," to use Kay Shelemay's phrase, does not, in fact, seem to be one of many issues, but a primary issue, a fundamental process, a given of music making, and this model acknowledges that by elevating the study of change to the highest analytical level of the model.[11,12]

Processes of social maintenance have been particularly well documented by ethnomusicologists in the years since Merriam's *The Anthropology of Music*, and it is easy to construct at least a partial list of the way music is sustained, maintained, and altered by socially constructed institutions and belief systems: ecology, economics, and the patronage of music; the social structure of music and musicians; protest, censorship, and the politics of music; performance contexts and conventions; beliefs about the power and structure of music; music education and training; and so on. The study of the processes by which these social systems impact music and, conversely, how music impacts these systems has been one of the most fruitful areas of research in the last twenty years, whether expressed in terms of context, causal relations, homologies, or deep-structural relations.

Emphasis on the individual is probably the most recent and as yet weakest area of development in ethnomusicology. While the study of individual composers and individual acts of creation is well entrenched in historical musicology, such studies have remained until very recently suspect in ethnomusicology. The antagonism and even fear of humanistic, historical, or individual approaches is exemplified in this statement of Judith and A. L. Becker (1984: 455):

A move toward the study of particularities nudges ethnomusicology away from the social sciences into the realm of the humanities where uniqueness is legitimate. Our discipline has historically been allied with the social sciences; we take our paradigms from the social sciences. Any step toward the humanities also feels like a step toward the approaches of traditional

11. Bielawski (1985) attempts to develop a full-blown theory of historical perspectives in ethnomusicology and emphasizes them—perhaps not surprising for an Eastern European—in his statement of basic goals for the field: "To study music from various historical points of view should be the aim of contemporary ethnomusicology" (p. 14). He goes on to argue that systematic and historical perspectives are "supplementary and interdependent," but like so many other claims along this line, he does not go on to say how precisely this might work.

12. McLean (1980: 53): "The one means of compiling a 'history' of Oceanic music is to begin with music styles as currently practised." The study and description of musical styles on the modern map is the beginning of an attempt to reconstruct history (see Nattiez [1982] for an example of a theoretical map with historical density).

historical musicology with its outworn methodology and unexamined assumptions.

They then invoke another paradigm they call literary criticism, ironically an approach deeply rooted in the humanities but that has recently been taken over by social science. The interpretive anthropology of Geertz and others seems to move the social sciences in the direction of the humanities and drastically reduces the need for the fear and trembling one senses on both sides of this apparently once-formidable division. This model, in fact, does move ethnomusicology closer to the humanities and historical musicology (and might have the effect of moving historical musicology closer to ethnomusicology), but without giving up an essential concern for the social bases of musical life and experience or a general scholarly concern for generalization and comparison.

John Blacking has emerged as a clear advocate of approaches to the study of the individual in a number of recent articles, but he too betrays a fear of individuality when he argues that it is not Mozart's uniqueness but his capacity to share that is important (1979). A balanced approach must be willing to acknowledge the extent and importance of individuality and uniqueness in particular societies, and finding a balance between historical, social, and individual processes should be an important part of "the interpretation of [musical] cultures." The work of Ellen Koskoff (1982), Dane Harwood (1976), Bruno Nettl (1983), Klaus Wachsmann (1982), Steven Feld (1984), and the writers of *Worlds of Music* (1984) has moved us substantially in the direction of increased consideration of individual creativity and personal experience as legitimate objects of scholarly enquiry.

Some of the issues that might be discussed under individual creativity and experience include composition, improvisation, and performances of particular pieces, repertories, and styles; perception of musical form and structure; emotional, physical, spiritual, and multisensory experience mediated by music; and individual cognitive structures for organizing musical experience and associating it with other experiences. If interest in the individual and individual experience continues to grow, then eventually the history of ethnomusicology might be interpreted as having moved successively through the three stages of this model, from a concern with historical and evolutionary questions in its early "comparative musicology" stage, to a concern for music in social life after *The Anthropology of Music*, to a concern for the individual in history and society in the most recent or next phase.

In fact, the work actually being done in the field today is rather well balanced between these approaches. The articles in *Ethnomusicology* in the eight-year period from 1979 to 1986 contain a good balance among these approaches. The largest group predictably emphasizes social processes, but a perhaps surprising number look at individual processes as well:

| | |
|---|---|
| general theory and method | 13% |
| surveys | 4% |
| music analysis | 10% |
| history/change | 22% |
| social processes | 34% |
| individual processes | 17% |
| Total | 100% |

Thus, it seems that this model rather effectively reflects not just the current theoretical atmosphere in the field but also the balance in the actual work we are doing. It is an accepting model in which virtually everyone in the field can find a place for his or her work.

## INTERPRETATION IN THE MODEL

Perhaps the most exciting feature of this model is the richness of interpretation that it suggests, hardly surprising since it was originally sparked by a book entitled *The Interpretation of Cultures*. In fact, the model suggests four hierarchical levels of interpretation (Figure 1.2).

To be effective, a model should be dynamic or cogent; that is, it should imply or suggest ways to relate the parts of the model to one another. In fact, this model strikes me as particularly dynamic in the sense that its parts can so easily be shown to interlock and interrelate. If the levels easily interrelate, then the move from description to interpretation and explanation, which bedevils the Merriam model, should be straightforward and in fact a feature of this model.

The main interpretive problem set up by the Merriam model was to find ways to relate music sound to conceptualization and behavior, and I have already written about some of the pessimism about what we have achieved. A striking recent statement of the difficulty of interpretation presented by the Merriam model comes from *Worlds of Music*, which uses it. Speaking of dividing music cultures into "parts" along the lines of the Merriam model, Titon et al. (1984) write: "At best, isolating parts of a music-culture for study is an oversimplification; at worst, an untruth. But given the limitations of courses and textbooks, it is our only recourse" (p. 9).

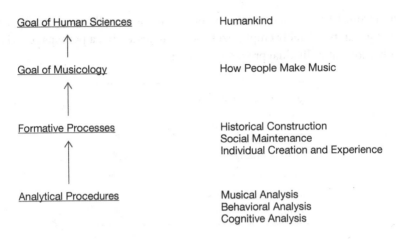

| Goal of Human Sciences | Humankind |
| Goal of Musicology | How People Make Music |
| Formative Processes | Historical Construction<br>Social Maintenance<br>Individual Creation and Experience |
| Analytical Procedures | Musical Analysis<br>Behavioral Analysis<br>Cognitive Analysis |

**Figure 1.2** Hierarchy of levels in the model.

All of us sympathize with their dilemma precisely because it is not just a dilemma of courses and textbooks, but a dilemma for ethnomusicology as a whole. J. H. Kwabena Nketia (1985) called for "the development of an integrative technique that enables the scholar to group and regroup his data" (p. 15) and for "methods of synthesis that bring together the different aspects of music and music making in a meaningful and coherent manner" (p. 18). He called this a "challenge" for ethnomusicology, and this model is an attempt to respond to that challenge.

At the first and lowest level of interpretation, I suggest that instead of or in addition to seeking to relate the levels of Merriam's model to each other through cause, homologies, or correspondences, we embed them within the levels of this model and ask how they contribute to the formative processes we have identified (Figure 1.3).

A rich story could presumably be told about how changes in sound, concept, and behavior contribute to the historical construction of a particular kind of music (e.g., Cavanagh 1982). Another story might revolve around the social forces that maintain sound structures, assign them meaning and value, and generate behaviors consistent across both musical and nonmusical domains. A third story might treat the range of individual variation in ideas, behaviors, and music in a given musical culture. In this model, Merriam's analytic levels can still be used, but the way they are related to one another is a little more flexible and varied than a monolithic search for causes and homologies, and thus easier to achieve. Furthermore, instead of sanctioning formal descriptions of either sound, cognition, or behavior, as interesting as they might be, this model demands an interpretation of what our descriptions imply about our knowledge of fundamental formative processes. For example, a formal

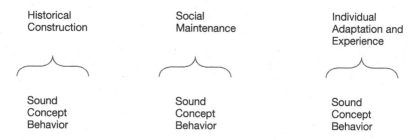

| Historical Construction | Social Maintenance | Individual Adaptation and Experience |
| --- | --- | --- |
| Sound Concept Behavior | Sound Concept Behavior | Sound Concept Behavior |

Figure 1.3 Merriam's levels embedded in this model.

analysis of the "music sound itself" might yield interpretations of a piece's importance in the historical construction of the style, of individual creative processes as evidenced in the piece or performance, or of elements in the cultural or social system that affected elements of form. Good writing in ethnomusicology already does these sorts of things, and that is why I claim that the interpretations demanded by this model are relatively easy and enormously varied. It is a rich model allowing for a variety of perspectives, not a narrow model with a single perspective.

Moving to a second, higher level in this model, we can ask how its parts interrelate to generate interpretations. Two main structural problems with Merriam's model have led to problems of interpretation, whereas this model solves them. First, in the Merriam model, music sound is directly contrasted to behavior and cognition. Having separated music from context in this artificial way, we have struggled ever since to put this particular Humpty-Dumpty back together again. In the model proposed here, the analysis of music, the study of the music sound itself, is demoted to a lower level of the model, while people's actions in creating, experiencing, and using music become the goal of the inquiry. Instead of trying to find homologies between unlike things—sound, concepts, and behaviors—this model tries to integrate and relate like things, namely, three formative processes.

The second structural problem with Merriam's model is that the relations between his analytic levels go only in one direction and relate one level to only one other (see Figure 1.1). In this model, on the other hand, each level is connected to the other two in a dialectical, or two-way, relationship. There are simply more relationships in this model and thus more possibilities for interpretation. Each process can thus be explained in terms of the other two (Figure 1.4). Historical construction can be explained in terms of both changes in patterns of social maintenance and individual creative decisions. Individual creation and experience can be seen as determined partly by historically constructed forms as learned, performed, and modified in socially maintained and sanctioned contexts. Social maintenance can be seen as an ongoing interaction

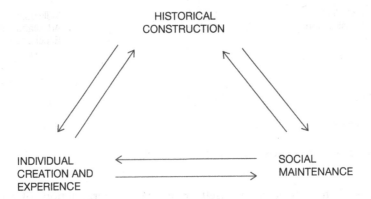

**Figure 1.4** Relationships in the model.

between historically constructed modes of behavior (traditions if you will) and individual action that recreates, modifies, and interprets that tradition. Thus, the levels in this model are on a metaphorical "rubber band": they can be pulled apart to be analyzed but they keep wanting to snap back together. This gives the model a certain dynamic, interpretive energy, to extend the metaphor, and allows the telling of many interesting stories. In general, application of this model demands a move from description to interpretation and explanation and provides a flexible, varied, and rather easy way to do it, or at least to imagine how to do it.

If we are able to identify and relate fundamental formative processes in particular ethnographic situations, then this should lead us to the third level of interpretation in the model, which is a concern for general statements about how people make music. The model thus leads us to a comparative stance with respect to music. If we can keep before us an image of fundamental formative processes that operate in many cultures, this should lead us to create microstudies that can be compared to other microstudies, as opposed to the detailed, independent, and insular studies that seem to proliferate in the ethnomusicological literature at present.

One example of how the model was used in a particular situation and had a comparative effect was a paper by Stephen Satory, a graduate student at the University of Toronto, who decided to use the model in his report of fieldwork in the Hungarian community in Toronto for the 1985 Niagara chapter meeting of the Society for Ethnomusicology. Subtitling his paper "The Role of History, Society and the Individual," he analyzed the musical life of Hungarians in Toronto, and particularly the position and importance of the dynamic revival movement involving improvised dancing called *tanchaz*, or "dance house," begun in the early 1970s in Budapest. Although he could have focused on any part of the model, he chose to address all three parts of it. Having committed himself to the model, he was constantly forced by it to move beyond a description of what he had observed to interpretations of broader processes. In his discussion of historical construction, he periodized immigration patterns, discussed the rise of community social institutions in Toronto to support cultural expression, and distinguished five types of transmission of the tradition, many of them involving specific individual actions. As for social maintenance, he compared this tradition in three locales: in the villages of Transylvania where the forms originated, in Budapest, and in Toronto. He interpreted its lack of popularity in Toronto, compared to its importance in Hungarian venues, as a consequence of the differing political, social, and intellectual climate in the three places, concluding among other things that the unstructured, improvisational aspects of the tradition do not correspond to the goal and work-oriented values of Hungarian immigrants to Toronto. In spite of its lack of popularity and community support, however, the tradition lives in Toronto through the agency of a relatively small number of individuals who value it variously as a means of ethnic group identity, nostalgia for village life, a source of friendships, exercise, and the aesthetic pleasure of skill and virtuosity. Using the model allowed Stephen to rework his material from a number of different perspectives, and the interpretations he made of his particular data linked his work to the work of many others.

At the Niagara meeting, his paper was one of four papers on immigrant musical traditions in North America. In the discussion that followed, Stephen's paper became the focus of comment not because it was the best researched, had the richest data, or concerned the most colorful tradition, but because it was the only paper that went beyond description to interpretation. The interpretations linked his specific research to wider issues that all of us were interested in and could discuss. Perhaps we should not ask much more from a model than that it increases the possibilities for communication among us.

The fourth level of interpretation would eventually identify what is shared and what is unique about music in the repertoire of human behaviors. Something like this level was suggested by Blacking (1979: 11): "the aim of ethnomusicological analysis is to reveal what is peculiar to the process of making and appreciating music, as distinct from other social activities." At this level ethnomusicology would contribute to comparative studies in many cognate fields and to our knowledge of humankind in general. If the fundamental formative processes in music are conceived as historical, social, and individual, then the eventual identification of musical processes will connect music to the rest of human behavior and music study to the rest of the academic world.

## RELATIONS TO OTHER DISCIPLINES

Finally, this model of an ethnomusicology that includes historical, anthropological, and psychobiological components and concerns could be a model for a unified, rather than a divided, musicology. This is a satisfying conclusion because it reflects the direction in which some ethnomusicologists have wanted to move for years. Ethnomusicologists often possess a sort of missionary zeal that they have a corner on the best, most proper, and widest perspective on music and that ethnomusicology is in fact musicology.[13] But it is not helpful to downplay or ignore the significant achievements of historical musicology in favor of a claim that we have all the right answers. Historical musicologists have much to teach ethnomusicologists about historical and individual creative processes, just as we have much to teach them about the powerful forces of contemporary culture on musical sound structures and the social and cognitive bases of musical experience.

When ethnomusicologists speak of musicology, they seem to regard its primary methodological stance as analytical and product oriented (e.g., Qureshi 1981), but at least some historical musicologists seem to work from perspectives not incompatible with those of ethnomusicologists. Anthony Seeger (1985: 349), in his review of the *New Grove* coverage of the many "ologies" of music, points out that Vincent Duckles, in his article on musicology, "at least raises the serious possibility that . . . all musicology becomes ethnomusicological in focus"

---

13. What will this discipline be called? Gilbert Chase (1976), in a pointed and delightful polemic on the relationship between history, anthropology, and musicology, decries the divisions within the discipline and points out a terminological shift since the days of Adler (1885) and Haydon (1941), and a significant retreat from the promise held out by the Harrison, Hood, and Palisca volume of 1963 entitled simply *Musicology:* "We have not yet—unfortunately—reached that point in time at which the term *musicology* is generally accepted as signifying the *total* study of music in human culture . . . *musicology,* without any qualifier, has been tacitly appropriated by the historical branch of that discipline" (pp. 231–232). The terminological situation since the mid-1970s has not improved, although one could cite the 1977 International Musicological Society meeting in Berkeley and the *New Grove* as evidence of a theoretical improvement. If usurpation of the term *musicology* was tacit in the mid-1970s, it is explicit in the 1980s with the publication of Kerman's *Contemplating Music* and the formation in 1982 of the *Journal of Musicology,* which, although it has an ethnomusicologist on the editorial board, pointedly ignores ethnomusicological concerns in its statement of purpose: "A quarterly review of music history, criticism, analysis, and performance practice."

and calls part of the article "an excellent summary of an important ethnomusicological perspective." As he points out, "no single perspective [on music] will ever be more than a perspective" (p. 351). The model proposed here may solve this problem of isolation and of unitary perspective by demanding the integration of perspectives at one level of interpretation.

The historical musicologist Richard Crawford likens his approach to that of a mapmaker in search of it all, as opposed to a prospector in search of a few treasures,[14] and Friedrich Blume, in his 1972 essay on "Musical Scholarship Today," defines a musicology that "embraces all fields of musical activity in all periods of history and all peoples and nations" (p. 16). He regards himself as a historian and musicology as a branch of history in much the way that many ethnomusicologists regard themselves as anthropologists, with ethnomusicology as a branch of that discipline. As a consequence of his view that musicology is a branch of a discipline with much wider social and cultural concerns, in his case history, he speaks about a musicology that has a broad reach, rather than a narrow analytic focus. Among other things, he calls for a study of "the mental processes shaping [sounds]" (p. 16) and regards as "dangerous" an isolated view of music that forgets "the impact of music in our social life and the role played by music in humanity" (p. 27).

If historical musicologists with deep roots in the discipline of history have such ethnomusicologically orthodox views, it would seem to follow that a complete musicology—one concerned with integrating our knowledge of music into our knowledge of mental, social, historical, and spiritual processes and with the music of all peoples and nations—might best be imaged with roots in three far-reaching disciplines: history, anthropology, and psychology. Claims about whether the resulting discipline is humanistic or scientific in its orientation could perhaps be left aside once and for all. Blacking and Gourlay, in their search for what is life enhancing about music; Feld, in his search for the sources of emotional content in music; and the Beckers, in their desire to interpret rather than explain musical cultures, have adopted value-based, personal, and difficult-to-compare orientations traditionally associated with the humanities. Some historical musicologists, on the other hand, perhaps

---

14. Richard Crawford (1985: 2), speaking for the field of American music studies, also carves out an orientation very close to ethnomusicological principles: "For scholars of American music in recent years have more and more looked beyond the selective, aesthetically dominated perspective of the concert hall and begun to consider any kind of music made in America as potentially significant. They have broadened their focus from Music with a capital M to *music-making*: in John Blacking's phrase, from product to process." He goes on to propose a journalistic who-what-where-when-how model, very similar to one proposed by Anthony Seeger (1980), that gets at issues dear to the hearts of ethnomusicologists.

taking their cue from developments in history generally and also in ethno-musicology, write about studying music "in the past" rather than "of the past" (Treitler 1982); the "vast masses" and their lives and music, as well as the great heros and great masters; and the social life and mental processes of music—orientations traditionally associated with the social sciences. We seem to be living in an ecumenical age when the disciplines to which we are "sub" are moving closer together. Musicology must take part in that movement. We can both benefit from it and contribute to it. Such a musicology also has a much better chance than our present divided versions of making significant contributions to our knowledge of humankind.

If we are able to create a unified musicology willing to make bold interpretive statements about the nature of the formative processes in music, the result would be a new and stronger discipline.[15] Musicology, which now has a rather limited profile and impact in the wider academic world, could take its proper place alongside its cousins in the other humanities and social sciences as a discipline making engaging and coherent claims about people and their artistic, social, and intellectual behaviors.

## REFERENCES

Adler, Guido. 1885. "Umfang, Methode und Ziel der Musikwissenschaft." *Vierteljahrsscrift fur Musikwissenschaft* 1: 5–20.

Becker, Judith and A. L. Becker. 1984. "Response to Feld and Roseman." *Ethnomusicology* 28(3): 454–456.

Béhague, Gerard. 1984. "Introduction." In Gerard Béhague, ed., *Performance Practice: Ethnomusicological Perspectives*. Westport, CT: Greenwood Press, pp. 3–12.

Bielawski, Ludwik. 1985. "History in Ethnomusicology." *Yearbook for Traditional Music* 17: 8–15.

Blacking, John. 1971. "Deep and Surface Structures in Venda Music." *Yearbook for International Folk Music Council* 3: 91–108.

———. 1977. "Some Problems of Theory and Method in the Study of Musical Change." *Yearbook of the International Folk Music Council* 9: 1–26.

15. Helen Myers (1981: 43) calls for a rigorous scientific approach based on Popper's notions of falsifiability: "What is required of us is to pose adventurous and imaginative conjectures and then strengthen them by systematically attempting to prove them false." While I share her enthusiasm for "adventurous and imaginative conjectures," the interpretive approach advocated here may not lead to directly falsifiable statements (Dentan 1984), but rather to complex "stories" that can only be compared using criteria such as completeness, cogency, inclusiveness, and so on.

————. 1979. "The Study of Man as Music-Maker." In John Blacking and Joann Keali'inohomoku, eds., *The Performing Arts: Music and Dance*, The Hague: Mouton, pp. 3–15.

Blum, Stephen. 1975. "Toward a Social History of Musicological Technique." *Ethnomusicology* 19(2): 207–231.

Blume, Friedrich. 1972. "Musical Scholarship Today." In Barry S. Brook et al., eds., *Perspectives in Musicology*. New York: Norton, pp. 15–31.

Cavanagh, Beverley. 1982. *Music of the Netsilik Eskimo: A Study of Stability and Change*. Ottawa: National Museums of Canada.

Chase, Gilbert. 1976. "Musicology, History, and Anthropology: Current Thoughts." In John W. Grubb, ed., *Current Thought in Musicology*. Austin: University of Texas Press, pp. 231–246.

Crawford, Richard. 1985. *Studying American Music*. Special Publications No. 3. New York: Institute for Studies in American Music.

Dentan, Robert Knox. 1984. "Response to Feld and Roseman." *Ethnomusicology* 28(3): 463–466.

Erdman, Joan. 1982. "The Empty Beat: *Khali* as a Sign of Time." *American Journal of Semiotics* 1(4): 21–45.

Feld, Steven. 1982. *Sound and Sentiment*. Philadelphia: University of Pennsylvania Press.

————. 1984. "Communication, Music, and Speech about Music." *Yearbook for Traditional Music* 16: 1–18.

Geertz, Clifford. 1973. *The Interpretation of Cultures*. New York: Basic Books.

Gourlay, Kenneth. 1982. "Towards a Humanizing Ethnomusicology." *Ethnomusicology* 26(3): 411–420.

Harrison, Frank Ll., Mantle Hood, and Claude V. Palisca. 1963. *Musicology*. Englewood Cliffs, NJ: Prentice-Hall.

Harwood, Dane. 1976. "Universals in Music: A Perspective from Cognitive Psychology." *Ethnomusicology* 20(3): 521–533.

Haydon, Glen. 1941. *Introduction to Musicology*. New York: Prentice-Hall.

Herndon, Marcia, and Norma McLeod. 1979. *Music as Culture*. Norwood, PA: Norwood Editions.

————. 1980. *The Ethnography of Musical Performance*. Norwood, PA: Norwood Editions.

Kerman, Joseph. 1985. *Contemplating Music*. Cambridge, MA: Harvard University Press.

Koskoff, Ellen. 1982. "The Music-Network: A Model for the Organization of Music Concepts." *Ethnomusicology* 26(3): 353–370.

McLean, Mervyn. 1980. "Approaches to Music History in Oceania." *The World of Music* 22(3): 46–54.

Merriam, Alan P. 1964. *The Anthropology of Music*. Evanston, IL: Northwestern University Press.

Myers, Helen. 1981. " 'Normal' Ethnomusicology and 'Extraordinary' Ethnomusicology." *Journal of the Indian Musicological Society* 12(3–4): 38–44.

Modir, Hafez. 1986. "Research Models in Ethnomusicology Applied to the *Radif* Phenomenon in Iranian Classical Music." *Pacific Review of Ethnomusicology* 3: 63–78.

Nattiez, Jean-Jacques. 1982. "Comparisons within a Culture: The Examples of the *Katajjag* of the Inuit." In Robert Falck and Timothy Rice, eds., *Cross-Cultural Perspectives on Music*. Toronto: University of Toronto Press, pp. 134–140.

———. 1983. "Some Aspects of Inuit Vocal Games." *Ethnomusicology* 27(3): 457–475.

Nettl, Bruno. 1983. *The Study of Ethnomusicology: 29 Issues and Concepts*. Urbana: University of Illinois Press.

Nketia, J. H. Kwabena. 1981. "The Juncture of the Social and the Musical: The Methodology of Cultural Analysis." *The World of Music* 23(2): 23–31.

———. 1985. "Integrating Objectivity and Experience in Ethnomusicological Studies." *The World of Music* 27(3): 3–19.

Qureshi, Regula Burckhardt. 1981. "Qawwali Sound, Context and Meaning." PhD Dissertation, University of Alberta, Edmonton, Canada.

Robertson, Carol. 1984. "Response to Feld and Roseman." *Ethnomusicology* 28(3): 449–452.

Sawa, George. 1983. "Musical Performance Practice in the Early 'Abbasid Era." PhD Dissertation, University of Toronto, Canada.

Seeger, Anthony. 1980. "Sing for Your Sister: The Structure and Performance of Suyá Akia." In Marcia Herndon and Norma McLeod, eds., *The Ethnography of Musical Performance*. Norwood, PA: Norwood Editions, pp. 7–42.

———. 1985. "General Articles on Ethnomusicology and Related Disciplines [in the *New Grove*]." *Ethnomusicology* 29(2): 345–351.

Seeger, Charles. 1977. "The Musicological Juncture: 1976." *Ethnomusicology* 21(2): 179–188.

Shelemay, Kay Kaufman. 1980. " 'Historical Ethnomusicology': Reconstructing Falasha Ritual." *Ethnomusicology* 24(2): 233–258.

Shepherd, John. 1982. "A Theoretical Model for the Sociomusicological Analysis of Popular Musics." In Richard Middleton and David Horn, eds., *Popular Music 2: Theory and Method*. Cambridge: Cambridge University Press, pp. 145–178.

Shumway, Larry. 1986. "Review of *Worlds of Music*." *Ethnomusicology* 30(2): 356–357.

Stone, Ruth. 1982. *Let the Inside Be Sweet*. Bloomington: Indiana University Press.

Thomas, Lewis. 1974. *Lives of a Cell*. New York: Viking Press.

Titon, Jeff Todd, general ed. 1984. *Worlds of Music*. New York: Schirmer.

Treitler, Leo. 1982. "Structural and Critical Analysis." In D. Kern Holoman and Claude V. Palisca, eds., *Musicology in the 1980s*. New York: Da Capo Press, pp. 67–77.

Wachsmann, Klaus. 1982. "The Changeability of Musical Experience." *Ethnomusicology* 26(2): 197–115.

Wade, Bonnie. 1984. "Performance Practice in Indian Classical Music." In Gerard Béhague, ed., *Performance Practice: Ethnomusicological Perspectives*. Westport, CT: Greenwood Press, pp. 13–52.

Yung, Bell. 1984. "Choreographic and Kinesthetic Elements in Performance on the Chinese Seven-String Zither." *Ethnomusicology* 28(3): 505–517.

———. 1987. "Historical Interdependency of Music: Case Study of the Chinese Seven-String Zither." *Journal of the American Musicological Society* 40(1): 82–91.

Zemp, Hugo. 1978. " 'Are'are Classification of Musical Types and Instruments." *Ethnomusicology* 22(1): 37–67.

# 2

# Toward a Mediation of Field Methods and Field Experience in Ethnomusicology

Fieldwork is so central to contemporary ethnomusicology that I would suppose nearly every graduate program devoted to training ethnomusicologists has a course on it, probably with a title containing the phrase "fieldwork methods." The three nouns in these courses' titles (*method, field,* and *work*) speak volumes about our collective understanding of theory and method in ethnomusicology, and thus provide the place where I would like to begin this reflection on fieldwork. I hope to show the limits of the usefulness of this phrase and the possibilities for an alternative view of where the field is and what happens in the field, a view that balances method and working with experience and playing. To do so, I move narratively between theoretical or philosophical reflection and some of my own fieldwork experiences, just as I do in practice.

## FIELDWORK METHODS: EPISTEMOLOGICAL SOLUTIONS TO AN ONTOLOGICAL PROBLEM?

### Method

The word *method* implies both a preexisting theory and a concern with the epistemological problem of finding, verifying, and knowing the truth within the frames of reference defined by theory. A course with the title "fieldwork methods" implies that ethnomusicology has a theory or theories for which fieldwork methods have been developed to test, and the existence of such courses implies that these methods can be taught. But does ethnomusicology have such theories, and, if so, what are they, and what are their associated methods?

One view of ethnomusicology is that it has been rather untheoretical in its orientation, especially since the mid-1950s when, in the United States, it broke away from comparative musicology and its theories of evolution and diffusion. This view is expressed by those who question whether ethnomusicology is a discipline (presumably disciplines have theories) and who, on the contrary, assert that it represents merely a domain of interest shared by a community of scholars. Those who support this theoryless view of ethnomusicology need only cite the myriad idiographic studies of individual musical cultures that dot the ethnomusicological landscape and the relative paucity of attempts to posit and test explicit theories. From this perspective, what passes for theorizing in ethnomusicology amounts for the most part to retrospective catalogs of what has been done and prescriptions for what might be done rather than statements of relationships to be explored in the field. This sort of theoryless ethnomusicology would have no use for methods; indeed, methods, whether applied in the field or in the laboratory, are impossible to define in the absence of theory. Perhaps professors with such views don't offer courses called fieldwork methods; rather, a title such as "things to do in the field" would suffice.

A second view of ethnomusicology acknowledges that, although no single theory predominates, ethnomusicologists currently work with many theories and have woven a "polyphonic" theoretical fabric. If a discipline requires a single, unifying paradigm (Kuhn 1962), then ethnomusicology still might not qualify, but at least each of its contrapuntal theoretical lines would require a disciplined method. A multiplicity of theory would account for the plural form of the course title, "fieldwork methods." The polytheory view is advanced by those who claim that no descriptive work of the sort that minimally constitutes ethnomusicological writing can take place in the absence of some sort of theory. Alan Merriam made this point repeatedly in the definitional debates of the 1950s and 1960s. Bruno Nettl's *The Study of Ethnomusicology: Twenty-Nine Issues and Processes* (1983) provides a "book of lists" of ethnomusicological theories, although some of them predate the 1960s, when the idiographic, intensive studies based on extended fieldwork in one place, called for by Mantle Hood and others, became the norm.

To illustrate the point that multiple theories exist along with the correlative methods they require, I give three examples. One informal theory, for example, maintains that musical practices disappear, which leads to methods aimed at their accurate preservation as sound, film, or video recordings. A corollary of this theory-and-method combination is that a practice has been preserved when converted into a recording, that is, into a fixed text or monument—perhaps analogous to the way jam preserves fresh fruit. A second theory that undergirds some of our activity would state, if made explicit, that music exists as a "sound fact" to be interpreted and compared, at least by ethnomusicologists, using ordinary language description and Western musical notation. The main methodological questions raised by this theory concern accuracy (are the rhythmic durations and intervallic pitch relations correct?), systematicity (are the descriptive tools logically consistent and unambiguously understood?), and replicability (would others using the same tools produce comparable results?). A third theory states that music is a form of human behavior created within a coherent cultural system, and therefore possesses structures analogous or homologous to other culturally constructed forms encoded as art, architecture, everyday speech, ideas about natural sounds, and cosmological or religious beliefs about the nature of the world. The methods characteristic of this theory involve describing and then finding ways to compare radically different formal structures and behaviors, typically through a reduction of those differences to a common structural model borrowed from linguistics and semiotics or through the elicitation of native metaphors and key symbols that link two or more cultural domains into a coherent ethnoaesthetic (Ortner 1973). This theory minimally requires fieldwork methods that go beyond the accurate preservation and description of music as an isolated cultural domain to the observation, recording, and analysis of other cultural domains as well.

The third view of the field holds that a large number (but certainly not all) of its practitioners share a core set of theories or beliefs that constitute the field as a discipline. Even Bruno Nettl, whose list of twenty-nine issues fits his view that ethnomusicology may be less a unified discipline than a field of interest, boldly asserted ethnomusicology's "central question" (1983: 234) and offered a four-part ethnomusicologist's credo (1983: 9), both of which, although he probably didn't intend them as such, could provide a place from which to search for our discipline. The credo seems particularly suggestive as a source for theories and methods that unify the discipline. In analyzing it, I will not question whether these beliefs are in fact widely shared, but rather show what they reveal about the link between theory and method in ethnomusicology.

According to the first part of Nettl's (1983: 8–11) credo, we believe that music systems can be compared, so we need methods to determine "what is typical of a culture" and distinguish those items from "the personal, the idiosyncratic, the exceptional." Whether the methods would be applied as analytic tools in the lab or as social measures in the field he doesn't say. Second, "we believe that music must be understood as a part of culture," but he provides no shared belief about the methods that would elucidate this theory, aware as he is of the methodological counterpoint on this problem. Furthermore, he acknowledges that "many pieces of research do not directly address this problem," which amounts to the troubling admission that, in ethnomusicology, method (as actualized in "pieces of research") bears no coherent relation to a shared theory. Third, we believe that fieldwork, particularly "intensive work with small numbers of individual informants," is an indispensable method, even in the absence of any theory that it might test. If theory and method seem unlinked or incoherent in the second aspect of the credo, in the third aspect theory disappears altogether, although, to be fair, this belief in extended fieldwork should probably be linked to the theory that music is a part of culture. Fourth, "we believe that we must study all the world's music."

Two theories support Nettl's credo. The first states that music derives its value as an object of study not from the complexity of its formal properties or its association with privileged social and historical groups, but by virtue of being a human activity—and all humans and all their behaviors are properly the object of scholarly inquiry. The second theory states that any claims about music that pretend to be universally true, or even true for a particular culture, have to account for all music, whether considered globally in broadly comparative studies or locally in characterizations of musical practice in a single culture. These two theories require methods that capture and consider all music within a culture and in the world, rather than methods designed to assess the relative value of particular genres, works, or musicians.

So what does ethnomusicology as a unified discipline, with its associated fieldwork methods, look like from the perspective of this credo? First, we need methods to collect and study all the world's (and a culture's) music so that we can make general, even universal, claims about the nature of music. We need methods to distinguish the typical from the idiosyncratic in the music we collect, presumably so that our comparative statements and universal claims have some statistical relevance. The methods we use during our extended, intensive fieldwork in one place, presumably to explain our theory that music is a part of culture, are apparently so disparate that they must be excluded from a shared credo. In fact, it may be possible to understand this relationship between music and culture in the absence of method, just by being there. If none of these theories appeal, then ethnomusicologists just churn out "pieces of research" in the absence of theory, and probably method as well. Read this way, Nettl's credo has the advantage of catholicity, but it returns us, ironically through shared beliefs, to a polyphonic understanding—and possibly an accurate one at that—of ethnomusicology without much shared method to go along with three shared theories. The one method we do share, extended fieldwork in one place, exists, according to this credo, unconnected to any particular theory.

In the 1990s, a case for a view of ethnomusicology as a unified discipline would probably be built around Nettl's credo that music is a part of culture (or is culture) but with the explicit continuation that fieldwork methods, including extended, intensive work in one place, exist or must be developed to demonstrate that relationship. This theory, that music is a part of culture, necessarily rests on a theory or theories of culture imported primarily from anthropology.

Anthropologists have "vexed" each other, to use Geertz's telling phrase, over the proper definition of culture, how it is manifested, and how it can best be observed and studied. At least three concepts seem in some sense primordial to the culture concept, though even these features have not escaped critique. First, culture, however defined, has to do with what is shared among a people. Second, cultures are bounded in space and often in time by the "ethnographic present"; we speak routinely and metaphorically of cultural boundaries that apparently block easy intercultural understanding. Third, bounded cultures contain insiders in relation to which the researcher, whether anthropologist or ethnomusicologist, is an outsider. Attempts to understand music as a part of culture involve specifying methods for border crossings to live and work among insiders long enough to apply other methods designed to elicit the shared musical, speech, and other behaviors that would demonstrate this music-as-culture theory. It is probably not too bold to claim that the most frequently cited research in ethnomusicology since the late 1970s has attempted to define and apply methods designed to work out the implications of this theory.

## The Field

In this review of the role of methods in relation to theory in ethnomusicology, the field emerges as the place where data are collected to test theories. It is a bounded place filled with insiders who share views about music, musical practices, and a host of other things. It is the place where we outsiders must go to encounter these insiders and their culture, and explain to other outsiders the relationship between music and culture posited by our theories. It is, above all, the primary place of knowing in ethnomusicology, a place privileged epistemologically by the theory that constructs it as the locus where methods will be applied to demonstrate the truth of our theory that music is a part of culture.

However, in this review of theory and method, there was a suggestive alternative to this epistemological vision of fieldwork, an alternative that seemed unconnected to theory, that by implication left method behind. It was the third aspect of Nettl's credo: we believe in fieldwork. Fieldwork for what? Not apparently as a place to test and work out theory, an experimental place in other words, but a place to become an ethnomusicologist, an experiential place. This third aspect implies the belief that the experience of fieldwork, whatever its methods or even in the absence of methods, constitutes the sine qua non of the state of being an ethnomusicologist. In this credo we have the privileging of ontology (being there) over epistemology (knowing that), and the beginning of a potentially fruitful turn away from fieldwork methods toward fieldwork experience. According to this credo, sometime during or after fieldwork, one becomes an ethnomusicologist. In effect, the self is transformed and reconfigured in the act of understanding one's own or another culture.

The view outlined here that the field is a place of experiment and that fieldwork is an epistemological process exists in parallel and unconnected to the view that the field is a place of experience and that fieldwork is an ontological condition. It would be easy and tempting to demand that we choose one or another of these views; indeed, both sides could and have been the subjects of merciless critiques. But instead of choosing between the two positions, it may be more profitable to attempt a mediation between them. Could, for example, the transformative moment in one's "being in the world"—in one's self, as it were—from nonethnomusicologist to ethnomusicologist be understood as a particular example of more general transformative experiences during fieldwork that lead to new understandings? If the self rather than method were the locus of explanation and understanding (not, by the way, the solipsistic object of understanding), might this realignment contribute to the reformulation of theory and method? On the other hand, could theory and method, which take for granted a fixed and timeless ontological distinction between insider and outsider, be reordered within an ontology that understands both researching and researched selves as potentially interchangeable and as capable of change through time, during the dialogues that typify the fieldwork experience? Although such a mediation may be too ambitious for this chapter, it is on its horizon.

## Work

The emphasis on theory and its accompanying epistemological problems helps to account for the term *work* in our hypothetical course title, "fieldwork methods." Aside from the way "work" valorizes the enterprise as possessing at least the potential for generating both symbolic and economic capital within our own social and economic system (Bourdieu 1991), work must surely be necessary if an outsider is to cross cultural boundaries and enter a conceptually distant field—this last metaphor itself configures a place of unremitting physical drudgery—filled with another category of beings, insiders, whose workings with music as culture must be explained. But if fieldwork is reconceptualized as an ontological project, would the term *work* still be appropriate? When one *is* in the field, isn't existence also fun and playful, at least from time to time? And don't we, as human beings, enter into caring, as well as working, relationships with other human beings while in the field, even as we do our research, apply our methods, and test our theories? Could we not search for another mediation, along the lines of the one suggested earlier, between the epistemological, methodological work of explanation in the field and the ontological understandings of human and musical experience in the field? Would we whimsically retitle our course, "life-experience understandings in ethnomusicology"?

## PLAYING, CARING, EXPERIENCE, AND THE UNDERSTANDING OF BULGARIAN MUSIC

### At Home in the Field

My own sense that concepts such as the insider–outsider dichotomy, the impermeability of cultural boundaries, and even that the field as the privileged place of ethnomusicological understanding might need rethinking began not with reflections on theories and methods like those earlier but with various attempts to understand Bulgarian music, both in and outside what ethnomusicology traditionally defines as the field. The most important event that led me to rethink these ethnomusicological givens occurred when, after a long and unsuccessful period of trying to learn to play the Bulgarian bagpipe (*gaida*) from one of Bulgaria's finest pipers, Kostadin Varimezov, I suddenly understood the basic kinesthetic principles that would allow me to play somewhat adequately in what I think is fair to call a virtuosic instrumental tradition (Rice 1985, 1994, 1995).

As part of my research on Bulgarian music, I decided that I should learn to play a traditional wind instrument, either the *kaval* (an end-blown, rim-blown flute) or the *gaida* (a mouth-blown bagpipe with one melody and one drone pipe). When I began this project, I was working on a dissertation topic; one of my goals was to discover native terminology used by women to describe their polyphonic musical practice (Rice 1977, 1980, 1988). I was distanced by gender and methodological stance from participating in what was essentially a women's singing tradition. In learning to play an instrument, I had no particular research questions I was asking, but as a musician I wanted to learn to play and participate in this tradition. In retrospect, I realize that I separated fieldwork from fieldplay at this early stage of my career in a rather unprofitable way. Epistemological methods and questions were associated with the former, and the ontological process of becoming a musician was the goal of the latter.

At the time I gave no thought to whether and how these two positions might be linked or mediated.

Some years later I was able to invite Kostadin to come to the University of Toronto, where I was teaching at the time, as an artist-in-residence for the academic year. During this period we, along with his wife, Todora, cocreated a "field" in which collecting and interviewing work and learning to play were conjoined. I recorded their repertoire of instrumental music, song, and dance in the manner of epistemologically oriented fieldwork and continued to learn to play, dance, and to a lesser extent sing in Todora's monophonic tradition, which was open to male performance. Even though I acted methodologically in the collection process, I didn't know where it would lead me theoretically, since I was more interested in music-as-culture questions than in music-as-sound fact, and I couldn't really observe music in Bulgarian culture in Toronto. In fact, I collected for two existential reasons. First, I imagined that the items I recorded would provide the repertoire for my existence as a musician, which it did. Second, I worried that, far from their close-knit, extended family, time would weigh heavily on them. I reasoned that spending time with me recording their repertoire and their life stories would make their stay more pleasant, which it did. My collecting in this case resulted from caring for them, not from theory or method. In retrospect, I would say that I had created a fieldwork situation that was structured ontologically rather than epistemologically, and with no particular expectation of a connection or a productive mediation between the two positions. It is probably unnecessary to add that even in the more typical situation of fieldwork far from home, there is no field there; the field is the metaphorical creation of the researcher.

The oddness, as fieldwork, of my research in Toronto only increased when the Varimezovs returned to Bulgaria and left me alone to continue on the path of becoming a musician in this tradition. (In Bulgaria, at least before World War II, little boys who would be musicians were sent to a real field to learn on their own, out of hearing range of adults; I was, at home, metaphorically in just such a field, one rather different from the one constructed by ethnomusicologists.) Under Kostadin's supervision I had mastered certain aspects of the playing technique; I could play melodies in a number of different pentachordal modes and in the famous Bulgarian asymmetric meters (5/8, 7/8, 11/8, etc.), and I could separate melody notes one from another by creating low-pitched "crossing noises," to use the pejorative Scottish bagpiping expression, with the appropriate closed-fingering technique. (These noises are necessary because the bagpipe's sound cannot be stopped with the tongue, as on most wind instruments.) However, I had failed to understand how to create the characteristic high-pitched ornaments that seemed so crucial to the bagpipe's style. Kostadin could not explain them to me in words, gestures, or musical notation the way he could melody, rhythm, and articulation, and, whenever I tried to insert them by lifting my thumb before the melody note, he would complain that I had "lost the style" and that I didn't yet have "bagpiper's fingers" (*gaidarski prŭsti*).

If I wanted to *become* a musician, I now had to do so in the presence of the tradition in what I would now call its textualized form—as both recordings of Kostadin and my memories of lessons with Kostadin—rather than in the presence of informants and insiders. Again, in retrospect, I would argue that this apparent liability, as understood from the perspective of traditional fieldwork, imitates, in fact, one of the experiences of acquiring culture generally. All of us who grow up in culture and acquire its traditions do so only partly as a result of direct, pedagogical intervention of the sort commonly associated with scolding by parents, teaching by teachers, or informing by informants; culture and its traditions are also acquired by observing, mimicking, and embodying shared practices (Bourdieu 1977) and by appropriating, understanding, and interpreting shared, symbolic actions (Ricoeur 1981) without the direct intervention of parents, teachers, informants, and insiders.

Without Kostadin, but still determined to learn to play the *gaida* adequately, I analyzed the recordings by slowing the tape down, only to discover that the high-pitched ornaments were richer and more varied than I had imagined. Moreover, I realized that my mental image of how to move the thumb and forefinger of my top hand could not under any circumstances produce this dense ornamentation. Still, I struggled gamely on, trying to play with some, if not all, the ornamentation and to approach the speed with which Kostadin and other Bulgarian musicians played. Then, one day I began to think about one of what I now call the "textualized traces" of Kostadin's attempt to teach me to play. He had told me that the key to the ornamentation was in the *razsvirvane* (the "playing around"), a series of melodic phrases as the bagpiper fills the bag with air and starts the reeds of the melody and drone pipes. Each phrase begins with a long note on the highest pitch of the *gaida*, followed by an ornamented descent. To play the long note, the player lifts simultaneously the thumb and two or three fingers of the top hand off the instrument. It suddenly dawned on me that if I did the same when I played the ornamentation, that is, if I lifted all my fingers simultaneously rather than, as I had been doing, the thumb first followed by the fingers necessary to produce the melody note, then I could produce the complexity and variety of ornaments that had proved so perplexing. This new kinesthetic understanding allowed me to play faster and more relaxed, and include more ornaments, than I ever had before. It sounded to me as if I had found "the style" I previously had "lost," acquired the elusive "bagpiper's fingers," and solved *le mystère des doigts bulgares*.

## Between Insider and Outsider

It was this learning experience, at home in the Bulgarian version of the field to which children are sent to become instrumentalists, that caused me to reflect on some of the basic tenets of ethnomusicological theory and method. One of the most troubling questions was simple: where was I? And I didn't mean the question just in spatial terms—that is, where is the field? Where was I in relation to ethnomusicological theory? And where was "I" in the temporal trajectory of myself becoming an ethnomusicologist and musician?

Until I found *"gaida* player's fingers" in the early 1980s, I had been strongly influenced by the methods provided by cognitive anthropology to develop a theory of culture as mental activity. Cognitive anthropology uses the elicitation of language terms to make inferences about internal rules, categories, and distinctions that "natives" employ when acting culturally and socially. Its positing of a contrast between "etic" (from phonetic) and "emic" (from phonemic) analyses seemed particularly attractive to me and other ethnomusicologists, who feared that Western-style (etic) analyses might ignore, misunderstand, or even violate important (emic) principles operating within a culture. Given that ethnomusicologists think and talk a lot about music, it seemed an attractive way to discover how natives think and talk about music, and thus gain insight into a supposed insider's perspective on musical and other forms of cultural practice. When I distanced myself from music making and tried to understand the Bulgarian insider perspective through words about music, I was happy with the results and felt that they represented significant advances over an outsider's etic analysis (Rice 1980, 1988). However, when I fully engaged with the music, overcame my scholarly distantiation, and attempted to appropriate the style to the point where I could not just talk about it but play it as well, I ran into the limits of this language-based method and its associated theory of culture. I encountered precisely the "linguocentric predicament" that Charles Seeger (1977: 47) would have predicted for me.

Starting with etic musical analysis and working with a native musician whose vocabulary for talking about music was limited, I had approached an understanding of the tradition, but there still was a significant gap between where I was as an outsider to the tradition and where insider instrumentalists were. They knew it and, worst of all, I knew it too. Bulgarians have a theory to explain this gap: how could I ever really understand their tradition when it wasn't "in my blood"? And some ethnomusicologists have a comparable theory; outsiders are forever doomed to partial understandings compared to insiders, never mind that most Bulgarians can't play the *gaida* either.

When I finally solved the mystery of bagpiper's fingers, I did so in dialogue with Kostadin's tradition of playing, preserved in recordings, after my conversations with him had ended. In the process, I believe I moved to a place untheorized by the insider–outsider distinction so crucial to much ethnomusicological thinking. After talking to a cultural insider, which took me in the direction of an emic understanding of the tradition but not all the way there, I confronted the tradition directly as a sound form and kinesthetic activity, and made it my own in an act of appropriation that transformed me, my self, into something I hadn't been before, a person capable of playing in this tradition with at least minimal competence. This transformation did not, however, make me into a cultural insider; I was not, at least it seemed to me, a Bulgarian. While Kostadin couldn't explain his ornamentation to me in enough detail to make me understand it, I came to be able to explain it to myself and to others; I now understood the finger movements and other mental processes necessary to produce the *gaida*'s characteristic ornamentation. My understanding was neither precisely that of an outsider nor that of an insider. Although the linguistic methods of cognitive anthropology had helped me narrow the gap between emic and etic perspectives, I could not in the end close that gap completely. When, on the other hand, I abandoned those methods and acted musically, it seemed as if I fell right into the gap between insider and outsider, into a theoretical "no place" that felt very exciting, if not exactly like a utopia. I was neither an insider nor an outsider.

The perspective I had acquired in the process of learning to play competently (not necessarily well) was neither emic nor etic. It was my own. I could now supply from my own self-understanding verbal explanations of the complex mental processes necessary to generate this music, explanations that at least one insider, Kostadin, had been unable to supply. If emic understandings are located in other people's heads and given to us in their language reports, then my understanding wasn't emic. On the other hand, if etic understanding involves applying objective analytic methods to sounds without regard for their cultural salience, then my understanding wasn't etic either. I felt as if I had achieved a mediation between these two theoretical categories, these two ontological conditions, and that this mediation challenged fundamentally one of the most important theoretical foundations of our discipline. If I was right, I would eventually need to search for new foundations. But before doing that, I needed to return to Bulgaria and put my new understanding to the test by playing for Bulgarians.

## Playing in a Field of Expanding Horizons

When I returned in the mid-1980s to Bulgaria, the ethnomusicological version of the field to which outsiders are sent to become experts, I was delighted

when Kostadin and others confirmed my self-assessment of my understanding in a number of direct and indirect ways. He stopped asking me to leave
out the high-pitched ornaments, and we worked on inserting them into all the
necessary places. He could now show me where in the melody to use them by
gesturing in midair with his "bagpiper's fingers" as I played—and I understood
what he meant. One of his sons, an amateur player himself, noticed that the first
finger of my top hand, crucial to the ornamentation, moved just like his father's;
that is, he saw as much as he heard one of my "bagpiper's fingers," which I had
acquired not from observation of his father's finger but in a metaphorical dialogue with his father's recordings. A younger bagpiper, who had also learned,
as I had, by listening to Kostadin's recordings rather than by being taught and
informed directly by him, recognized in my playing Kostadin's ornamental
style: "It is as if you are listening to Varimezov."

I was, of course, pleased and excited by their comments, but one of the most
touching moments for me occurred at a celebratory gathering of their extended
family in a village near Burgas in the foothills of the Strandzha Mountains,
the area where Kostadin and Todora came from and in which their tradition
flourished. We sat outside under a grape arbor on either side of the traditional
*dŭlga trapeza* (long table) that provides the locus of all Bulgarian celebratory meals. As we ate and drank, Kostadin played the *gaida* and Todora and a
younger woman sang songs. During the evening an elderly neighbor, with an
impressive mustache of the type worn mainly by older villagers, approached
and sat down across from me. Kostadin introduced me as the professor who
had invited him to Canada for a year and told the man that I played the *gaida*.
"Hah, an American plays the *gaida*," he almost spat out in surprise and disbe-
lief. He then turned to me and ordered, "Play, and I will tell you whether you
are a *gaidar* [bagpiper]." I thought, "Oh brother, there is no way I can satisfy this
guy," particularly since my playing usually went to pot when I was nervous, as
he had made me. Kostadin handed me his *gaida*, and I reluctantly began playing. When I stopped, to my surprise he smiled, seemed pleased, and said, "You
are a *gaidar*."

In their comments and actions, these Bulgarians confirmed that my self-
understanding was now leading to recognizably Bulgarian musical behavior.
Although I wasn't a Bulgarian, I could act like a Bulgarian in the production of
a complicated musical form, and when I acted like a Bulgarian in this particular
way, they did too; that is, if the occasion were right, they danced. I could now
enter into a dialogue with Bulgarians not just in their language but in their
music and dance forms as well. Although I was no doubt an outsider ethnically,
weren't they accepting me as something like an insider musically and therefore culturally? (After all, music is culture, according to one ethnomusicological metaphor.) Actually, one Bulgarian took this connection between cultural

performance and ethnicity further than I was willing to. During a village fair in 1973, a man, whom I had noticed scrutinizing me intently as I talked and danced but whom I didn't know, called me over and demanded to know where I was from and why I was there. (I worried that he was a member of the state security apparatus, with whom I had had a number of unpleasant run-ins.) I explained that I was an American living in Bulgaria for a year or so "on a specialization" to study its folk music. "Hah," he said, "you lie! You speak Bulgarian, and you dance Bulgarian dances. Therefore, you are a Bulgarian."

These sorts of interactions "in the field" suggest that categories of insider and outsider may not be particularly helpful ways to describe the kind of dialogic relationships in language, music, and dance that develop between people who perform and appreciate traditions they have each made their own in varying degrees. Just as I had tried to enter into the horizons of their tradition, they now seemed to accept and include at least some of my actions within the horizons of their understanding of that tradition. Perhaps, I thought, now was the time to begin in earnest the search for new theoretical and even philosophical foundations for ethnomusicology.

## FIELDPLAY UNDERSTANDINGS: ONTOLOGICAL SOLUTIONS TO AN EPISTEMOLOGICAL PROBLEM?

### Remnants of Romantic Hermeneutics in Ethnomusicology

The recognition of a distinction between the knowledge of insiders to a culture and the knowledge of outsiders to that culture has been, since the early 1970s, an important, perhaps even central, aspect of method in, and a fundamental epistemological problem for, ethnomusicology. The distinction is usually traced to a book published in 1954 by the linguist Kenneth Pike, who distinguished between what he called etic accounts of language and culture, which were based on the categories of scientifically trained observers, and emic accounts, which sought to understand the categories and meaningful distinctions of native speakers and cultural insiders. Cultural anthropologists in the late 1950s and 1960s found the distinction useful, and it spawned a number of new research paradigms variously labeled ethnoscience, cognitive anthropology, and the ethnography of speaking. It was these trends that influenced a new stream of ethnomusicological research in the 1970s and 1980s, including my own.

Nearly forty years after Pike's work, ethnomusicologists continue to discuss it, reinterpret it, define research projects and methods in terms of it, and criticize the limitations of the work based on it. A panel at the 1992 Society for Ethnomusicology annual meeting took it up, and in 1993 the journal *The World of Music* devoted an issue to it. At some level the distinction seems axiomatic; after all, it is rooted in the very concept of culture and the concomitant notion of cultural boundaries. It is cultures with boundaries that define the positioning of insiders and outsiders. On the other hand, when we start analyzing this supposedly axiomatic distinction, we bore each other with questions and doubts. Isn't etic really a particular kind of emic? Is it a dichotomy or a continuum? Have we misinterpreted Pike's original idea? And on and on.

Pike's distinction has its roots in a philosophical tradition begun by René Descartes inquiring into the epistemological foundations of knowledge. Descartes felt that only by doubting being, both in its supernatural form as defined in the religious tradition of the day and in its natural form as the perceptible world, could he understand the conditions limiting human knowledge. His radical doubt of supernatural and natural being led him to conclude that only ego could be known to exist without doubt; his argument, *cogito ergo sum,* might be glossed, "I doubt therefore I am." Descartes's doubt of the possibility of knowing anything about the world set in motion the long history of Western Enlightenment philosophy devoted to the epistemological questions "what do we know?" and "how do we know it?" This stream of Western philosophy spawned a seemingly necessary set of distinctions between the ego and the Other, subject and object, objective knowledge of observed behavior and subjective knowledge of inner experience, mind and body, the natural and social sciences, and insiders and outsiders. In this Enlightenment view, knowledge of the world is dependent on methodologically precise, objective observation. In turn, the limitations of these methods prevent us from examining inner experience and the intentions and meanings of others—at least without experiencing what might be called methodological embarrassment.

I undertook my search for alternatives to the Enlightenment position that privileged epistemological problems while doubting being and the existence of a world as the result of my fieldwork experiences. But I came to realize that such a search had already been started by nineteenth-century Romantics, who were desperately interested in understanding the intentions, abilities, inner experience, and motivations of Others, especially those Others they believed to be geniuses. A theologian, Friedrich Schleiermacher (1977), and a philosopher, Wilhelm Dilthey (1989), are usually credited with founding Romantic hermeneutics to interpret and understand the works of genius produced by Others. But in keeping with the Enlightenment and the scientific revolution for which it provided the philosophical foundations, Dilthey in particular suggested that one would have to understand the Other by analyzing directly observable behavior. Today much work in the social sciences, including ethnomusicology, relies in large part on this Romantic hermeneutic tradition, where the Other is now not the genius of Romanticism but the exoticized Other, the insider, of fieldwork methods. This work is simultaneously reluctant to give up on the possibility of objectivity and possesses a new confidence that formal methods, like those of ethnoscience—a telling label, by the way, ethno*science*—can be applied to knowing something about the Other.

Although the Romantic hermeneutic tradition, which continues to influence much of the social sciences and ethnomusicology, fosters objective methods, much of twentieth-century philosophy, social sciences, and natural sciences—the last in the wake of the theory of relativity—has made us skeptical of even this much recourse to objectivity. It is now common to point out that the outsider stance is not objective but a particular kind of emic perspective with the backing of powerful institutions in powerful countries. But the opposite is also true; that is, we often continue to insist that claims to an emic perspective and to understanding the meanings assigned to behavior by insiders must be subjected to the same standards of validity and verifiability as objective inquiry. So, although many of us believe in something like multiple subjectivities and have abandoned the search for objective knowledge, we still tend to demand and trust in objective methods to demonstrate to colleagues our understandings of the Other's intentions, feelings, perceptions, distinctions, and rules. It is at this contradiction that we really have to seek a new philosophical foundation for our ethnomusicology and our social sciences and to try to mediate the dichotomies we have inherited from the Western Enlightenment and premodern scientific traditions.

## Phenomenological Hermeneutics as a Foundation for Ethnomusicology

The philosophical tradition that I have found most helpful in reinventing myself as an ethnomusicologist, because it seems to possess the potential for just such a productive mediation between experimental, objectivist strategies of observation and experiential, subjective knowledge of the force of meanings and intentions, goes by the name of phenomenological hermeneutics. It represents both a continuation and a break with the tradition of Romantic hermeneutics, which, in the work of Dilthey, has been so influential in the social sciences. The main thinkers and their works that have influenced me are Martin Heidegger's *Being and Time* (1978), Hans-Georg Gadamer's *Truth and Method* (1992 [1975]), and Paul Ricoeur's *Hermeneutics and the Human Sciences* (1981). Clifford Geertz's (1973, 1983) interpretive anthropology also participates in this philosophical project. I am going to review some of the main claims of this philosophical tradition, particularly those that radically challenge the Enlightenment tradition, which provides the foundation for so much of contemporary ethnomusicology.

As I do so, the sources for some of the language in the previous two sections should become clear.

In phenomenological hermeneutics, the world, far from being doubted by the subjective ego, is restored to its ontological and temporal priority over the ego or subject. The world—or in our terms, the culture or the tradition— exists and the subject/ego is "thrown" into it. According to Heidegger, "being in the world" is the ego's ontological condition before knowing, understanding, interpreting, and explaining. What the ego/subject comes to understand and manipulate are culturally and historically constructed symbolic forms such as language, dress, social behavior, and music. In hermeneutic jargon, the unbridgeable gulf between subject and object is mediated as the subject becomes a self through temporal arcs of understanding and experience in the world. The self, whether as a member of a culture or a student of culture, understands the world by placing itself "in front of" cultural works. This sense of understanding a world is rather different from the notion that the outsider as subject must, through the application of ethnoscientific methods, get behind the work to understand another subject's (the insider's) intentions in producing the work. In the hermeneutic view, the subject, supposedly freed from prejudice by method, is replaced by the self, who inevitably interprets and understands the world before any attempt to explain it can proceed. Understanding, in this tradition, precedes explanation rather than being the product of it, as it is in the Enlightenment tradition. This idea should be immediately attractive to ethnomusicologists, who have frequent opportunities to observe that highly sophisticated nonverbal musical understanding often exists in the absence of verbal explanations of it—precisely the case with Kostadin's knowledge of high-pitched ornamentation.

Since, according to this philosophical tradition, we understand our world in terms of preexisting symbols, like language, before we explain it, our explanations are always conditioned by preconceptions and preunderstandings given to us by those symbols. The self-conscious task of bringing that understanding to language involves what Ricoeur (1981: 164) calls a "hermeneutic arc." If we take music to be one such symbol system, we can say that the arc begins with preunderstandings of music, either as a performer or as a listener who finds it coherent, and passes through a structural explanation of music as sound, behavior, and cognition, to arrive at an interpretation and new understanding of the world or culture referenced by music acting as a symbol. Phenomenological hermeneutics thus helps to recast the problem of understanding the experience of musical symbols from a fruitless and methodologically unsound search for an unknowable, subjective, psychological inner quality in the subject or the Other to an interpretation of the world that music references by a self operating within finite but expandable horizons.

The metaphor of horizons, which we use routinely in our pedagogical work ("Let's study this music to expand our horizons") but often replace with boundaries in our scholarly analyses of cultures, has been theorized anew by Gadamer. Rather than cultures with boundaries, Gadamer explores the metaphor of a world with horizons. Like the physical world, the horizons of an individual's social and cultural world change as he or she moves through space and time. Whereas Enlightenment philosophy leaves us with a certain confidence in a rational and fixed subject moving through the world, analyzing and in some sense controlling it while keeping it at a distance, hermeneutics suggests that the subject becomes a self in the encounter with the world of symbols. In other words, I became a *gaidar* (and an ethnomusicologist) in the encounter with Bulgarian music and musicians. The notion of the subject as constant and above the world, as "reigning over objectivity," is an illusion (Ricoeur 1981: 190). It follows that, if such an independent subject existed, it would impose its interpretation on the world. In Ricoeur's view, on the other hand, the ego constructs itself as a self by being thrown into a world. In his view, appropriation, or "the act of making one's own that which was previously alien, . . . ceases to appear as a kind of possession, as a way of taking hold of." Rather, appropriation "implies instead a moment of dispossession of the narcissistic ego." Ricoeur continues, "By the expression self-understanding, I should like to contrast the self which emerges from the understanding of [symbols and symbolic action] to the ego which claims to precede this understanding. It is cultural works, with their universal power of unveiling, which give a self to the ego" (Ricoeur 1981: 192–193).

My appropriation of Bulgarian bagpipe performance, although it began as a selfish desire to learn the tradition for myself and what it could do for me in the American world of scholarship and amateur performance of Balkan music, went as far as it did because I cared for Kostadin. He in turn began to pressure me to appropriate the tradition completely, that is, to transform myself into a *gaidar,* for himself. My self-transformation had become meaningful and important to him and his self-definition and self-regard. He did not remain the inveterate insider, but transformed himself and expanded his horizons in his encounter with me and my world.

Marcia Herndon, in her 1993 article in *The World of Music* issue devoted to the emic/etic dichotomy, wrote, "I speak as myself; neither fully insider nor outsider, neither fully emic nor fully etic" (1993: 77). I believe that I got to this place vis-à-vis Bulgarian culture, but by a different route. Herndon attributed her ontological condition to "my mixed-blood status with Cherokee coming from both sides of my family" (1993: 77). In hermeneutic terms, however, all those who place themselves "in front of" recorded or performed musical works, whether or not they can claim any genetic relation to those who produced them, may be able to make this claim: I am neither insider nor outsider;

I speak as myself, a self formed, reconfigured, and changed by my encounters with and understandings of Bulgarian, and indeed all kinds of other, musical works and performances.

For Ricoeur, appropriation is the process by which a scholar, or anyone thrown into a world, "struggle[s] against cultural distance and historical alienation." Since, in this starkly un-Romantic view, access to the inner experience of the Other is neither attainable nor sought after, one is left to interpret symbols and symbolic behavior in terms of the world or worlds they potentially reference, an understanding that is finite, changeable, multidimensional, forced to compete with other interpretations, and limited by the expandable horizons of the individual. As Ricoeur puts it, "It is because absolute knowledge is impossible that the conflict of interpretations is insurmountable and inescapable. Between absolute knowledge and hermeneutics, it is necessary to choose" (1981: 193).

When, as in ethnomusicological research, a new world of music is encountered, new understanding results when the horizons of the researcher's world are expanded to include at least part of the world that the new music symbolically references. From this perspective, the researcher seeks to understand not so much the inner experience of people from another culture, but rather the world suggested by music sounds, performances, and contexts. Because ethnomusicologists often find themselves at some cultural or historical distance from the traditions they study, appropriation is the dialectical counterpart of that initial distantiation. Even so-called insider ethnomusicologists, those born into the traditions they study, undergo a productive distantiation necessary for the explanation and critical understanding of their own cultures. Rather than there being insider and outsider ways of knowing, all who place themselves "in front of" a tradition use the hermeneutic arc to move from preunderstandings to explanation to new understandings. Even an insider faced with a particular cultural work or performance may not interpret it in the same way as the insider who produced it and was "behind" it. In other words, not just scholars follow this hermeneutical arc. All individuals operating within tradition continually reappropriate their cultural practices, give them new meanings, and in that process create a continually evolving sense of self, of identity, of community, and of "being in the world."

## More Field Experience and Dialectical Strategies

Ricoeur is a master of dialectical thinking. First of all, he identifies seemingly irreconcilable oppositions, like the one between objectivity and subjectivity (or, in another essay, between history and fiction), demonstrates how each side partakes of qualities of the other, and then finds a way to mediate the opposition by resetting the terms in which the opposition was proposed and seemed so primordial. If ethnomusicologists adopt his philosophical stance, then we will be forced into such dialectical strategies. We will no longer be satisfied with identifying and then choosing between the oppositions we generate. Just such a mediation between insider and outsider was what I attempted in the previous sections.

Other oppositions await mediation as well. For example, the experience that I described earlier of becoming a musician through an encounter with the Bulgarian tradition suspiciously echoes Mantle Hood's 1960 call for acquiring "bi-musicality." In the 1960s, Mantle Hood and his students often seemed to acquire this "bi-musicality" to study and report on music "in its own terms" and for its own sake, with culture and history providing little more than a "context" in which music was made. Alan Merriam and his disciples, on the other hand, were calling for a study of music as culture that often seemed to ignore "the music sound itself" and to challenge the respectability, and certainly the relevance to music-as-culture studies, of the knowledge gained through "bi-musicality." As I mentioned, I was mainly interested in the music-as-culture metaphor when I began my study of the *gaida*. In touting the scholarly benefits of becoming a musician in a tradition I wish to understand, have I entered a vicious circle? Am I merely reproducing the oppositions of thirty years ago? I don't think so.

One payoff of my self-transformation into a *gaidar* superficially resembles Hood's emphasis on music in its own terms, and that is my ability to explain aspects of the sound structure of the music from the perspective of a performer using the language of Western music theory and notation. Some of the description in the second part of this essay was devoted to such explanations, but my emphasis on the state of "being in the world" with Bulgarian musicians also refocuses questions of music as culture beyond notions of the analogies and homologies that musical performances and other cultural actions possess to questions of the social and cultural relationships generated between the selves who make music in culture. When the field researcher begins to participate in meaningful cultural action, then the pragmatics of music and culture, that is, the study of the conditions underlying specific musical and cultural utterances, becomes the focus of investigation. When the field researcher engages in acts of musical interlocution, as I did, then the ontological condition of the self and other agents seems to compete with the ontological priority normally given to observable music and language behaviors and events in epistemologically driven ethnomusicological theory and method.

It was when I began to participate, even at my limited level, in musical conversations with Bulgarian musicians during field trips in the late 1980s that

I came to understand how Bulgarians, operating from a variety of social positions, interpreted the structures of musical utterances as referencing a world. Bulgaria in the 1980s experienced the death throes of communism. As the society divided itself along political and ethnic lines (the latter in the form of severe government-imposed sanctions against the Turkish and Gypsy Muslim minorities), musical practice participated in the contestation. Where the Communist Party had once dictated the public forms of musical production, during the 1980s those in opposition to the party sought new musical forms to express their distaste for the party's policies, practices, ideology, and aesthetics. Musicians played and listeners heard enormous variations in musical style and often seemed to make aesthetic choices based on political preferences. It was in this political context that Todora said to me, as we listened to an outstanding *kaval* player on the radio, "May it fill your soul." There are a number of questions that her expression of enthusiasm raised for me. Why is the soul the locus of aesthetic pleasure? What in music filled her soul? Why did that performance fill her soul?

I can't yet answer the question of why the soul is the locus of aesthetic pleasure, except with the rather banal suggestion that it may have something to do with self-identity as Orthodox Christian Slavs (even when people like Kostadin and Todora are not particularly religious), but in musical conversation I began to get an inkling of the what and why of soul-filling performances. The precise pitch and presence or absence of the barely audible ornaments and "noises" between melody notes in instrumental performances, which had presented me with so many technical and musical problems, turned out to be crucial to the identity of the player and the playing style. And questions of identity—whether one was Bulgarian, communist, anticommunist, Muslim, Gypsy, Turkish, Western leaning, or backward looking—were what was at stake for most Bulgarians in the late 1980s. Kostadin's way of playing the ornaments was "Bulgarian" and even regionally distinctive, a marker of "authenticity." Muslim Gypsy musicians, on the other hand, used a slightly different style of ornamentation, and some younger *gaida* players tried to imitate it, primarily because it was flashy and fashionable, even when they didn't care to link it to its possible political references. I learned to play one such tune "in conversation" with Kostadin's nephew, who for the most part followed Kostadin's example, but when I played this tune for Kostadin he insisted that I replace an ornament his nephew had played below the melody with one above it. The way his nephew and I played the phrase was "empty," according to Kostadin. Though the quantity of ornaments didn't change, one version created for Kostadin an aesthetically empty response, whereas the other one was capable of filling his soul. Fieldwork in Bulgaria had taught me that his preferred way of playing was filling because it referenced a familiar, comfortable world of previous experience, a world dominated by Bulgarians and the progress and security provided by the Communist Party. His nephew's way was empty aesthetically because it referenced a world of change, threat, and potential instability. Without that participatory experience of music making and living in Bulgaria, the explanation of what at first glance seemed a rather mystical link between aesthetics and metaphysics—"May it fill your soul"—would have been impossible. That. nearly imperceptible ornamental tone was not just a feature of musical style but a source of soul-filling (or empty) aesthetic experience and, through its capacity to reference a world, of social and political experience.

Throughout this chapter I have exposed a number of oppositions: studies of music "in its own terms" versus music as culture; explanations based on methods versus understandings based on experience; and insiders and outsiders. I have held out the hope for some sort of mediation, rather than a choice, between them. This study follows the temporality of my experiences with Bulgarian music and with ethnomusicology, and in so doing reveals that it is almost surely in the temporal dimension that the mediation between these oppositions will occur. Heidegger's insight that the fundamental ontological condition of "being in the world" was its temporality is probably also the place to seek the kinds of mediations demanded by these oppositions. An initial understanding of musical style and production became the ground on which I in time built an understanding of music as culture. Instead of bracketing experience while focusing on experiment as our methods require—or glorifying experience while abandoning method as our dissatisfaction with positivism grows—Ricoeur's phenomenological hermeneutics suggests bringing experiment within the framework created by experience. Instead of explanation for the natural sciences and experience for the human ones as Dilthey suggests, Ricoeur brings explanation within the framework of experience in his "hermeneutical arc." Instead of immutable outsiders, the hermeneutical arc may provide a pathway from the outside, with its cultural alienation, toward the inside by means of appropriation and understanding. Instead of generalized insiders, the hermeneutical arc may provide another path from the inside, with its cultural engrossment, toward the outside by means of distantiation and explanation.

In this chapter I illustrate two hermeneutical arcs that mediate between method and experience and between explanation and understanding by moving through time. The first began with my understanding of many elements of Bulgarian musical style, as well as an understanding of the limits of that understanding as far as ornamentation was concerned. Further attempts to appropriate the tradition led to an explicit, verbalized explanation of how those ornaments must be produced and to corresponding problems of the appropriate methods to use in their description. The arc ended, "for the time being," when explanations led back to an understanding of how to play the instrument to produce sounds that were understood by me and interpreted by Bulgarians as adequate representations of Bulgarian musical style. The second arc began with this new understanding of musical style, moved through an explanation of the locus where musical style accounted for aesthetic satisfaction (the exact position of particular ornamental notes), and ended, again for the time being, with an understanding and interpretation of how and why this musical style references the politically charged Bulgarian world of the 1980s. These temporal arcs from understanding through explanation to new understandings contain the possibility for the mediation between field methods and field experience posited at the beginning of this chapter.

## REFERENCES

Bourdieu, Pierre. 1977. *Outline of a Theory of Practice.* Cambridge: Cambridge University Press.

——. 1991. *Language and Symbolic Power.* Cambridge, MA: Harvard University Press.

Dilthey, Wilhem. 1989. *Introduction to the Human Sciences,* edited by Rudolf A. Makreel and Firthjof Rodi. Princeton, NJ: Princeton University Press.

Gadamer, Hans-Georg. 1992 [1975]. *Truth and Method,* 2nd rev. ed. New York: Crossroad.

Geertz, Clifford. 1973. *The Interpretation of Cultures.* New York: Basic Books.

——. 1983. *Local Knowledge.* New York: Basic Books.

Heidegger, Martin. 1978. *Being and Time,* translated by John Macquarrie and Edward Robinson. Oxford: Blackwell.

Herndon, Marcia. 1993. "Insiders, Outsiders, Knowing Our Limits, Limiting Our Knowing (Emics and Ethics in Ethnomusicology)." *The World of Music* 35(1): 63–80.

Hood, Mantle. 1960. "The Challenge of Bi-Musicality." *Ethnomusicology* 4(2): 55–59.

Kuhn, Thomas S. 1962. *The Structure of Scientific Revolutions.* Chicago: University of Chicago Press.

Nettl, Bruno. 1983. *The Study of Ethnomusicology: Twenty-Nine Issues and Processes.* Urbana: University of Illinois Press.

Ortner, Sherry. 1973. "On Key Symbols." *American Anthropologist* 75: 1338–1346.

Pike, Kenneth. 1954. *Language in Relation to a Unified Theory of Structure and Human Behavior.* Glendale, CA: Summer Institute of Linguistics.

Rice, Timothy. 1977. "Polyphony in Bulgarian Folk Music." PhD dissertation, University of Washington, Seattle.

——. 1980. "Aspects of Bulgarian Musical Thought." *Yearbook of the International Folk Music Council* 12: 43–67.

——. 1985. "Music Learned but Not Taught." In *Becoming Human through Music.* Reston, VA: Music Educators National Conference.

——. 1988. "Understanding Three-Part Singing in Bulgaria: The Interplay of Concept and Experience." *Selected Reports in Ethnomusicology* 7: 43–57.

————. 1994. *May It Fill Your Soul: Experiencing Bulgarian Music.* Chicago: University of Chicago Press.

————. 1995. "Understanding and Producing the Variability of Oral Tradition: Learning From a Bulgarian Bagpiper." *Journal of American Folklore* 108(429): 266–276.

Ricoeur, Paul. 1981. *Hermeneutics and the Human Sciences*, edited and translated by John B. Thompson. Cambridge: Cambridge University Press.

Schliermacher, Friedrich. 1977. *Hermeneutics: The Handwritten Manuscripts*, edited by Heinz Kimmerle, translated by Jame Duke and Jack Forstman. Missoula, MT: Scholars Press for Theory of Structure and Human Behavior.

Seeger, Charles. 1977. *Studies in Musicology: 1935-1975.* Berkeley: University of California Press.

# 3

# Reflections on
# Music and Meaning

*Metaphor, Signification, and Control
in the Bulgarian Case*

The question of whether and how music has meaning has vexed musicologists for years. I recall a visceral encounter with the problem in 1974 during my first year of university teaching. A young colleague about my age but trained in historical musicology relished quashing all our students' attempts to suggest any referential meaning or expressive significance for music, citing as evidence contradictory interpretations of, say, the key of G minor as happy or sad. He preferred to describe what he thought was knowable in music—namely, its structural properties. Having been trained in ethnomusicology, I found this reduction of music to form and structure senseless, and yet at the time it proved difficult to articulate a coherent, rather than a felt, response. Then ethnomusicologists were struggling with how to formulate ideas about music's meaning (see Feld 1974 for a contemporaneous, critical review of approaches based on language analogies), and we continue to wrestle with this theme.

In the intervening quarter century, ethnomusicologists and so-called new musicologists have become much more confident in proclaiming the meaning of music in particular situations and for particular people—so confident, in fact, that such discourse seems to have become a taken-for-granted feature of our discipline.[1] I became aware of this at a 1993 conference, organized by

---

1. McClary (2000), in taking up the question of musical meaning, positions her work explicitly in opposition to discourses on historical musicology that overlook (or at least underemphasize) music's capacity for reference. As she puts it, "Music studies have a . . . history . . . that has long denied signification in favour of appeals to the 'purely musical'" (pp. 7–8).

Mark Slobin and sponsored by the Center for Russian and Eastern European Studies at Yale University, on the role of music in the political transition in Eastern Europe. During the closing discussion a professor of comparative literature claimed to be astounded by the assembled ethnomusicologists' unproblematized assertions of music's referential meaning when in his field the notion that literature had meaning was under attack! (The published versions of those papers are contained in Slobin 1996.)

If these personal experiences are indicative of more general trends, ethnomusicology has made important strides in understanding the nature of musical meaning. Yet there is surely need for further work and clarification in this area.

Since I have not engaged in a systematic review of the literature on music and meaning as developed in ethnomusicology, philosophy of music, and historical musicology, I offer here some reflections on the topic influenced by some reading in ethnomusicology and semiotics, Paul Ricoeur's writings on phenomenological hermeneutics, George Lakoff and Mark Johnson's ideas about metaphor, Pierre Bourdieu's analysis of practice, Michel Foucault's ideas on discourses of knowledge/power, and my own and other colleagues' research on Bulgarian music.

I make four principal points whose originality, if any, is more in pulling them together and applying them to a specific case than in their newness. First, what we mean by meaning still needs clarification. I turn to the dictionary and thesaurus to point out that there are at least three meanings for *meaning*, and we confuse ourselves when we fail to distinguish between them. Second, I posit the notion that musical meaning—that is, music's significance as human experience—is expressed metaphorically in claims about the nature of music. Third, using categorizations derived primarily from semiotics, I review some of the ways music seems to signify referentially. Fourth, I examine attempts to control music's signification and significance within hierarchies of power. In all these instances except the first I give examples from the Bulgarian musical tradition.

## THE MEANING OF MEANING

Martin Clayton's (2001) introductory essay to a volume of the *British Journal of Ethnomusicology* inspired the following thoughts. He asks, quite reasonably, what do we mean by meaning? As I understand it, he wants to maintain a broad definition, and to do so he segues into a useful disquisition on the ontological status of music and how a clearer understanding of that status (as thing or imaginary form or meaningful action) will inevitably impact our claims about musical meaning. He goes on to distinguish between "meaningful" in some broad experiential sense and what must, by implication, be the narrower "structural, syntactical and semiotic aspects of meaning described by musicologists" (p. 5). I think he is right that, as I will discuss in the next section, our understanding of the ontological status of music is almost universally expressed in metaphors and that claims about musical meaning in his broad sense are linked intimately to our implicit or explicit understandings of its ontological status. However, I found myself still asking what musicologists mean by meaning. The problem is that we seem to be using "meaning" in a number of senses. These need to be pulled apart and distinguished to make our discussions of musical meaning if not clear, then at least less ambiguous.

*Meaning*, as a quick look at my modest home dictionary and thesaurus reveals and as we know intuitively, has minimally three distinct meanings. (I shudder at the prospect of how consulting the *Oxford English Dictionary* might complicate this.) The first meaning given is "what is . . . signified, indicated, referred to, or understood." Close synonyms for this sense are words like *signification, sense, import, purport*, and *message* and phrases like *semantic meaning* and *referential meaning*. This seems to be Clayton's narrow sense of the word *meaning*. The second dictionary meaning of *meaning* suggests an array of linked synonyms like *significance, importance, value*, and *merit*. (Complicating this simple dichotomy, one of the meanings of *significance* is signification.) Such a sense of meaning seems to provide a basis for the broader concept of meaning, which Clayton, appropriately, wants to keep before us. Third, *meaning* means intention or purpose. We hear this sense of the word in quizzical responses to avant-garde art and music: What does it mean? What, in other words, was the artist trying to achieve? What did he or she intend? Though we may hear this question most often in response to difficult works of art and music, such turns toward intention are probably a very frequently used interpretive strategy, used even when the interpreter is faced with common behaviors and works that are fully integrated into culturally shared practices and styles.

Another, perhaps more sophisticated version of the question, one that avoids the so-called intentional fallacy, might be: How am I to interpret this work? How am I to understand its formal logic, its references to worlds, and its artistic, cultural, and social significance and value? This question yields a fourth sense for the word *meaning*, one somewhat undeveloped in my dictionary: meaning refers to (means) interpretation and understanding. (This question and the concepts of interpretation and understanding used here are developed in Ricoeur's 1981 essays on phenomenological hermeneutics.) Both these last two senses— meaning as intention and meaning as interpretation and understanding—seem to me to combine the narrow and broad senses of meaning in a fruitful (even broader?) way and locate the concept of meaning not in the thing or the form or the action but in the people who make and reflect upon them.[2]

If *meaning* has multiple meanings, then, when we speak about music and meaning, we either have to be careful to specify the sense in which we are using the term or abandon its use altogether. It would be hard to argue that one or another sense is preferable in the abstract, though in particular instances one meaning may be more convenient rhetorically than another. For example, in a context devoted to musical reference, it may make sense to refer to musical meaning in its limited sense of signification and use the words *significance, value,* or *function* to refer to other aspects of music, musical performance, and musical experience. In another context devoted to music's importance in human life, the opposite may be true: it might make more sense to use musical meaning to refer to a broad range of its functions and values while concurrently employing terms like *signification, indication, index, icon, representation,* and *symbol* for one aspect of its significance. Some, faced with this problem, may prefer to abandon the phrase *musical meaning* in favor of contrasting terms such as *signification* and *significance, reference* and *importance,* or *semantics* and *value,* realizing that in each case the former term is one aspect of the latter one. I try this last tack in most of what follows.


## METAPHORS AND THE NATURE OF MUSIC

It seems to me that all human beings, including ethnomusicologists, understand the nature and significance of music (its meaning in the broad sense) by making metaphors that link music to other aspects of human experience. Each such metaphor makes a truth claim about the ontological status of music: music is art, music is meaningful action, music is humanly organized sound, and so forth. I would like to suggest that, as researchers, we not critique some of these metaphors as false while proclaiming others as the keys to the musicological kingdom: "music is not a thing at all but an activity" (Small 1998: 2). Rather, ethnomusicologists should take seriously all musical metaphors they encounter, whether of their own making or that of their research subjects, and for what they are: fundamental claims to truth, guides to practical action, and sources for understanding music's profound importance in human life. Rather than true or false, each claim, it seems to me, is merely limited, one of many possibilities.

---

2. Feld (1984: 2–3) writes usefully on meaning situated in intention and interpretation. Pointing out that, in communicative interactions such as musical performance, we assume that others have "subjective intentions," he writes: "We cannot speak of meaning without speaking of interpretation (whether public or conscious). . . . Meaning fundamentally implicates interpretation."

A given metaphor probably achieves some goals and makes some sense in certain situations but fails to account for the full range of music's possibilities and significance. I further suggest that multiple musical metaphors probably guide action and thought in individual lives, in society, and through time. Sometimes, I suppose, they happily commingle; at others they may become alternative, competing strategies.[3]

If we look broadly at music cultures around the world, many culturally specific metaphors suggest themselves. For example, among the Navajo of the southwestern United States, music is medicine, a form of therapy; it is performed to heal the sick. It doesn't represent something; it does something (McAllester 1954; Witherspoon 1977). Among some strict Muslims, music is the work of the devil; its performance and appreciation signify apostasy and contribute behaviorally to it. For some African American jazz musicians, a musical performance is a story and, if you are not telling a story, no matter how technically accomplished you may appear to be, your playing is not part of the tradition. Such metaphors may be as endless as the cultures we study, and each tells us something important about the nature of music in that society (cf. Merriam 1964: 63–84 on "concepts" of music).

Musicologists also base their studies of music on metaphors that make fundamental claims about music's nature and significance. Among the common metaphors in current use and therefore applied cross-culturally are music as art, as entertainment, as emotional expression, as social behavior, as commodity, as referential symbol, and as text for interpretation. Our analyses are predicated on the truth of one or some of these metaphors—truth claims we perhaps too often champion to the exclusion of others we aren't using at the moment or have rejected for some reason. I would also argue that we sometimes demonstrate but often simply imply the truth of our favored metaphors for our research subjects. We claim, explicitly or implicitly, that they behave as if our musicological metaphors were true for them as well. I look at a few of them here.

The music-is-art metaphor suggests that the nature of music is first and foremost about its making and the results of that making: the processes of performing and composing music and the musical products (dare I say "things") resulting from that process. This metaphor leads us to consider how music is

3. Bohlman (1999) deals with the ontological status of music in ways similar to and different from this analysis. Like this chapter, he champions the analytical utility of keeping before us multiple ontologies of music, particularly as they may manifest themselves in other cultures. Unlike this chapter, he is less interested in the role of metaphor as a mechanism for positing and recognizing the ontologies of music, though he points out that music as object is one of the most recognizable claims about the nature of music in the West, along with the seemingly opposing notion that it "exists in conditions of process" (p. 18).

made (its techniques and forms and structures) and how effectively it is made (with craft, balance, virtuosity, and beauty).[4] Music is so powerful as an art, its techniques of production so formidable, and the pleasures of its reception so enrapturing that such considerations can easily eclipse other views of the nature of music—that is, other metaphors, including the metaphor that music is a referential symbol or text. While ethnomusicologists have been at pains to move beyond the shadow of the music-as-art metaphor to others, we need to recognize that it informs the experience of music for those raised not just in the traditions of European aesthetics but in most musical traditions we study.

A second metaphor, which has been developed mainly by ethnomusicologists, claims that music is social behavior. (Recent ethnomusicological monographs advancing this metaphor include Seeger 1987, Sugarman 1997, Turino 1993, and Waterman 1990.) Working with this metaphor, ethnomusicologists have tried to demonstrate that, because music is made and understood by people in society, every performance of music is also a performance of social structures or social relations. Musical performances may enact past or present social structures, or they may model alternatives to existing structures and help to imagine future ones. Music's status as a performance of social relations lies within the domain of practice, often unremarked on and beyond discourse until a musicologist analyzes them (Bourdieu 1977). We have shown how musical practices mirror existing social structures, how they enact them, and how they reinforce or challenge them in some way.

A third metaphor that has challenged ethnomusicologists in recent years has been the idea that music is a commodity. We have encountered this mainly in our fieldwork, as our subjects engage the commercial world of the music industry and as we take more interest in that world as a locus for our research. The reality of this metaphor is manifested in the ability of musicians to exchange their performances and the products resulting from those performances for money or other marketable commodities.

A fourth metaphor states that music is emotional expression. It claims that music either is the surface manifestation of inner emotions, and therefore expressive of them, or is generative of emotions. In other words, music doesn't simply reference emotions as a symbol might; it expresses or manifests them directly. This metaphor, while very powerful in Western cultural experience, has remained somewhat on the periphery of ethnomusicology. However, Turino

---

4. A selection of recent ethnomusicological monographs that attend to the experience of music as art, usually among other things, includes Bakan (1999), Berliner (1994), Brinner (1995), and Tenzer (2000). Perhaps not coincidentally, all these books concern musically complex traditions (jazz, Javanese, and Balinese music) that reward a certain analytical engagement with music forms and structures and their apprehension and appreciation.

(1999: 221) recently challenged "the next generation" of ethnomusicologists "to develop a theory of music in relation to what is usually called 'emotion.'"

Metaphors are not simply literary devices. They are constructions that help us to understand our world. When we take them as true, they powerfully inform our view of the world and our actions in it (Lakoff and Johnson 1980: 156–184). When we are faced with five common and possibly cross-culturally useful metaphors about the fundamental nature of music (as symbol or text, as art, as social behavior, as commodity, as emotional expression), a number of important questions arise.[5] First, how do our subjects deploy these metaphors? Are some or all of them kept in some kind of balance or always kept in mind? Or do people bring one into the foreground while pushing the others into the background? Or does one actually eclipse the others, making them disappear at least for a while? In other words, we may want to consider how and whether our subjects use metaphors of music's nature and significance strategically to their benefit.

To move the discussion out of the abstract, let me give some examples from the traditional and neotraditional music of Bulgaria, where I have done field research off and on between 1969 and 2000.[6] This music has its roots in a rural society, based on subsistence farming, most of whose members were illiterate until about 150 years ago. Elaborate discourses of the sort one finds in many literate cultures on music as art or as emotional expression do not exist traditionally, but Bulgaria has been modernizing for the past 150 years, and such discourses now exist in the country and have been applied to the music and its practices.

When one observes Bulgarian music being performed in traditional social contexts—for example, at weddings and gatherings of friends—the music-as-social-behavior metaphor stands out strikingly. In such settings the most prominent social structures and relations being performed through music are

---

5. An anonymous reader was struck by the similarities between this list of metaphors and Merriam's (1964: 209–227) chapter on uses and functions of music. In fact, my list of metaphors was not inspired by Merriam's chapter—though his book and that chapter, in particular, need to be credited as seminal for broadening ethnomusicological discussions of the significance of music, including this one. I didn't make the connection because metaphor and function are different. Merriam's functions flowed from a structural-functionalist paradigm, were analyzed by the observer rather than by those under study, and served the goal of social cohesion and stability. Metaphors are "ways of understanding and experiencing one kind of thing in terms of another" (Lakoff and Johnson 1980: 5), guide the actions of individuals operating in society, and serve understanding and experience.

6. I apologize to readers who have already encountered these stories in my previous publications, especially Rice (1994, 1996). I hope I am putting these old data into a slightly different analytic frame.

gendered behaviors and kinship structures. Such performances were undoubtedly more important to social life and social structuring before rapid modernization began after World War II, but I had the good fortune to observe it at
work among a family of musicians with deep roots in prewar village musical
practice. Kostadin Varimezov, a skilled bagpiper (*gaidar*), moved in 1956 with
his wife, Todora, who knew hundreds of songs, from their village in southeastern Bulgaria to become a professional musician in one of Bulgaria's new professional folk ensembles.[7]

They continued to maintain their family structure through musical performance. In particular, it seemed to me that they understood themselves as a
family at least in part through informal gatherings that included the performance of instrumental music, song, and dance. By attending such gatherings
and engaging in singing, playing, and dancing, they and their extended family
of children and grandchildren, brothers and sisters, and cousins, nieces, and
nephews performed their membership in the family. For example, at one such
family get-together in 1988, Kostadin and Todora and some of their children
and grandchildren were joined by a young man in his thirties who had married the daughter of Todora's sister. The young couple had traveled across the
entire breadth of the country to join in the festivities on a national holiday. He
in particular was anxious to learn some songs from Todora and to sing with his
cousins-in-law as a way to cement his relationship to them and bring his membership in their extended family vividly to life (Rice 1994: 289–291). The wives
of Kostadin's and Todora's own sons behaved in a similar way. Though they
came from the western region of the country around the capital, Sofia, they
had learned the dances of the southeastern Strandzha region where Kostadin
and Todora had been born so they too could become effective members of this
family. Another nephew had married a professional singer with a distinctive
style from yet another region in central Bulgaria. After marrying into the family, she learned Todora's style and repertoire and taught them to her daughter
as one way to insert herself into the extended patrilineal family structure that
characterizes Bulgarian kinship.

When music enacts social behaviors, structures, and relations, it often does
so, as in this example, in the domain of practice, a domain beyond discourse
(Bourdieu 1977). In this domain music is social behavior, not a symbol or

---

7. Rice (1994) amounts to a lengthy biography of the Varimezovs in the context of transformations in Bulgarian society from a prewar, rural economy to a postwar communist command
economy. Buchanan (1991, 1995) writes in detail about the process of the professionalization
of traditional musicians. She points out that their transformation from prewar, unpaid village
"players" (*svirachi*) to postwar, paid, urban "musicians" (*muzikanti*) accompanied and facilitated many changes in traditional musical practice and signification.

representation of it. When this metaphor is operating, the power and effectiveness of music lie precisely in its existence as a performance of social behaviors, structures, and relations beyond discourse.

Musical performance as social behavior can turn into a symbol or text when something happens that calls for commentary—that brings the behavior into the domain of discourse. For instance, interpretation and commentary may be generated when something goes wrong or something happens that transgresses the unspoken norms of behavior otherwise enacted at the event.[8] At the 1988 Varimezov family gathering, for example, a neighbor—also a professional musician and player of the traditional bowed fiddle (*gŭdulka*)—and his wife attended. He joined Kostadin in playing instrumental music to accompany the singing and dancing, but his wife, in contrast to everyone else there, participated in neither activity. After the event Kostadin and Todora regarded her behavior as strange enough to warrant interpretation. With their commentary they moved her behavior from the domain of practice and social behavior into the domain of text requiring interpretation. They interpreted her nonparticipation in the singing and dancing as evidence that she felt estranged from them, that she was probably angry about a perceived slight of her husband by Kostadin. In other words, if she were a friend, she would perform as a friend by joining in the singing; her lack of participation must have been a sign that she was no longer a friend.

This woman's musical nonparticipation then occasioned further reflection on and interpretation of the behaviors of members of the family, especially in-laws who had married into the family. Kostadin and Todora expressed their delight at the willingness of their children's spouses to sing and dance at social occasions and commented favorably on the in-laws who had married into the family. One exception, however, caused much anguished discussion. A nephew had married a woman who was "silent," who didn't join the "fun." From Kostadin and Todora's point of view, her silence at family celebrations indicated that she did not respect the family even though she had married into it.[9] Her musical inaction put the family's future in jeopardy. In these instances of reflection and

8. Cowan (1990: 206–224), in a chapter entitled "Aphrodite's Table," makes this point and gives a wonderful example of a party with music and dancing that ended unhappily. She interviewed participants afterward to illustrate the conflicting interpretations that helped each explain and interpret the party's failure.

9. Sugarman (1997: 59) comments on similar attitudes at Albanian weddings: "Guests are expected to express their happiness in the occasion being celebrated . . . through their singing and perhaps also dancing . . . . As an important means of asserting one family's respect for another, singing is regarded as a moral act"—yet another culturally specific metaphor about music's essence.

interpretation, social behavior is transformed into meaningful behavior, that is, a text worthy of commentary (Ricoeur 1971). In this instance, music as text is the flip side of music as social behavior. Often something special or unusual or troubling happens to cause people to turn over the record.

The metaphors of music as art and as symbol became especially important and the object of extensive discourse when the Bulgarian state took over as the principal patron and organizer of traditional music, song, and dance after World War II. The communist government in power from 1944 to 1989 appropriated village music to advance its ideological agenda.[10] Prominent on this agenda was the idea that all people—but especially the working classes, including peasants—should be exposed to great art as part of the Communist Party's progressive goals for the betterment of humankind under communism. For the communists, village music was a two-edged symbol. On the one hand, having been created, according to them, under conditions of feudalism and capitalism, it was a symbol (with a negative valence) of the very social and economic conditions the communists were trying to eradicate. On the other hand, at least since the national renaissance and the birth of ideas of independence from the Ottoman Empire in the mid-nineteenth century, traditional music, song, and dance had been viewed by intellectuals in urban centers as symbols of the Bulgarian people and therefore of the Bulgarian nation (Buchanan 1991). The communists understood the potential positive effect they could accrue to themselves by exploiting this positive symbol of the nation. Their problem was how to mediate the positive and negative valences of traditional music as symbol and create a new symbol to reference the progressive goals of the Communist Party.

The answer lay in transforming traditional music into an art by adding to it layers of Western art music such as harmony, counterpoint, and orchestral and choral textures; replacing traditional variation and improvisation with fixed compositional form through the use of musical notation; and demanding new standards of intonation and precision in performance. (These moves are delineated in Buchanan 1991, 1995.) Such art, understood by communists to be one of the highest intellectual achievements of humankind, could then also act as a symbol of the goals of the party for the spiritual advancement and progress of the working and peasant classes. Thus, the communists manipulated traditional music, song, and dance away from the metaphor of music as social behavior; embraced the metaphor of music as art; and assigned completely new meanings to it partially through the alteration of its form as a sign.

10. This section condenses an extensive literature by American scholars writing about changes to tradition and the politics of music under communism in Bulgaria. A selection of these works would include, among others, Buchanan (1991, 1995), Levy (1985), Rice (1994: 169–233), and Silverman (1982, 1983).

The communist state also created the possibility for traditional music to exist as commodity for large numbers of Bulgarians. In the villages of precommunist Bulgaria, supported mainly by subsistence farming, instrumental music, song, and dance were important parts of social life, but the economy did not generate enough money to support large numbers of professional musicians. A few land-less Roma (Gypsies) earned small amounts of money playing music, but for Bulgarian peasant farmers who supported their families by working the land and caring for animals, this path was not a possibility and was even negatively marked (Buchanan 1991: 314–318, 1995: 386; Rice 1994: 52–53). As the com-munists actively created their new symbols for the state, including new ways of making traditional music, they needed a cadre of instrumentalists, singers, and dancers capable of advancing and performing their symbolic vision of the future under communism. The mechanism for achieving this was the formation of professional ensembles of folk music, song, and dance at the national radio and television station and, eventually, in nearly every city and town of any size, a total of fourteen such ensembles by the 1980s (Buchanan 1995: 388). Skilled instrumentalists, singers, and dancers from the villages of Bulgaria could now sell their skill to the state, in the process transforming a social behavior into a commodity with new artistic values and new symbolic meanings.

This commodification of the tradition also changed traditional social struc-tures. As Buchanan (1996b: 195) has pointed out, "The incorporation of women into the state folk ensembles [as paid singers and dancers] during the 1950s flew in the face of the patriarchal social norm. . . . The participation of women . . . symbolized musical excellence, the emergence of music professionalism . . ., and the construction of socialist society." In the 1950s, professional musical performance gave village women, probably for the first time, an independent source of income and status outside the traditional family structure. Women's performance as professionals in state ensembles effectively restructured social relations within the families of participants.

Availing oneself of this new commodity value, however, was not always a sim-ple matter. In Strandzha in 1988, I met a fine singer who, after I complimented her on her singing and asked why she was not a professional, told me that her husband—presumably realizing the social implications of such a move—had prevented her from joining an ensemble. Todora, and I presume many other excellent singers, were so involved in the social life of the family, especially rais-ing children, that they couldn't free themselves to employ their skills in this new way. Instead, they continued to perform music primarily as an aspect of prewar forms of social behavior, many of which continue to the present.

Performing music professionally and also in village amateur "collectives" (*kolektivi*) was clearly a social behavior, in particular a way to perform fealty to the ideals of the communist state. (Levy 1985: 167–174 and Silverman 1982,

1983 describe these village collectives.) Buchanan (1995: 391) describes how the dominance in state ensembles of conservatory-educated conductors and arrangers over mainly provincial musicians with a deeper, experiential knowledge of the tradition "implement[ed] the value-laden hierarchy of power associated with the Western symphony." I assume that for these musicians this musical hierarchy probably felt like a synecdoche for power hierarchies of the totalitarian state (though they wouldn't have put it that way). Furthermore, "the non-traditional emphasis on precision playing [achieved under the direction of conductors and aided by musical notation was] a trademark of West European music professionalism" and thus "iconic of the socialist philosophy of cultural progress" (Buchanan 1995: 391). In the terms of the present discussion, I interpret Buchanan as suggesting that musical performance operated in this case semiotically both as icon and trademark and, through performative implementation, as social behavior. The musicians in effect performed in practice their social subordination to the state as represented by conductors and arrangers, a performance that could be read as text and interpreted symbolically by fellow Bulgarians and visiting ethnomusicologists.

What these Bulgarian examples illustrate is that these four qualities of music as social behavior, as symbol or text, as art, and as commodity coexist in complex relationships. Sometimes they seem to exist together, as they did during the communist period. At other times they follow serially one after another, as when a social behavior is subjected to interpretation to become a text. And sometimes one metaphor can seem to eclipse the others, as when in the communist period the social significance of music for various types of rural social structuring was almost completely erased by music as political symbol and commodity. It seems to me that questions about music and its significance (its meaning) for human life should be asked with these kinds of metaphoric shifts in mind.

## MUSICAL SIGNIFICATION

In this section I turn in more detail to one metaphoric claim about music, namely, that it is a symbol with referential meaning or a text for interpretation. The terms *symbol* and *text* have been developed in different discursive traditions. The implications of the term *symbol* have been worked out in detail in semiotics. As for *text*, I have applied Ricoeur's (1971) notion of meaningful action having textual properties to musical performance and claim that music is sometimes understood as a form of action interpretable for its reference to a world. Here I conflate these two ideas because they both make the claim that music can have referential meanings to things, ideas, worlds, and experiences within and outside itself.

When considering music as symbol or text, three obvious questions suggest themselves. How do musical symbols acquire their signification? What types of musical signification are there? Why does music seem to have multiple and changing references?

Without citing the literature in detail, it seems to me that semiotics has established that someone always makes music's symbolic reference—that is, symbols always signify something to someone. In other words, musical signification is always constructed; it is not simply there in the music. Because people construct references, music's semantic meaning varies from person to person, from place to place, and from time to time. As people move through social and historical space or when they occupy different spaces, their interpretations will differ and change. In the case of Bulgarian music, for example, we have already seen how the meaning attributed to village-style music making changed from the prewar to the postwar period when the cultural and social system changed.

If people create musical signification, it seems to me that they do so in at least four ways: (1) by recognizing its identity or similarity to other musical forms, (2) by positing its iconicity or resemblance to forms outside music, (3) by noticing its association with other things or ideas, and (4) by inferring a reference (a meaning) when two musical forms contrast with one another. In the spirit of my fourth definition of meaning, I want to focus on categorizing processes of interpretation rather than sign types, as is often done in semiotics.[11]

The identity or similarity of two performances of music, through either quotation or repetition, sets up the possibility for a signification generated by what some might call intertextuality. When a piece of music, its performance, or some of its parts are identical or similar to other pieces, performances, or parts, this identity or similarity—to those who recognize it—sets up an intertextual reference to that piece, performance, or part.[12] In the Bulgarian tradition, for example, such intertextual references are recognized between instrumental

11. Feld (1984: 8) calls similar processes of interpretation "interpretive moves," and his list of types, which moves beyond semiotics and combines ideas about the significance and signification of music, includes locational, categorical, associational, reflective, and evaluative moves.

12. As Turino (1999: 226–227) points out, in C. S. Peirce's trichotomy of sign types into icon, index, and symbol, such intertextuality or quotation would be classified as an icon, "a sign that is related to its object through some type of resemblance between them." Peirce further subdivides icons into three classes: image, diagram, and metaphor. Such musical intertextuality would be image-icons because of their "simple properties shared." In my classification of symbolic processes I have chosen to reserve the term *icon* for resemblances between musical and nonmusical things, that is, where the qualities shared may not be so simply apprehended. In Peircean terms this type of icon would probably be classified as a metaphor-icon. So the distinction I am making in this section between identity/similarity and iconicity/ resemblance would, in Peircean terms, be that between image-icon and metaphor-icon.

tunes and song tunes and between nearly identical tunes in different meters. In the former case instrumentalists borrow song tunes, transform them rhythmically by adding subdivisions of certain durations, and, in the process, create the basis for much of the instrumental repertoire. As Kostadin told me, referring to this process, "The richness of Bulgarian instrumental music is thanks to the wealth of songs" (Rice 1994: 103). For those who hear this association, the instrumental tune calls forth the associations or meanings of the song text and the contexts in which the song may have been heard. For those who don't hear the association, this aspect of musical signification is absent. Instrumentalists also use tunes in one meter to create new tunes in another meter. As a composer of instrumental tunes, Kostadin called it "his secret," even though many musicians know it (Rice 1994: 198). This means that a new tune in 7/8 can reference its original in 6/8, creating for those who recognize it a type of reference for the new tune.

Iconicity refers to a perceived resemblance between a musical structure or performance, whether an entire piece or some part of it, and something nonmusical, such as a religious belief, a political ideology, a kinship structure, or a social practice. Positing music's iconicity with other domains has been a particularly fruitful area of recent ethnomusicology writings. The results have included Judith and Alton Becker's (1981) claim that the cyclical structure of Javanese gamelan music—marked by gongs sounding shorter cycles within longer cycles—is iconic of (i.e., bears a resemblance to) more general Javanese conceptions of time, particularly a complicated calendar system with weeks of different lengths (e.g., five, six, and seven days) embedded within one another. The simultaneous sound of many gongs at certain moments in the gong cycle is an icon of the "full days" that result when the first days of many weeks coincide. Feld (1988) has shown that the Kaluli of Papua New Guinea sing in an overlapping style ("lift-up-over sounding") that is iconic of conversational style and the soundscape of the forest they live in, leading him to conclude that "the music of nature becomes the nature of music" (p. 102). The scholars pursuing this line of interpretation argue that such iconic relationships, often left uninterpreted by members of the culture and therefore requiring interpretation by ethnomusicologists, are a source of the affective power of music.

In the Bulgarian case, recall Buchanan's claim, cited earlier, that during the communist period many features of arranged ensemble playing, including its precision, were iconic of socialist ideas about progress and submission to state control. In this area of iconicity the link between aesthetics and ethics becomes clearest. A good way of making music, in other words, is often also a good way of being socially in the world. Turino (1993), for example, has demonstrated this clearly for the Ayacucho Indians of the Andean highlands in Peru, for whom large and out-of-tune ensembles iconically represent and enact an ethics of community participation that overrules narrower, more strictly musical aesthetics; that is, musical performance seems to be simultaneously a symbol and a social practice.

Association refers to the attribution of meaning to a musical form through some kind of co-occurrence. In Peircean semiotics, such a musical sign belongs to the class of signs called "index"—"a sign that is related to its object through co-occurrence in actual experience" (Turino 1999: 227). When an interpreter notices this co-occurrence, I label the interpretive process that results an association. In Bulgaria, the association of folk music with the state was made clear at performances in which symbols of the state were prominent aspects of the stage setting (see Rice 1994: 277–278 for a description of such an event). For example, the Bulgarian and Soviet flags might be flown prominently or the backdrop of an outdoor stage might consist of a drawn portrait of Todor Zhivkov, long-time head of the Bulgarian Communist Party, or sometimes of the entire politburo. In such cases it was impossible to escape the intended meaning, accomplished through created associations, that well-performed Bulgarian traditional music, properly selected and arranged, was an index of the good things the party was promising and of the bright, progressive future it held out for the people. In more traditional, localized instances one person might so often request a given instrumental tune that it effectively became his index, an association that would often be ratified in the naming or renaming of the tune as, say, "Ivan's tune." And when the tune was played the now-referential tune would evoke thoughts and memories of Ivan.

Contrast is, in some sense, the opposite of identity and similarity, but it refers to a more complex semiotic process. Instead of a perceived identity or similarity between two symbolic forms (or signs), they appear to contrast over one or many features. By focusing on contrast in the forms, people associate different, often opposite, meanings to the two forms. The "symbolic logic" here is that if sign A refers to an object B through identity, resemblance, or association, then its opposite (sign –A) can refer to objects that are the opposite of object B, that is, –B, even in the absence of identity, resemblance, or association between sign –A and object –B. In this case, the signs move into the Peircean sign class of symbols. Turino (1999) argues that a symbol in the Peircean scheme is a sign "related to its object through the use of language, rather than being fully dependent on iconicity or indexicality" (p. 227). Sign contrast, in other words, creates signification that flows from the relation between signs rather than from the identity, resemblance, or association of a sign with its object.

Musical change and the history of music, it seems to me, have often come about when people rather self-consciously develop new forms of music that contrast with old forms to articulate with, comment on, reference, or serve new social formations and new cultural understandings. In Bulgaria, as we have seen, the contrast between traditional solo playing and singing and modern choral singing and orchestral playing was created as a way to represent a new meaning for folk music—namely, a modern, communist ideal in contrast to the older style, which represented the feudal, capitalist, and Ottoman societies that supported it before the communists came to power. Orchestras and choruses may be iconic of socialist ideas and indexical of (associated with) modernity. They also gain those references from the semiotic contrast between older forms of village music as indexes of the traditional, the backward, the past, and the national. The pairing of musical signs, with their contrasts of solo/group, monophonic/harmonic, variable tuning/fixed tuning, and so forth, creates the possibility that the new sign can be interpreted as a symbol (in addition to an icon or index) of modernity, the progressive, the future, and the cosmopolitan.

In the 1980s, Bulgarian music performed at weddings evolved into a performance style that contrasted in almost every respect with the state-supported version of the music (Buchanan 1991, 1996a; Rice 1994, 1996; Silverman 1989). Although in many respects the melodies, song lyrics, meters, and rhythms were the same in the two types of music, wedding music evolved into a highly improvised, chromatic form with amplified Western instruments performed by small ensembles featuring minority Rom musicians. This style contrasted with the emphasis in the state's arranged folklore on composition, acoustic traditional instruments, diatonicism, and ethnic purity. This contrast in the form of the sign suggested to some Bulgarian listeners that wedding music could stand for the opposite of what the state's music referenced through association. As the communist system declined in the 1980s and the state was viewed in more negative terms, this contrast in musical style seemed to reference symbolically a contrast between a present, outmoded, totalitarian, oppressive political system and a hoped-for vibrant, democratic, and free political system. There are, of course, some iconic elements in wedding music as a sign. Improvisation, virtuosity, and loudness could be interpreted as icons of freedom, individuality, and lack of control, respectively. But these icons become more convincing as interpretations within the symbolic frame created by the contrast between the forms of musical signs.

The third question—why can music bear so many meanings simultaneously?—has at least five answers.

First, music itself is made up of many elements that occur simultaneously: melody, rhythm, timbre, loudness, and textural interplay between simultaneous voices to name but a few. Each of these elements can have different meanings associated with them simultaneously. As Turino (1999: 237) asserts, "The multi-componential aspect of music can not be overemphasized as a basis for music's affective and semiotic potential." For example, traditional Bulgarian melodies and meters can reference a nation and its supposed ancient history, while the harmonies that accompany it can simultaneously reference the modern world beyond the nation and aspirations for progress from a dim, impoverished past to a bright, prosperous future. Thus, the complexity of the musical sign itself opens up the possibility of multiple meanings.

Second, since musical meaning may arise from at least four processes (identity, iconicity, association, and contrast), each of these processes may contribute its own meaning to the musical sign.

Third, the passage of time means that each new performance of music has new potential for meanings to be assigned to it, whether in relation to previous performances or in association with the new events in which it occurs. For example, traditional unaccompanied Bulgarian singing performed in a village before World War II may have been interpreted as a symbol of appropriate social behavior; the same singing after the war became a symbol of the nation and, specifically, of its imagined past rather than its gritty present or glorious future.

Fourth, the sign's form can change over time, opening up the possibility of new meanings. When Bulgarian instrumental music based on traditional diatonic melodies with a range of a sixth absorbed chromaticisms and arpeggiations over an octave range in the second half of the twentieth century, the new forms signified a striving for modernity of a rather different kind from that envisioned by communist-inspired aesthetics (Buchanan 1996a; Rice 1996).

Fifth, as music is performed in many different contexts, with different people interpreting it, it can take on new meanings. Bulgarian music performed by a family at home may be interpreted as evidence of a desire to realize a family's potential to create good feelings among its members; performed at a state-sanctioned holiday, it may be interpreted as evidence of the family's support of the state's policies in areas beyond the musical domain.

So the answer to the question of whether music has referential meaning is not no, as my former young colleague claimed, apparently frustrated by its malleability compared to what he supposed, probably incorrectly, are the more permanent and shared significations of language utterances. Rather, the answer is a resounding yes. And music can have a wonderful surfeit of meanings at that. Part of the power of music surely lies in its capacity to absorb and refract multiple meanings, sometimes simultaneously, sometimes serially.

## THE CONTROL OF MEANING

Since interpreters assign signification to music, we need to ask: In particular situations, who gets to assign meaning to music? Are such assignments of meaning policed and controlled, and if so, how and why? If different people or groups assign different meanings to music, then to what extent does this give rise to discord or contestation? These questions are inspired to some extent by Foucault's (1980) equation of knowledge and power and his critique of discourse as a domain where power in the guise of knowledge is exercised.

The obvious answer to the first question is that everyone who comes in contact with a given piece or performance gets to assign a meaning or meanings to it. When music functions as a text or symbol, the author, composer, or performer of that text is only its first reader, its first interpreter. Though listeners and subsequent performers of it may want, as a matter of curiosity, to divine its meaning in relation to its author's intentions, they are under no obligation to do so. They may prefer to assign their own meanings to it, in the process making the music a significant, signifying aspect of their own lives. It is in the nature of music as text or symbol that composers and performers cannot control its interpretation and the meanings that subsequently accrue to it. When dissatisfaction with the communist government reached its peak in the 1980s, the positive valence the state applied to its arranged versions of traditional music took on a negative valence for the growing number of people unhappy with their lot and no longer optimistic about their future under communism.

If music can attract to itself an efflorescence of interpretation and signification, how and when are they contested? Within local communities, it seems to me that very often it is the community and its values, acted out in countless unremarkable, quotidian activities, that tend to dominate individual interpretations in the space where meaning is assigned to particular performances of music. At the national level, governments and their representative institutions—ministries of culture and education, for example—actually have some power to strongly influence, even if they can't quite control, music's interpretation and meaning. Totalitarian states in the twentieth century have been especially interested in controlling music production and meaning, perhaps understanding, better than even some scholars do, music's affective power and therefore the emotion that goes along with its interpretation.[13] In the Bulgarian case the government had at its command all the symbolic techniques I listed earlier, coupled with its control of the organizations of power and propaganda, including the ministries of culture and education and state-run radio, television, and the recording industry. They appropriated folk music as a symbol because of its identity with the music of the past experience of a majority of Bulgarians, who had grown up in rural environments and for whom this music represented the comforts of home and

13. One of the major points of Turino's (1999) article on Peircean semiotics is that it may provide the foundation for an understanding of musical affect, emotion, and sentiment. In particular, he claims that music operates at the level of icon and index in ways that are prelinguistic and that even block conscious symbolic analysis of meaning.

childhood. Through their control of educational and cultural institutions they altered its form to bring it into line with more modern forms of music, setting up the possibility that it could reference (through identity, resemblance, association, and contrast) both the rural past and a hoped-for progressive future. They controlled the means of dissemination of this new form, ensuring its ubiquitous presentation and reception, to the exclusion of other, competing signs of modernity borrowed, for example, from jazz and popular music. The beauty, sophistication, and polish of arranged folklore thus became an icon of the good life promised by the communists in the future. Finally, they controlled the meanings that accrued to arranged music by its association with signs of the state on national holidays, public ceremonies, and state-controlled media. In sum, these political meanings were inescapable, though not unassailable.

Even though the state created the musical signs and controlled many of the events at which meanings were made evident through association, the meaning of music is too elusive for even totalitarian states to control. Kostadin, for example, who became a professional bagpiper in a state-sponsored orchestra of folk instruments, tried to ignore the other instruments that, as he put it, "howled" around him so that even arranged music could continue to be associated with (i.e., be an index of) his past life in the village. In a similar vein, Buchanan (1995) provides a nuanced account of the complex interactions of "webs of symbolic discourses" (p. 382) during the communist period, which included a negotiation between musicians' "individual and localized worldviews" and the "reality constructed by their government" (p. 384).

The state also could not control the valence of the meanings it tried to assign to music. When in the early years of the communist period people's attitudes to the state were largely positive, the valence of this music seems to have been largely positive (Buchanan 1995: 396; Rice 1994: 183). But in the 1980s, when negative attitudes to the party and state were ascendant, the valence of this music became rather negative. And the state couldn't control people's attention to their music to receive its intended meanings. People disenchanted with the state and its music turned their attention to other forms of music, including foreign music from Serbia and other neighboring countries; wedding music, which was evolving outside state control; and rock music and jazz. (The state's somewhat futile attempts to control wedding music as one response to its extraordinary popularity are documented in Buchanan 1991, 1996a; Rice 1994: 250–255; and Silverman 1989.)

These kinds of music, in my view, became signs of freedom from totalitarian control, and the state was powerless to control them and their meanings (cf. Buchanan 1996a: 225; Rice 1996). Technology, especially radio from foreign countries and a burgeoning new technology—amateur recordings on audiocassette—effectively operated outside state control (Silverman 1983). The state tried to control these new musics and meanings through state-sponsored festivals of wedding music and even the arrest of the most prominent musician in this genre, Ivo Papazov (Buchanan 1996a). But these efforts proved feckless, and wedding music and its meanings became one of the early warning signs of the demise of the totalitarian state.

Music, with its possibilities for multiple meanings and its ability to generate affect, is an emotion-laden form rich with possibilities for ideological model-ing and control and yet able, in many instances, to wiggle free of that control, either because of the uncontrollability of the electronic technologies in which it is disseminated, the multiplicity of references inherent in music as a semiotic form, or the claim by its makers and listeners that it is, after all, not a sign that signifies at all, but an art.

## CONCLUSION

I have tried to outline three important dimensions of music and meaning in this chapter and illustrate them with references to Bulgarian music. First, one way to approach musical meaning in its broad sense (i.e., its significance for human life) is to focus on the claims to truth about music made through meta-phorical predication: music is art, social behavior, commodity, symbol, text, and many more. Second, music operates as a symbol or text in at least four basic ways: when interpreters recognize (1) identity or similarity with previous pieces or performances; (2) iconicity with something beyond music, such as an ideational or social system; (3) an association with individuals, events, ideas, or institutions; and (4) formal musical contrasts that imply different referential meaning. Third, music always means something to someone, and therefore its meanings are inevitably multiple and contestable and, in some instances, con-trollable. Music and meaning appears to be an especially rich area of research, partly because of the multiple stories people and institutions operating from vastly different social, historical, and geographical positions tell about it and partly because its essence escapes every attempt to corral and control either its significance or its signification.

## REFERENCES

Bakan, Michael. 1999. *Music of Death and New Creation: Experiences in the World of Balinese Gamelan Beleganjur.* Chicago: University of Chicago Press.

Becker, Judith, and Alton Becker. 1981. "A Musical Icon: Power and Meaning in Javanese Gamelan Music." In W. Steiner, ed., *The Sign in Music and Literature.* Austin: University of Texas Press, pp. 203–215.

Berliner, Paul. 1994. *Thinking in Jazz.* Chicago: University of Chicago Press.

Bohlman, Philip V. 1999. "Ontologies of Music." In N. Cook and M. Everist, eds., *Rethinking Music.* Oxford: Oxford University Press, pp. 17–34.

Bourdieu, Pierre. 1977. *Outline of a Theory of Practice.* Cambridge: Cambridge University Press.

Brinner, Benjamin. 1995. *Knowing Music, Making Music: Javanese Gamelan and the Theory of Musical Competence and Innovation.* Chicago: University of Chicago Press.

Buchanan, Donna A. 1991. "The Bulgarian Folk Orchestra: Cultural Performance, Symbol, and the Construction of National Identity in Socialist Bulgaria." PhD dissertation, University of Texas, Austin.

———. 1995. "Metaphors of Power, Metaphors of Truth: The Politics of Music Professionalism in Bulgarian Folk Orchestras." *Ethnomusicology* 39(3): 381–416.

———. 1996a. "Wedding Musicians, Political Transition, and National Consciousness in Bulgaria." In M. Slobin, ed., *Retuning Culture: Musical Changes in Central and Eastern Europe.* Durham, NC: Duke University Press, pp. 200–230.

———. 1996b. "Dispelling the Mystery: The Commodification of Women and Musical Tradition in the Marketing of *Le mystère des voix bulgares.*" *Balkanistica* 9(2): 193–210.

Clayton, Martin. 2001. "Introduction: Toward a Theory of Musical Meaning (in India and Elsewhere)." *British Journal of Ethnomusicology* 10(1): 1–17.

Cowan, Jane. 1990. *Dance and the Body Politic in Northern Greece.* Princeton, NJ: Princeton University Press.

Feld, Steven. 1974. "Linguistics and Ethnomusicology." *Ethnomusicology* 18(2): 197–217.

———. 1984. "Communication, Music, and Speech About Music." *Yearbook for Traditional Music* 16: 1–18.

———. 1988. "Aesthetics as Iconicity of Style, or 'Lift-up-Over Sounding': Getting Into the Kaluli Groove." *Yearbook for Traditional Music* 20: 74–114.

Foucault, Michel. 1980. *The History of Sexuality. Volume 1: An Introduction.* New York: Vintage.

Lakoff, George, and Mark Johnson. 1980. *Metaphors We Live By.* Chicago: University of Chicago Press.

Levy, Mark. 1985. "The Bagpipe in the Rhodope Mountains of Bulgaria." PhD dissertation, University of California, Los Angeles.

McAllester, David P. 1954. *Enemy Way Music.* Cambridge, MA: Peabody Museum, Harvard University.

McClary, Susan. 2000. *Conventional Wisdom: The Content of Music Form.* Berkeley: University of California Press.

Merriam, Alan P. 1964. *The Anthropology of Music.* Evanston, IL: Northwestern University Press.

Rice, Timothy. 1994. *May It Fill Your Soul: Experiencing Bulgarian Music.* Chicago: University of Chicago Press.

———. 1996. "The Dialectic of Economics and Aesthetics in Bulgarian Music." In M. Slobin, ed., *Retuning Culture: Musical Changes in Central and Eastern Europe.* Durham, NC: Duke University Press, pp. 176–199.

Ricoeur, Paul. 1971. "The Model of the Text: Meaningful Action Considered as a Text." *Social Research* 38: 529–562.

——. 1981. *Hermeneutics and the Human Sciences*, edited by J. B. Thompson. Cambridge: Cambridge University Press.

Seeger, Anthony. 1987. *Why Suyá Sing*. Cambridge: Cambridge University Press.

Silverman, Carol. 1982. "Bulgarian Lore and American Folkloristics: The Case of Contemporary Bulgarian Folk Music." In W. W. Kolar, ed., *Culture and History of the Bulgarian People: Their Bulgarian and American Parallels*. Pittsburgh, PA: Tamburitza Press, pp. 65–78.

——. 1983. "The Politics of Folklore in Bulgaria." *Anthropological Quarterly* 56(2): 55–61.

——. 1989. "The Historical Shape of Folklore in Bulgaria." In Dunja Rihtman-Augustin and Maja Povrzanovic, eds. *Folklore and Historical Process*. Zagreb: Institute of Folklore Research, pp. 149–158.

Slobin, Mark. 1996. *Retuning Culture: Musical Changes in Central and Eastern Europe*. Durham, NC: Duke University Press.

Small, Christopher. 1998. *Musicking: The Meanings of Performing and Listening*. Hanover, NH, and London: Wesleyan University Press.

Sugarman, Jane C. 1997. *Engendering Song: Singing and Subjectivity at Prespa Albanian Weddings*. Chicago: University of Chicago Press.

Tenzer, Michael. 2000. *Gamelan Gong Kebyar: The Art of Twentieth-Century Balinese Music*. Chicago: University of Chicago Press.

Turino, Thomas. 1993. *Moving Away from Silence: Music of the Peruvian Altiplano and the Experience of Urban Migration*. Chicago: University of Chicago Press.

——. 1999. "Signs of Imagination, Identity, and Experience: A Peircian Semiotic Theory for Music. *Ethnomusicology* 43(2): 221–255.

Waterman, Christopher Alan. 1990. *Juju: A Social History and Ethnography of an African Popular Music*. Chicago: University of Chicago Press.

Witherspoon, Gary. 1977. *Language and Art in the Navajo Universe*. Ann Arbor: University of Michigan Press.

# 4

# Time, Place, and Metaphor in Musical Experience and Ethnography

What kind of a world do ethnomusicologists and the people we study live in? What questions are we asking of that world, of ourselves, and of music makers and music making? It seems to me that for many years ethnomusicologists have been moving toward ever new answers to these questions and that that movement demands yet a third question: what sorts of theoretical frameworks might help us answer the questions we are asking about music in the world as we understand it?[1]

One venerable theoretical framework, dating from Alan Merriam's 1964 *The Anthropology of Music,* seems to construct, in line with the anthropology of the day, a relatively simple world of bounded, isolated, shared cultures and relatively static social structures. The primary questions that arise for ethnomusicology

1. The ideas in this chapter were first developed in response to an invitation from T. M. Scruggs of the University of Iowa to speak in a lecture series he organized in 1996 on globalization, nationalism, and the commodification of music. Later versions were presented at the University of California, Santa Barbara (1998); Florida State University (2000); the University of Valladolid, Spain (2002); and the University of Texas at Austin (2002). I am grateful for all these invitations and the stimulating suggestions of students and faculty on each of these occasions. Versions were also presented as an invited keynote address to the Third Triennial Meeting of the British Musicological Societies (1999); at the Thirty-Fifth World Conference of International Council for Traditional Music in Hiroshima, Japan (1999); and at the annual meeting of the Society for Ethnomusicology (2000), where Salwa El-Shawan Castelo-Branco, David Elliott (a music educator), Andrew Killick, and Ellen Koskoff provided thoughtful responses. I am also grateful for the helpful comments on a previous draft of this chapter by Jonathan Stock and Veit Erlmann. The research for the third story, about Bulgarian popfolk in the summer of 2000, was supported by a Short-Term Travel Grant from the International Research and Exchanges Board (IREX).

from this worldview concern the relationship of music to other domains of culture and its role (as mirror or agent) in the maintenance or change of social systems. This framework still usefully guides a significant portion of our research, even as we have moved beyond the oversimplified view of the world that it supports. Most ethnomusicologists understand that today's world, the world in which we and our subjects make, understand, and experience music, is more complex than it used to be or we are realizing that it was always complex and our ways of thinking about it were too schematic and blinkered.

If we now understand our world as not so simple, but rather as a complex of unbounded, interacting cultures and as consisting crucially of the rapid movement of people, ideas, images, and music over vast distances, then what sorts of questions arise? Ethnomusicology has developed as an omnivorous intellectual arena for asking nearly every conceivable question about music, so a short list of questions will hardly do. But here are a few that respond, in some measure, to our understanding that music making today occurs in a complex, mobile, dynamic world. In what ways does musical experience change through time? Why do two people living in the same time and place experience the same music so differently? Why do people of the same ethnic group make such different kinds of music? What happens to musical experience as mediated musical sound shuttles through space? Under what conditions does music change from a pleasant aesthetic experience to a repulsive symbol of a loathsome politics? Why do totalitarian states repress, censor, and even liquidate artists who merely make music and sing songs? When does it become necessary to create a new musical style? Why do Korean American youth living in Los Angeles love African American music?

It seems to me that these sorts of questions invite us to move in two directions simultaneously: first, toward more atomized studies of individuals and small groups of individuals linked for perhaps just a moment in time and place by shared beliefs, social status, behaviors, tastes, and experiences of the world (and perhaps not at all by ethnicity), and second, toward understanding these individual beliefs and actions as taking place within a "modern world system" of some sort, a system that at the least challenges, and in some cases seems nearly to obliterate, cultures and societies as traditionally understood. Although some will be moved to analyze the structure and function (and perhaps culture) of this modern world system, my list of questions points in the direction of individual or small-group musical experience. I seek answers to the general question, how do individuals experience music in modernity, in modern life, in the modern world system?

To help answer this question and the kinds of questions listed earlier, I propose in this chapter a "three-dimensional space of musical experience" that should help us write what I call "subject-centered musical ethnography."

I suggest that a move away from culture to the subject as the locus of musical practice and experience may provide a fruitful approach to some of the questions about music that our encounter with the modern world leads us to ask.

## THE BACKGROUND IN THEORY AND PRACTICE

The broad intellectual context in which many ethnomusicologists now work and which frames this proposal begins with anthropologists' own critique of the culture concept, encapsulated in Lila Abu-Lughod's evocative 1991 article titled "Writing against Culture," and worked out in detail by postcolonial and feminist scholars and critics of ethnographic writing. These critics argue for tension, strain, and contestation among different social and temporal "subject positions" within culture and against the ethnographic construction of an idealized, shared culture among, for example, undifferentiated Balinese or Nuer (see Borofsky et al. 2001 for a recent manifestation of this argument). This translates into a hypothesis that, while aspects of musical experience may be shared by a sociocultural or ethnic group, important differences will be observed that can be understood through a fine-grained analysis of the shifting temporal, social, and cultural bases of that experience.

A second influential line of thought from anthropology has been the re-envisioning of the world and the call for a reorientation of its study by such scholars as Arjun Appadurai and James Clifford. Appadurai (1996) argues for a newly complex world, one that is "deterritorialized," increasingly made up of wandering migrant laborers, political exiles, war refugees, transnational businesspeople, hopeful immigrants, and bourgeois tourists. If "locals" are dislodged by forces beyond their control, those who remain behind are increasingly subjected to products, organizations, and mass-mediated images circulating in an ever more globalized economic system. Even though many studies have documented intercultural contact, movement, and subjugations of the local in the more or less distant past (e.g., J. L. Abu-Lughod 1989; Braudel 1981–1984; Curtin 1984; Wallerstein 1974, 1980, 1989), Appadurai (1996) prefers to argue that earlier forms of translocal processes and capitalist and colonial world systems differ fundamentally from the current situation. In particular, he claims that new technologies of travel and documentation have allowed us to enter a "new condition of neighborliness," where we need theories of "rootlessness, alienation, and psychological distance" driven by "fantasies (or nightmares) of electronic propinquity" (p. 29). Clifford (1997: 5), on the other hand, stresses the continuity between past and present conditions of travel and rootlessness and is instead critical of older anthropological paradigms that ignore them, in particular the "classic quest—exoticist, anthropological, orientalist—for pure traditions and discrete cultural differences. Intercultural connection is, and has long been, the norm." If traditional methods were blind to these interconnections, he proposes a new focus on routes rather than roots, on travel rather than dwelling, and on a serious ethnographic encounter with the agents and territories that anthropologists (and ethnomusicologists) encounter on their way to their imaginary, isolated locales: international travel, the city, and the cosmopolitans who visit or reside there, people such as school teachers, missionaries, doctors, government officials, traders, and producers of commercial sound recordings.

While these theoretical repositionings in anthropology have been useful to ethnomusicologists, our understandings have also been reconstituted by our own practice, or more precisely by the practice of those we work with and study, who have caused us to think about the "world of music" in new ways. In particular, the commercial genre known as "world music" has challenged those who study it (e.g., Erlmann 1993; Guilbault 1997; Monson 1999). Veit Erlmann has opened up the problem most succinctly for my purposes by positing a dichotomy between accounting for a world system of global/local dialectics and accounting for the experience of that system, which he acknowledges are not the same. His theoretical proposals seemed aimed primarily at understanding and critiquing the system, while my interest in subject-centered musical ethnography represents a proposal for approaching the other side of the dichotomy, experience. In doing so I hope to avoid "the romanticization and mythologization of individual experience and agency" (Erlmann 1993: 7), which in this proposal is neither a stand-in for the local and therefore tradition as against modernity nor a hopelessly optimistic place for antihegemonic thought and action and a "diversity [that] subverts homogeneity" (p. 5). In the end I imagine we would both agree that this dichotomy needs to be resolved through a synthesis of some kind, and indeed he has moved toward achieving that synthesis in his more recent work (Erlmann 1999).

"World music" is not the only musical sign of modernity, however, nor are the challenges it poses to ethnomusicological theory unique to it. Modernity has also infiltrated, confronted, changed, and invigorated local forms of music making not yet fully engaged with the global marketplace. Not least among the problems for musical ethnography has been the challenge of following those we study as they travel around the world. Twenty years ago while living and working in Toronto, I received a request to borrow some recording equipment from an American graduate student studying Azorean song dueling. When I asked why he was not going to the Azores, he replied that the best singers in the tradition lived in Canada. Thomas Turino (1993) traveled between the Andean highlands and Lima, Peru, just as those he studied did. Theodore Levin's (1996) quest to understand Central Asian music led him to Queens, New York. Jane

Sugarman (1997) used her own observations and Albanian-made videotapes to create a seamless narrative of the role of wedding music in the creation of Albanian culture in a diaspora that took her to western Macedonia, Toronto, and Detroit. Helen Rees (2000) accompanied local Naxi musicians from China's southwestern border province of Yunnan back to her native England to translate for their first international tour. She summarizes neatly the temporal, spatial, and conceptual arc of one musical practice, writing that *Dongjing* music from Lijiang

> has been exalted ritual music, refined secular entertainment, funeral music, tool of patriotic and political propaganda, object of musicological interest, emblem of place and ethnicity, and an economic asset in the socialist market economy and the tourist trade. Over the last fifty years it has also traveled a trajectory of geographically widening recognition and significance. . . . Before 1949 a music of purely local significance, it gradually gained sporadic recognition at provincial and national levels, and since 1988 has achieved national and international acclaim through tourist performances, commercial recordings, and concert tours to Canton, Beijing, Shanghai, Hong Kong, Taiwan, and six European countries. (p. 193)

Such changes in the uses of music through time and its transportation through space are increasingly reflected in the textures of the musical ethnographies ethnomusicologists are writing.

Equally noteworthy is the jumble of musical and cultural styles we encounter in one place. Bruno Nettl (1983) has long been an advocate of studying all the music of a society, but the conjunction of cultural experiences and musical forms enabling and influencing Kheli Fiedjoe, a fifteen-year-old piano prodigy in Lomé, Togo, challenges us in new ways. The son of two doctors and the student of a teacher educated in philosophy at the Sorbonne, his world consists of "Tupac Shakur meeting Pushkin to a tune by Saint-Saëns, orchestrated by Salif Keita."

> This is the scene: Kheli is in the living room trying to practice. His mom is up on the roof pounding manioc for the fufu [a staple dish] while she recites Buddhist mantras. His dad is sitting in the paillotte [a traditional straw-thatched gazebo] with grandpa, reading The New England Journal of Medicine. His sister is off in France, letting her native Mina [the local language] grow rusty while she pursues a master's degree in business English and Portuguese. His school principal is singing spirituals in a classical soprano, straight out of the Harlem Renaissance. His Lycee Francais buddies are getting ready to go out dancing to soukous and Eurotechno at

Privilege, the Lebanese-run disco. The poor boys in his neighborhood are playing barefoot soccer, calling out the names of Nigerian stars who play for top-ranked Dutch clubs. Their sisters are in the market, selling water for four cents a bag from trays on their heads, humming Ivorian makossa, Ghanaian gospel, local traditional Mina tunes, French hip-hop, American R & B. (Steinglass 2001: 20)

This mix of cultural and musical styles, in versions now endlessly available around the globe, is made possible by colonialism in the first instance and the ubiquity of electronic media in the second. The simultaneity of every place in one place is another marker, in addition to travel in timespace, of modernity all over the world. Although ethnomusicologists are increasingly narrating such stories, the implications of such narratives for theory and method are just beginning to be elucidated. In what follows, I would like to make some suggestions as a contribution to that discussion.

One of the most ambitious attempts in ethnomusicology to make some general sense of the complexities of music making in the kind of world I have just encapsulated anecdotally is Mark Slobin's *Subcultural Sounds: Micromusics of the West* (1993), a rare and laudable attempt to move beyond the particularism of so many of our musical ethnographies to "frameworks, guidelines, [and] categories" that might aid "a future comparative method" and yet are "open-ended enough to allow for substantial revision and extension" (p. 6). Slobin seems most intent on accounting for the shifting variety of small-group interactions at the local level, while acknowledging that this microlevel, the subcultural as he calls it, is increasingly penetrated by influences at the intercultural and supercultural macrolevels. Below the subcultural level he is interested in the individual musician or music lover whose musical experience is formed at the intersection of these three types of "-cultures" (p. 11). He hopes that readers "will modify, elaborate, or even discard my proposals in a spirit of dialogue" (p. 13).

In that spirit, the proposal I present later responds to four basic issues that arise for me in Slobin's suggestions. First, though Slobin seems as fascinated by "lived musical experience" as he is by local "musical scenes," the narrative weight falls on the scenes and "the dynamics of subcultural life" (Slobin 1993: 38) rather than on individual experience. His characterization, following Appadurai, of "a planet in flux" (p. 15) seems to capture a fragmentation of experience that might make a focus on individuals fruitful, and I take as my starting point Slobin's suggestive epigram, "we are all individual music cultures" (p. ix). Second, his division of the world into subcultures, intercultures, and supercultures and his lists of units under these broad categories is helpful: at the subcultural level are the family, the neighborhood, the organizing committee, the ethnic group (p. 36), and gender and class; at the intercultural level are the music industry, diaspora, and affinity groups; and at the supercultural level are regions, transregions, nation-states, and, after Appadurai, ethnoscapes, technoscapes, financescapes, mediascapes, and ideoscapes. In my view, these units (and others that might be suggested) are not simply cultures and cultural but social and geographical (or sociogeographical) locales in which individuals experience music, along with other things. Third, many of the conundrums that Slobin uncovers within and between "-cultures" can be clarified and even resolved by more careful attention to temporality. Tellingly, only in the "closing thoughts" of the last chapter does he introduce time systematically, in a three-part classification of the length of "intergroup contact: long-standing, medium-range, and quite recent" (p. 112), and time's absence is a felt gap throughout the book that I would like to fill in here. Fourth, Slobin lists the enormous variety of uses and experiences associated with music. As he puts it, "Music is at once an everyday activity, an industrial commodity, a flag of resistance, a personal world, and a deeply symbolic, emotional grounding for people in every class and cranny the superculture offers" (p. 77). This is an important theme and in what follows I try to push this line of thinking a bit further.

## SUBJECT-CENTERED MUSICAL ETHNOGRAPHY

My proposal concerning the possibilities for and the structure of subject-centered musical ethnographies takes seriously Slobin's notion that we are all individual musical cultures. Although Erlmann (1993: 6) worries that such an approach will result only in "a random collection of ethnoaesthetics," I think such ethnographies may have some useful theoretical payoffs. One of the goals of modeling these ethnographies would be to bring some narrative coherence to the complex and seemingly fragmented world that many social theorists, cultural critics, and ethnomusicologists are writing about. That coherence would be situated in subjects' biographies and in the interaction of people occupying slightly different subject positions but interacting in time and place. Structuring musical ethnographies similarly using a model such as I propose later would introduce a modest level of systematicity and reduce the randomness of such an approach. What I emphatically am not suggesting is that subject-centered ethnographies are preferable to those that employ other analytic foci. Rather, it seems to me that it might be one of many ways to bring some order to our research in the crazy quilt of a world described by Appadurai and Clifford and experienced by many of us.

Since my proposal begins with the notion of subject, some discussion of that concept is necessary. Contemporary social theory uses a number of somewhat equivalent terms: person, individual, self, subject, agent, and actor. Different theoretical perspectives inevitably favor one or another of them, and they have different referents and relevance in different cultures (see, e.g., Ochs and Capps 1996). It is beyond the scope of this chapter to tease out the senses in which these terms are used in different discursive traditions, and in what follows I am going to use them somewhat interchangeably. In general, however, I claim that the subject, self, or individual around whom musical ethnography might be centered is a thoroughly social and self-reflexive being. It is this idea that makes subject-centered (or self-centered!) musical ethnography productive.

In this view, experience is not an inner phenomenon accessible only via introspection to the one having the experience. Rather, experience begins with interaction with a world and with others. For Maurice Merleau-Ponty, experience begins socially and prelinguistically with a body-subject that is "sentient and sensible, it sees and is seen, hears and is heard, touches and is touched" (Crossley 1994). The self is made through an encounter with symbols in the world into which it is "thrown" (Gadamer 1975), the process reaching its culmination with the learning of language, always already given socially, and the development of self-awareness, self-reflexivity, and awareness of others. It is this thoroughly social self, subject, or person that is amenable to the kinds of social analyses favored by ethnomusicologists. Biography or subject-centered ethnography then becomes not a documentation of individuality and creative genius (though it could be that) but an account of the social "authoring" (to use Bakhtin's trope) of the self.

If the self is inherently social, Anthony Giddens (1991: 1) extends the argument relevantly for my project by claiming that self-reflexivity and narratives of the self are conditions of "high" or "late" modernity in which traditional "habits and customs" are "undercut." In his view tradition gave to people their habitus, status, and roles, in the process limiting their ability to structure a self outside these given frameworks. Modernity, on the other hand, knocks down these traditional underpinnings and requires all of us to construct reflexively our biographies from a wide array of choices not available in traditional societies. Lifestyle choice becomes not a trivial accoutrement of the bourgeoisie but crucial for everyone living in modernity (p. 5). "What to do? How to act? Who to be? These are focal questions for everyone living in circumstances of late modernity—and ones that, on some level or another, all of us answer, either discursively or through day-to-day social behaviour" (p. 70). The self-reflexive project of self-identity in modernity, understood as a social process, provides the rationale and foundation for subject-centered musical ethnography. Not coincidentally, the acknowledgment of our self-reflexivity as scholars has shifted the focus of some recent musical ethnographies to individuals (or sets of individuals), their self-understandings, and the interpretation of their musical practices by interested others (e.g., Bakan 1999; Friedson 1996; Rice 1994; Stock 1996; Titon 1988; see also Stock 2001 for an overview of issues concerning the ethnomusicological study of individuals).[2]

## THREE DIMENSIONS OF MUSICAL EXPERIENCE

My proposal for subject-centered musical ethnography posits for each subject, person, or individual a three-dimensional space of musical experience. The three dimensions of this imaginary, ideal space are time, location, and metaphor (Figure 4.1). This space is ideal in two senses. First, three or more orthogonal dimensions define and construct "space" in formal, mathematical terms, a concept of space given to us by Newton and Leibniz. Second (and a corollary of the first point), it is an ideational space for thinking about musical experience, not the place in which musical experience happens. Musical experience occurs "really" in a material world of sonic vibrations, interacting bodies, and socially organized physical places and locales, a concept of space given to us by Aristotle as natural and by Kant as constructed (Curry 1996). So in this chapter I use "space" in its abstract mathematical sense to define an arena of analysis, not in its common usage as "distance extending in all directions." "Location" is the name of an axis in this abstract "space" of musical experience, and "place" and "locale" refer to real ("natural") and constructed nodes along the location axis.

That time and place are foundational for human existence, and by extension musical experience, was established in the European philosophical tradition during the first half of the twentieth century through the independent work on human existence in Bakhtin's dialogism (Bakhtin et al. 1990 [1919]), Martin Heidegger's ontology (1962 [1927]), and Merleau-Ponty's phenomenology (1989 [1945]). To account for specifically musical experience, we need a third dimension. This dimension, I suggest, consists of metaphors that make

2. Michel Foucault can be understood as mounting an attack on phenomenological projects such as the one proposed here. Foucault was clearly more interested in how practice defined practitioners than in the practitioners themselves. However, the subject remains for him a bracketed yet necessary being. If discourses are "sites of struggle" and each side gives different meanings to the same discourse, then this claim presupposes intersubjectivity and subjects who use the same discursive means variously to control, to oppose control, and to fight for their rights (Crossley 1994: 120). Foucauldian studies of the genealogy of discourses and discursive categories may not need the subject and intersubjectivity, but if we want to understand how these discourses are deployed and resisted in the present, as I do, then we need a notion of the self similar to the one outlined here. "Situated subjectivity and intersubjectivity provide a necessary, unexplicated background for Foucault's foreground or figural concerns. And like the background of any image, they too can become figural without changing the picture" (Crossley 1994: 159–160).

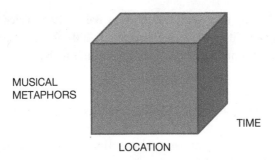

MUSICAL
METAPHORS

TIME

LOCATION

Figure 4.1  A three-dimensional space of musical experience and ethnography.

claims about the nature of music and that bring music closer to other domains of human experience. These metaphors ideologically ground the behavioral, interpretive, and discursive strategies that put those claims into practice. Using such a three-dimensional model as a heuristic position or lens through which to view musical experience from different subject positions and to follow the life histories of individuals encountering the social in an ever-lengthening and often changing dimension from the local to the global (and back again), we should be able to ask and answer the kinds of questions listed previously.

Here is a brief overview of each of these dimensions.

## Location

Social theory in the last fifteen years or so has been characterized in part by a renewed interest in ideas of space, place, and location, perhaps because the comfortable spatial constructs of traditional disciplines no longer seem adequate. The anthropologists' society or village and the sociologists' class or nation-state have been exceeded by the movements of those they study. Geographers are reshaping their discipline by no longer taking space as natural, immutable, and fixed but understanding it as a social construction, as a projection of the social in space, and as dynamic as time itself (May and Thrift 2001).

Since ethnomusicologists typically have gone to a place to study (though multisited ethnographies such as those cited earlier are increasingly common), our practice or conceptualization of practice may blind us to the realization that we and our subjects increasingly dwell not in a single place but in many places along a locational dimension of some sort. Musical experience may be the product of and contribute to the making of many "places" in space (Feld and Basso 1996; Stokes 1994). My proposal responds to the growing understanding that our and our subjects' experiences are no longer contained within local, isolated cultures or even within nation-states but are and have been shaped by regional, areal, colonial, and global economics, politics, social relations, and images. The global and the local have become a cliché of recent locational analysis in ethnomusicology, but the locational dimension contains many other positions that powerfully impact musical experience (for recent examples, see Berrian 2000 and Forman 2002).

At least three ways of viewing space, in the sense of distance or expanse, have been proposed recently. Appadurai (1996: 46), for example, thinks the shape of space in the modern world is "fundamentally fractal," not Euclidean, and therefore needs to be explained by something close to chaos theory. Second, geographers speak of space itself as fundamentally multidimensional: as real and perceived, as phenomenal and behavioral, as ideal and material, as container or network or grid (Curry 1996: 3). Third, Edward Soja (1989: 149) speaks of "the nodality of social life, the socio-temporal clustering or agglomeration of activities around identifiable geographical centers or nodes." Here he has in mind a set of nested "locales" that

> provide settings of interaction.... These settings may be a room in a house, a street corner, the shop floor of a factory, a prison, an asylum, a hospital, a definable neighbourhood/town/city/region, the territorially demarcated areas occupied by nation-states, indeed the occupied earth as a whole. Locales are nested at many different scales and this multilayered hierarchy of locales is recognizable both as social construct and a vital part of being-in-the-world. (pp. 148–149)

"Locale" and "place," the latter as explicated by Edward S. Casey (1996), have similar meanings and import in the location dimension posited here.

The location dimension I am proposing responds best to this last image of nested settings, places, locales, and nodes of social and musical behavior, but it keeps in mind the dialectic of real and imagined suggested by the second approach. From the point of view of the subject, these locales can be material and face to face or they may constitute "imagined communities" in extralocal settings from the regional to the national to the diasporic to the global. Other potentially productive locales, imagined by scholars, might be used in the model as well: border areas as cultural spaces; Appadurai's "-scapes"; the center and the periphery; and so forth. The crucial aspect of this dimension is that we and our subjects live and experience music socially in multiple locales, and our musical ethnographies must take this into account. Equally important, this sociogeographical dimension is not a procrustean bed of naturally given places. It is rather a way to think about and plot out the multiple social settings in which people produce, experience, and understand music. This "sense of place" varies from person to person, time to time, and narrative to narrative.

Understanding this dimension as in flux, nested, dynamic, multiple, and constructed is one way to deal with real-world complexity without giving in to Appadurai's fractals and chaos theory.

In using this framework, the nodes on this dimension will inevitably vary with each application. For example, for my analytic purposes, I have found it useful to posit a set of nested nodes that seem to influence musical experience, on one hand, and to themselves be constructed in part by musical practice on the other: the individual, subcultural, local, regional, national, areal, diasporic, global, and virtual (Figure 4.2). Though these spaces can refer to on-the-ground realities, they may be equally important for musical experience as constructed mental locales in which musicians and their audiences imagine themselves experiencing music.

Most of these locales or places are self-explanatory, but I will comment on each of them briefly here. The individual comes into play when selves or subjects understand themselves as isolated or unique, perhaps in opposition to culture and society or in an especially creative moment; a variant of this notion at this level of analysis might be the body considered as a node of musical experience. The subcultural refers to parts of societies, defined socially by gender, class, race, ethnicity, age, occupation, interests, and so on. Geographically this position includes the "locales" or "places" where these subcultural behaviors are performed: the home, the workplace, the neighborhood, the schoolyard, the market, the club, and the dancehall. The local is a geographical metaphor for the social and cultural units traditionally studied by ethnomusicologists, particularly in places that enable face-to-face interaction: for example, a people, a culture, a society,

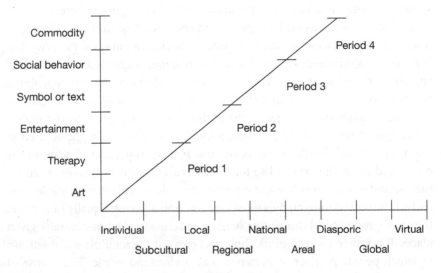

**Figure 4.2** Some nodes in a space of musical experience.

a village, or a town. The regional refers to extralocal constellations of villages or groups that are constructed by scholars or reported on by locals: for example, the South, Northumberland, or the Prairies. The national refers to the nation-state, its policies and practices, and the discourses that allow its citizens to imagine it. The areal refers to parts of the world that are thought to have a shared historical experience such as Latin America, the former French colonies of Africa, and formerly communist Eastern Europe. The diasporic refers to the sense of connectedness among populations with a common origin but dispersed widely across the globe, the Jewish people providing the archetypal case (Shelemay 1998). The global refers to connections facilitated by commerce, travel, and electronic media among otherwise different people around the world. For example, "Real Punks" produce very similar-sounding music whether from the United States, England, Japan, South America, Bulgaria, or Indonesia; publishing their views in a fanzine called *Punk Planet,* they "do not conceive of themselves as having an imagined homeland," but rather as "an inherently global community that supersedes local and national boundaries" (Rodel 2002). The virtual refers to the possibilities for a kind of disembodied existence and experience in places created by the electronic Internet, where, for example, musical communities coalesce in their devotion to "folk music" and the exchange of "mods," that is, binary music files created and played back on computer software (Bryant 1995; Lysloff 2003). These are merely suggestions, though perhaps this dimension has the advantage of bringing together and establishing possible relationships among a number of different locational foci in current ethnomusicological research.

## Time

There are minimally two ways to think about time. One is chronological and historical; the other is experiential and phenomenological.

History as conventionally written presupposes the ability of the writer to step outside time, observe it passing by, and create an orderly narrative of events. Periodization, which can vary from the microscopic to the macroscopic, is one of the conventional strategies of such an approach to time (Figure 4.2). Descriptions of musical sounds in succession (a chord progression or a formal analysis) represent a kind of periodization within a performance. Klaus Wachsmann (1982) periodized his listening experience into a first hearing of a piece and subsequent hearings. More typically we periodize musical styles, grouping a continuous succession of pieces or performances into categories spanning decades and centuries. Sometimes these histories of style are linked to changes in the social maintenance and cultural underpinnings of music. I take this approach when, for example, I divide the history of Bulgarian traditional music into three periods of economic and social maintenance: (1) the precommunist period of family farming to 1944; (2) the communist period from 1944 to 1989; and (3) the postcommunist, democratic, market-economy period from 1989 to the present (Rice 1996). Musical experience changes as these economic and political periods change.

Phenomenologically, musical experience in the present is partly conditioned by inveterate previous experience. People living in the present will have a very different experience of Bulgarian music if they knew it in the precommunist period than if they first encountered it in the communist or postcommunist periods. Bringing experience into periodized histories suggests that time doesn't simply pass in a straight, measured line, but in fact is a fundamental aspect of our being and experience in the world (Heidegger 1962 [1927]). Music may blandly proceed from beginning to end, from hearing to hearing, from piece to piece, and from style to style in the chronological perspective. But in the flux of time, rather than outside it, each new hearing, as Wachsmann pointed out of his hearing and rehearing of a Beethoven piece over many years, contains a new experience. His simple example illustrates the crucial role time plays in musical experience. When we think about longer spans of time, periodized by important social and cultural changes that affect nearly everyone in a particular society or even many of us around the world, the importance of time for musical experience takes on even greater significance.

The space of musical experience needs to take both views of time into account. The chronological, historical view is most easily represented graphically, as I do in Figure 4.2. But the way the experience of music changes as the subject moves through time and the way music gives us its own experience of time (measuring it, foreshortening it, stretching it out) need to be a part of the narratives created when using this space of musical experience.

## Metaphor

The third dimension consists of beliefs about the fundamental nature of music expressed in metaphors in the form "A is B"; that is, "music is x." These beliefs then become the basis for discourses about music, musical behaviors (including all aspects of creativity, reception, performance, and institutionalization), and strategies for deploying these beliefs and behaviors in self-interested ways.

The metaphors I have in mind are not literary tropes, rhetorical devices, or examples of fancy, decorative language. Rather, my view of metaphor is informed by a turn in twentieth-century analytic and continental philosophy away from a rhetorical view of metaphor toward the claim that it is a key element in human thought and therefore has important epistemological and ontological implications (Johnson 1981). I. A. Richards, a student of rhetoric, initiated this turn in 1936 when he claimed that "metaphor is the omnipresent principle of language.... Thought is metaphoric, and proceeds by comparison, and the metaphors of language derive from them" (Richards 1981 [1936]: 50–51). Max Black (1981 [1954–1955]), an analytic philosopher, extended Richards's ideas by arguing that metaphors are statements, not words, that extend the meanings of both the "primary subject" (A) and the "subsidiary subject" (B). These subjects are neither labels nor things but "systems of things" with "commonplace" attributes. Since metaphors suppress some details about their subjects while emphasizing others, they "organize our view" of the subjects, create new understandings of both subjects of the metaphor, and contribute importantly to epistemological issues in analytic philosophy. Paul Ricoeur, a philosopher in the continental tradition, elucidated the psychological processes at work when metaphor creates new understandings. He explains that "meaningful metaphoric utterances" occur when "things or ideas that were remote appear now as close.... What Aristotle·called . . . the transfer of meaning is nothing else than this move or shift in the logical distance, from the far to the near" (Ricoeur 1981 [1978]: 233). This shift provides the basis for the innovative nature of metaphor and its ability to help us imagine new relationships and construct new symbolic worlds. George Lakoff, a linguist, and Mark Johnson, a philosopher, were less interested in metaphors as the locus of conceptual innovation than in the way they guide the thoughts and actions of individuals operating in society and serve understanding and experience. When we take them as true, they powerfully inform our view of the world and our actions in it (Lakoff and Johnson 1980a: 156–184). "No account of meaning and truth can be adequate unless it recognizes the way in which conventional metaphors structure our conceptual system" (Lakoff and Johnson 1980b: 486). As Johnson (1981:43) puts it, returning to Richards's initial insight, "metaphoric process is an omnipresent principle of cognition.... All experience has an 'as' structure."

For the purposes of this proposal, I am interested in implied or explicit "metaphoric utterances" in the form A is B (music is x) that bring seemingly distant domains closer together and that organize, and in some cases shift, our view and experience of both subjects of the metaphor. If all thought is metaphoric, then this definition of metaphor requires us to revisit the distinction between literal and metaphoric meaning, because in this philosophical tradition both are capable of making true statements. In this view, what appear to be "literal expressions" are something more like "old," "conventional," "dead," taken-for-granted metaphors that powerfully inform our view of the world, but where the sense (or memory) of a shift in cognition or experience has been lost. Often their metaphoric sense has to be recovered through analysis and deconstruction: think, for example, of "music literature" or "feminine endings."

What appear to be "metaphoric expressions" per se have a quality of newness and require a shift in cognition and experience: think, for example, of "songs as waterfalls" or "music is the work of the devil." In this view of metaphor, much depends on context and subject position. That is, one subject's fresh and challenging metaphor may appear as literally true to another. Both evaluations capture the two sides of the coin of metaphor: its capacity to frame our understanding when taken as true, near, and obvious and its capacity to alter and reconfigure our understanding when taken as surprising, far, and insightful.

Such metaphors, whether obvious or surprising, are probably as endless as the cultures we study, and each tells us something important about the nature of music in that society (compare Merriam 1964: 63–84 on "concepts" of music). Some surely challenge ethnomusicologists' commonplace ideas about the nature of music. For example, among the Navajo, music is medicine, a form of therapy; it is performed to heal the sick. It doesn't represent something; it does something (Witherspoon 1977). This metaphor makes a Navajo truth claim, organizes their musical and ritual behavior, and is obvious and close to their experience. For some ethnomusicologists, this metaphor requires an act of imagination and analysis to bring the previously distant systems of music and clinical healing closer together and to understand its truth, a cognitive shift comparable to what Navajos must have gone through when David McAllester (1954) asked them questions about music as an aesthetic object. These sorts of differences in perspective on the truth of various musical metaphors not only provide a challenge to and locus for ethnomusicological research but also, when present in specific instances of social and cultural interaction, generate conflict over the nature of music and musical experience.

Not only do the people we study make metaphors to account for their experience of music, but also musicologists base their studies of music on metaphors that make fundamental claims about music's nature and significance. Among the common ones in current use, and therefore applied cross-culturally in our studies, are music as art, as cognition, as entertainment, as therapy, as social behavior, as commodity, as referential symbol, and as text for interpretation (Figure 4.2). Though in many cases these metaphors are left unspoken, I believe that our analyses in every case are predicated on the truth of one or some of these metaphors.[3] Furthermore, in advancing our arguments, we often imply

---

3. Daniel Neuman (1980: 27–28) makes a similar point about the role of metaphor in research: "The nature of the relationship between music and culture (or music and society or social system) has been expressed in a number of ways, but is based always, I believe, on one of three primary metaphors of relationships, which need to be made explicit." The first is music "as a component of sociocultural system"; the second is music "as model, microcosm, or reflection of a social system"; and the third is music "as commentary," as a "reflection on or about cultural systems."

that those we study behave as if these metaphors were true for them as well. I will discuss just four of these common metaphors to illustrate what I have in mind on this dimension.

The music-as-art metaphor suggests that the nature of music is first and foremost about the processes of performing and composing music, the musical products resulting from those processes, and the reception of those processes and products in perception, cognition, and interpretation. Here I purposefully conflate many separate domains of musicological study, including psycho-acoustics, music theory, style history, and aesthetics, as well as the conventional distinction between art and craft. This metaphor leads us to consider the techniques, forms, and structures of music and how those structures may be evaluated in terms of craft, balance, virtuosity, and beauty (see Bakan 1999, Berliner 1994, Brinner 1995, and Tenzer 2000 for recent examples that emphasize these themes, among others). Music seems so powerful as an art, its techniques of production so formidable, and the pleasures of its reception so enrapturing that such considerations can easily eclipse other views of the nature of music and even lead to denials that this is a metaphor at all. Ethnomusicologists have been at pains to move beyond the shadow of the music-as-art metaphor to the theoretical light of other metaphors, but we need to recognize that it or something like it informs the experience of music not simply for those raised in the traditions of European aesthetics but in nearly every musical tradition we study.

A second metaphor, developed by ethnomusicologists in part as a response to the music-as-art metaphor, claims that music is social behavior, a claim that seemed far from the understanding of musicologically trained ethnomusicologists in the 1960s. Ethnomusicologists demonstrated that, because music is made and understood by people in society, every performance of music is also a performance of existing or emergent social structures and social relations (see Neuman 1980, Seeger 1987, and Waterman 1990 for examples of this approach). Musical performances may enact past or present social structures, they may model alternatives to existing structures, or they may help to imagine future structures.

A third metaphor powerfully attractive to ethnomusicologists as an alternative to the music-as-art metaphor claims that music is a symbolic system or text capable of reference not only to already existing music but also to a world beyond music. The terms *symbol* and *text* are deployed in different discursive traditions, the former in semiotics and the latter in literary criticism and hermeneutics. Here I conflate these two metaphors because they both make the claim that music can have referential meanings to things, ideas, worlds, and experiences outside music itself (see Becker and Becker 1981 and Feld 1988 for examples of this approach).

A fourth metaphor, music as commodity, has challenged ethnomusicologists in recent years, if only because we, like many of our subjects, find the previous metaphors more palatable and less, well, cheap. In many sociogeographical locales, musicians can, literally and really, exchange their performances and their recorded products for money or other marketable commodities. This reality takes on a metaphorical quality when new possibilities for such exchanges challenge older, taken-for-granted ideas about music as art, as social practice, or as therapy and thus create a kind of cognitive dissonance in musicians. If we and our subjects prefer other metaphors, we and they have encountered this one as we all engage the commercial world of the music industry and as we increasingly make that world the focus of our research.

Though some debate centers around the relative merits of each of these claims and other ones as well, I suggest that ethnomusicologists take seriously every musical metaphor, whether of their own making or of their research subjects, for what they are: fundamental claims to truth, guides to practical action and discourse, ways of reconfiguring our understanding of the world, and sources for comprehending music's profound importance to human life. Though true from some subject's point of view, each may require others to reshuffle their conceptions of the nature of music. One can imagine a single subject employing many metaphors in different nodes of place and time to make sense of musical experience and many subjects contesting the nature of music at the intersection of their individual spaces of musical experience.

Musical metaphors also guide discursive and practical action in individual lives, in society, and through time. They guide individuals' use of music rather than specify its social functions (Merriam 1964: 209–227). Sometimes I suppose the metaphors happily commingle; at other times they may become alternative, competing strategies. When we are faced with multiple metaphors about the fundamental nature of music, a number of important questions arise (Rice 2001). How do our subjects deploy these metaphors? How are they discursively constructed? Or are they left implicit? Are they kept in balance, or are some brought into the foreground while others are pushed into the background? Or does one eclipse the others, making them disappear? When subjects' metaphors conflict or are contested, how are they used strategically to the subjects' benefit? How and why do societies and social institutions control musical metaphors and thus set the agenda for the significance and signification of music?

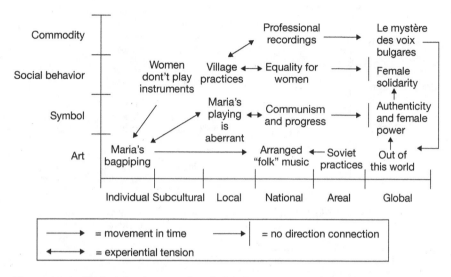

Figure 4.3  Individual, local, national, and global experience.

## THREE STORIES

To illustrate this abstract model, here are three necessarily schematic and simplified stories from my work on Bulgarian traditional music. For my Bulgarian examples I need seven locations, four metaphors, and a three-part periodization (Figures 4.3 and 4.4).[4] Others using this model would construct its specific nodes to suit their own narrative and analytical goals.

## A Female Bagpiper

The performance of Bulgarian music—indeed, the performance of all music—is the performance of some aspects of social structure and social relationships. Bulgarian music was and still is used, among other things, to bring kinship structures to experiential life and to enact traditional gender roles. For the first story, the crucial aspect of gendered musical behavior is that men traditionally played musical instruments and women did not.

When Maria Stoyanova decided to play her father's bagpipe, this shocked her family and everyone in her village (Rice 1994: 268–271). Though she was born in the 1950s and raised during the communist period, her parents still

---

4. My ability to represent three dimensions failed me in Figures 4.3 and 4.4, so I have used the "arrow of time" to indicate that dimension. These arrows refer simply to the passage of time and do not precisely reference the three periods that underlie these Bulgarian stories.

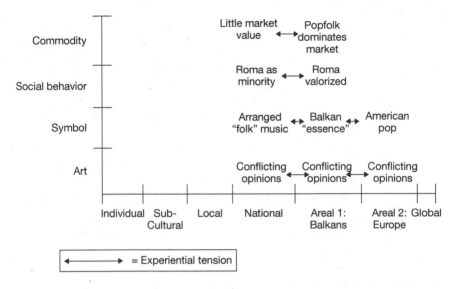

**Figure 4.4** Bulgarian musical experience in the year 2000.

used precommunist ideas about gender to justify taking the instrument away from her, one illustration of how time is a nested dimension of experience, that is, phenomenological as well as chronological. In the process, they treated her playing as a text ripe for interpretation and misinterpretation. Not only was the bagpipe indexical of male behaviors, but also its very construction, with three phallic tubes sticking out of it, was iconically male. So her playing of it could be read as representing some sort of public sexual display inappropriate for women. For Maria, her playing has nothing to do with sexuality, as interpreted at the local level using values in place before World War II. It has rather to do with art, supported by the communists' commodification of "folk music." This was the sound she loved and she, as an individual, was determined to play this instrument for its artistic value even if it meant flying in the face of older sub-cultural and local values. This conflict over the significance of music took place in a space whose temporal dimension allowed the co-occurrence of precom-munist and communist attitudes toward female music making.

The conflict, or experiential tension, between Maria's individual ideas about bagpipe music as art and local ideas about bagpipe music as acceptable only for men was resolved with the passage of time from prewar traditionality to post-war communist modernity. Between 1944 and 1989, the national government appropriated local music traditions and made them into symbols of national identity and the hoped-for progress of humankind under socialism, an art of "arranged folk music" influenced by Soviet predecessors, and a commodity based on new forms of music professionalism (Buchanan 1991, 1995; Levy 1985; Rice 1994: 169–233; Silverman 1982, 1983).

In the 1960s, when Maria auditioned on the bagpipe to study at the newly formed national high school for folk music, the jury of sophisticated urbanites was as shocked as the people in her village had been. One of those present told me they read the bagpipe's blowpipe as a phallus in her mouth, understood bagpipe playing as a male tradition, and wondered whether they should admit her to a school founded to support and preserve a tradition she seemed to be flouting. In the end, a Marxist ideology of equality for women won out, and she was admitted. She eventually became the principal bagpipe teacher at the national conservatory devoted to folk music and a sought-after soloist with many wedding bands. At the national level during the communist period, her playing functioned metaphorically as both a symbol of women's equality of opportunity in a socialist state and a social enactment of women taking a leading role in the previously male domain of instrumental music. New values at the national level trumped older values at the local level, empowering Maria in ways denied to her by tradition (see Rice in press for a fuller account of Maria's musical practice).

In Figure 4.3, the story begins with the "traditional" social behavior of women at the subcultural level and moves to Maria's appropriation of a male traditional behavior for her individual satisfaction, a move read at the local level as aberrant, which creates what I call "experiential tension." Maria's art, along with local practices and values, then take on completely new significance when they move, in the communist period, to the national level, a move that generates experiential tension between these new practices and older local ideas about the nature of music.

## Powerful Voices

A second story begins during the communist period when this new "national music" was firmly in place and had for the most part eclipsed local, precommunist values and practices. Significantly for this story, these national transformations of local music traditions were commodified during this period. For the first time, musicians, singers, and dancers could make a living wage (feed a household, as they said) from their performances on stage, for the radio, and in commercial recordings. These recordings then slipped through a "space hatch" from a Bulgarian space of musical experience into foreign conceptual spaces structured in the same three-dimensional way but with different nodes of time, location, and metaphor. In other words, the subjects of this story are not Bulgarians but their others, a subject position that might be called "foreign fans of Bulgarian music." In these foreign spaces, now conventionally but perhaps incorrectly called the "global," Bulgarian nationalized folklore commodified on recordings was interpreted first of all as art. For many listeners, including myself when I first heard it, Bulgarian women's choirs made wonderful-sounding music with no cultural referents except to the largely empty label "Bulgarian" (Figure 4.3).

Although this movement of Bulgarian recorded commodities began in the 1960s and even earlier, it reached its apotheosis in the United States during the late 1980s with a set of recordings released on Nonesuch with the title *Le mystère des voix bulgares*. Since in the West we often follow aesthetic experiences with questions about symbolic significance (What does it mean? What did the composer intend?), these recordings were also read symbolically in ways that were unconnected to the meanings associated with its production (see Buchanan 1996, 1997, 1998 for critical treatments of these recordings and their reinterpretation outside Bulgaria). In countless newspaper articles and in notes accompanying the recordings and the concerts, this state-sponsored arranged choral singing was read as exotic, even unearthly, music. The political context of its production did not travel with the recordings, and its relative newness as arranged music was intentionally obfuscated by producers and presenters in Western Europe and the United States to encourage its misreading as ancient, authentic, traditional, and "cosmic." Another interpretation without justification in local practice read the undeniably powerful female voices as the performance and symbolic representation of powerful females, although, as Donna Buchanan (1996: 195) points out, the professionalization of local musical practice at the national level gave the singers in these choirs a new social status and a quasi-independence denied them in local, patriarchal society. The early recordings and the responses to them circulated in a Slobinesque "microscene" of Balkan music enthusiasts who danced to, sang, and played this music (see Lausevic 1998 for a discussion of this scene). For decades since the release of the first commercial recordings of Bulgarian music in the 1960s, Bulgarian women's singing has continued to inspire imitators in the United States, Japan, and northern Europe. Bulgarian choral music presents young women in these places with a useful symbol of gendered behavior, one that sounds powerful and strong. By singing it in choirs they create a social situation in which to express and perform strength, female solidarity, and independence from men.

In one of the more amusing of the interpretations, or misinterpretations, of this arranged, state-sponsored choral singing, the syndicated television serial, "Xena, Warrior Princess," used, in early episodes at least, this style as a leitmotiv to accompany Xena into battle against her exotic and otherworldly foes. In 1995, I received a call from Joe LoDuca, the composer of the music for the series, asking for my help in finding singers for the recording sessions in Los Angeles. When I asked him why Bulgarian music, he told me that the producers had heard the *mystère* recordings and thought that this powerful female sound would be ideal for their powerful heroine. In other words, they mapped a powerful female sound onto the sound of a powerful female (see also Buchanan 1998).

One way to interpret this story in terms of the space of musical experience is to argue that the recordings moved outside a Bulgarian national locale (significantly not a local place) into a global locale. In both places the recordings are commodities with artistic, symbolic, and social significance. In the Bulgarian space they model new forms of social behavior in which women have relatively more equality of opportunity than they had at the local level, and they have a symbolic meaning associated with the propaganda goals of the party controlling the nation-state. Figure 4.3 illustrates the fact that only the recorded commodity passed into the global node of musical experience. The Bulgarian symbolic meanings and social significance were filtered out, it was appropriated as art, and all manner of new meanings and behaviors were attached to it. Although ethnomusicologists have tended to be critical of this process, lamenting the loss or distortion of the original meaning and critiquing the rather odd orientalist and new-age takes on "world music," we also must acknowledge and study the social utility, cultural production, and individual musical experience that occurs at the "global" level, or more precisely in the new local and subcultural locations, made possible by travel and shuttling media, as, for example, Mirjana Lausevic (1998) does in her study of the Balkan music scene in the United States.

## Postcommunist *Popfolk*

The third story brings us into the postcommunist period and is based on a brief period of fieldwork in the summer of 2000 (Rice 2002). Music in Bulgaria in the postcommunist period has become at least partly about location (Buchanan 1998, 1999; Peters 1998). Many Bulgarians I talked to that summer tended to interpret the music in Bulgaria and their musical preferences as answering the question, where are Bulgaria and Bulgarians located in today's world? The subjects of this story are, again, not individuals but groups of people who occupy three different subcultural positions and who therefore answer these questions differently. In Figure 4.4, the three subject positions might be labeled nationalists, Balkanists, and Europeanists. They are represented in locational terms as the national; areal 1: Balkans; and areal 2: Europe; the tensions between them in all four metaphoric domains are indicated by double-headed arrows.

During the communist period Bulgarian village music, in arranged forms, became—and still is—a symbol of Bulgarian national identity (Buchanan 1991). It put into practice an ideological bracketing of ethnic minorities within the country and an emphasis on difference from the neighbors on its borders. In 2000, Bulgarian nationalized folk music (*narodna muzika*) had virtually vanished from the airwaves and recorded media in the new, capitalist, commodity market for music. What was popular, what sold, was a new form of music called by various names, but most commonly in the year 2000 *popfolk* and *chalga,* a word whose connotations and implications might be captured in the expression "Bulgarianized 'Gypsy' music." It consists of Bulgarian-language cover versions and newly authored texts set to Rom (Gypsy), Turkish, Serbian, Greek, and Romanian folk and popular melodies. It is a kind of pan-Balkan, Rom-influenced popular music, commonly interpreted, by both its proponents and opponents, as a symbol of Bulgaria's areal location in the Balkans.[5] Proponents celebrate that fact, arguing that Bulgarians should not deny that part of their history and "nature."

Opposition to this style comes from two sides. Bulgarian nationalists are deeply offended that this style has eclipsed music that has identifiable, ethnically Bulgarian features and, even worse, that it glorifies a scorned ethnic minority, the *Tsigani* (to use a somewhat derogatory Bulgarian term), who originated the style and provide many of the most popular singers and instrumentalists in this new genre. In addition to being hated by narrow-minded nationalists, popfolk is also criticized by intellectuals, bureaucrats, and well-educated youth invested in moving Bulgaria away from its Ottoman and Soviet past, both of which isolated Bulgaria from cultural and economic centers in Western Europe. They hope to insert themselves and Bulgaria into the so-called European family, lobby for membership in the European Union and NATO, consume Western European and American images and products, and favor classical music and Europeanized and Americanized forms of popular music.

While the symbolism of the music is clear to all, arguments for and against it tend to be couched in aesthetic and commodity terms, and the performances themselves, recorded in music videos, sometimes model intimate relationships

---

5. That Bulgarians are using new genres of popular music to construct ideas about the Balkans has already been pointed out by Bulgarian and American scholars. In the mid-1990s a popular genre, referred to as "Pirin folk" after the region of southwest Bulgaria also known as Macedonia, was "about musically constructing Macedonia" (Buchanan 1999: 172; also Peters 1998). The musical construction of the Balkans was also the topic of a panel of papers by Donna Buchanan (1998), Jane Sugarman, and Martin Stokes at the 1998 Society for Ethnomusicology annual meeting. Buchanan (1999: 176) cites a Bulgarian musicologist, Rozmari Statelova, who claims that Pirin folk represents "the Balkans in Bulgaria." This story brings these earlier reports up to the year 2000 and places them in the context of my proposed space of musical experience.

between Roma and Bulgarians, idealized forms of social relationships rare in everyday life. Opponents call it "cheap" music, made solely for its commercial potential without redeeming artistic value. On the other hand, ethnic Bulgarians who participate in its making defend its artistry, pointing to some respected poets who have contributed song lyrics and to the university music educations of some of the musicians. Bulgaria today, in transition from socialism to capitalism, from totalitarianism to democracy, and from a regional Comecon to access to global markets, is a fascinating place where different subject positions are colliding over the meaning and value of music.

## THE SPACE OF MUSICAL EXPERIENCE AND ETHNOGRAPHY

The three-dimensional space of musical experience I have proposed here represents an attempt to model the encounter of ethnomusicologists and their subjects with modernity. Thus, it is the space of both musical experience and ethnography. In other words, both we and our subjects operate in similar spaces of the same structure. In this limited sense, the space I have proposed here is also postmodern insofar as it tries to capture recent late modern, postmodern, and postcolonial critiques of our modernist understandings of the relationship between scholars and their subjects.[6] Modernity understands itself in contrast to tradition. Under modernity, ethnomusicologists view themselves as cosmopolitan, moving about and operating freely in a global space largely inaccessible (at least in concept and method) to the inhabitants of those traditional, local cultures we often study (for a recent counterexample, see Turino 2000). In modernity, we could travel to their locales but they could not necessarily travel to ours. Their experiences were local, while ours were global. The space of musical experience and ethnography I am proposing here is shared, in structure at least, by us all; it is the conceptual space in which

6. Though postmodernism as a position beyond the modern/traditional dichotomy seems useful, I am not advocating postmodernism as a philosophical position. In fact, I am opposed to the pessimism of postmodernism, that is, its apparent ability to deconstruct the modernist project, but not to offer positive alternatives. To propose a space of musical experience as a heuristic device for future study, as I do here, flies in the face of the spirit of much postmodernist discourse. Similarly, while the idea of different subject positions inscribed in this model shares with postmodernism a rejection of the modernist idea of absolute truth, it is not antifoundational in the same sense. It holds out the possibility of comparison, judgment, and interpretation, and of the authoring of the self through music as a series of moral choices in social relationships with others; and it is founded on philosophical claims about the social nature of human "being-in-the-world" (Heidegger 1962).

musical ethnography and music experience co-occur for both scholars, musicians, and audiences and in that limited sense is postmodern. It is the space in which scholars, musicians, and audiences know the passage of time; savor music's differing essences, meanings, and metaphoric connections to other domains of culture; and feel the gradations of power as we move (if at times only conceptually) from locale to locale. It is a space in which those otherized by modernist ideologies now write their own ethnographies or participate dialogically in their writing. It is the space where the authority of omniscient authors and ethnographers is challenged by the realization that they are positioned within the same kinds of spaces as their subjects, not in a fundamentally different sort of space.

I further contend that an abstract space like this is fundamental to our studies of technology and media, on the one hand, and power and contestation, on the other. Travel technology, for instance, enables us and our subjects to move through this space, and electronic media function as "space shuttles" that bring near to experience the temporally and spatially distant, give us "schizophonic" ways of experiencing music, and help us construct and revise our "senses of place" and space (see, e.g., Manuel 1993 and Taylor 1997). Contestation occurs because individuals are situated differently in the space of musical experience. Power is negotiated and acted out along its dimensions in terms, for example, of who controls the (metaphoric) discourse, who has been there the longest, and who occupies the superior position (locale).

Finally, I suggest that this model of the space of musical experience and ethnography might provide us with an analytical tool to aid our understandings of individual encounters with modernity, as well as provide a framework for comparison between and among our idiographic studies.

In the present time, in the global space of commodified forms, where new meanings eclipse older ones, the experience of music may feel modern to some and postmodern to others. Musical ethnographies that trace the movements of subjects in location, metaphorical understanding, and time and the differing experiences such movements entail take on a fundamentally dynamic character responsive to the new or newly understood complexities of today's modern world.

## REFERENCES

Abu-Lughod, Janet L. 1989. *Before European Hegemony: The World System* A.D. *1250–1350*. New York: Oxford University Press.

Abu-Lughod, Lila. 1991. "Writing against Culture." In Richard G. Fox, ed., *Recapturing Anthropology: Working in the Present*. Santa Fe, NM: School of American Research Press, pp. 137–162.

Appadurai, Arjun. 1996. *Modernity at Large: Cultural Dimensions of Globalization*. Minneapolis: University of Minnesota Press.

Bakan, Michael. 1999. *Music of Death and New Creation: Experiences in the World of Balinese Gamelan Beleganjur*. Chicago: University of Chicago Press.

Bakhtin, Mikhail M. et al. 1990 [1919]. *Art and Answerability: Early Philosophical Essays*. Austin: University of Texas Press.

Becker, Judith, and Alton Becker. 1981. "A Musical Icon: Power and Meaning in Javanese Gamelan Music." In Wendy Steiner, ed., *The Sign in Music and Literature*. Austin: University of Texas Press, pp. 203–215.

Berliner, Paul. 1994. *Thinking in Jazz*. Chicago: University of Chicago Press.

Berrian, Brenda F. 2000. *Awakening Spaces: French Caribbean Popular Songs, Music, and Culture*. Chicago: University of Chicago Press.

Black, Max. 1981 [1954–1955]. "Metaphor." In Mark Johnson, ed., *Philosophical Perspectives on Metaphor*. Minneapolis: University of Minnesota Press, pp. 63–82.

Borofsky, Robert et al. 2001. "When: A Conversation about Culture." *American Anthropologist* 103(2): 432–446.

Braudel, Fernand. 1981–1984. *Civilization and Capitalism, 15th-18th Century*. London: Collins.

Brinner, Benjamin. 1995. *Knowing Music, Making Music: Javanese Gamelan and the Theory of Musical Competence and Innovation*. Chicago: University of Chicago Press.

Bryant, Wanda. 1995. "Virtual Music Communities: The Folk Music Internet Discussion Group as a Cultural System." PhD dissertation, University of California, Los Angeles.

Buchanan, Donna A. 1991. "The Bulgarian Folk Orchestra: Cultural Performance, Symbol, and the Construction of National Identity in Socialist Bulgaria." PhD dissertation, University of Texas at Austin.

——. 1995. "Metaphors of Power, Metaphors of Truth: The Politics of Music Professionalism in Bulgarian Folk Orchestras." *Ethnomusicology* 39(3): 381–416.

——. 1996. "Dispelling the Mystery: The Commodification of Women and Musical Tradition in the Marketing of *Le Mystère des Voix Bulgares*." *Balkanistica* 9(2): 193–210.

——. 1997. "Review Essay: Bulgaria's Magical *Mystère* Tour: Postmodernism, World Music Marketing, and Political Change in Eastern Europe." *Ethnomusicology* 41(1): 131–157.

——. 1998. "Ottoman Images and Oriental Imaginings in Bulgarian Popular Culture: Ethnopop, Mysterious Voices, and Xena, Warrior Princess." Paper presented at the 43rd annual meeting of the Society for Ethnomusicology, Bloomington, Indiana, October 21–25.

——. 1999. "Democracy or 'Crazyocracy'?: Pirin Folk Music and Sociocultural Change in Bulgaria. In Bruno B. Reuer, ed., *New Countries, Old Sounds?: Cultural Identity and Social Change in Southeastern Europe*. Munich: Verlag Südostdeutsches Kulturwerk, pp. 164–177.

Casey, Edward S. 1996. "How to Get from Space to Place in a Fairly Short Stretch of Time: Phenomenological Prolegomena." In Steven Feld and Keith H. Basso, eds., *Senses of Place*. Santa Fe, NM: School of American Research Press, pp. 13–52.

Clifford, James. 1997. *Routes: Travel and Translation in the Late Twentieth Century.* Cambridge, MA: Harvard University Press.

Crossley, Nick. 1994. *The Politics of Subjectivity: Between Foucault and Merleau-Ponty.* Brookfield: Avebury.

Curry, Michael R. 1996. "On Space and Spatial Practice in Contemporary Geography." In Carville Earle et al., eds., *Concepts in Human Geography.* London: Rowman and Littlefield, pp. 3–32.

Curtin, Philip D. 1984. *Cross-Cultural Trade in World History.* Cambridge: Cambridge University Press.

Erlmann, Veit. 1993. "The Politics and Aesthetics of Transnational Musics." *The World of Music* 35(2): 3–15.

———. 1999. *Music, Modernity, and the Global Imagination: South Africa and the West.* New York: Oxford University Press.

Feld, Steven. 1988. "Aesthetics as Iconicity of Style, or 'Lift-up-Over Sounding': Getting into the Kaluli Groove." *Yearbook for Traditional Music* 20: 74–114.

Feld, Steven, and Keith H. Basso. 1996. "Introduction." In Steven Feld and Keith H. Basso, eds., *Senses of Place.* Santa Fe, NM: School of American Research Press, pp. 3–11.

Forman, Murray. 2002. *The 'Hood Comes First: Race, Space, and Place in Hip-Hop.* Middletown, CT: Wesleyan University Press.

Friedson, Steven M. 1996. *Dancing Prophets: Musical Experience in Tumbuku Healing.* Chicago: University of Chicago Press.

Gadamer, Hans-Georg. 1975. *Truth and Method.* New York: Seabury Press.

Giddens, Anthony. 1991. *Modernity and Self-identity: Self and Society in the Late Modern Age.* Stanford, CA: Stanford University Press.

Guilbault, Jocelyne. 1997. "Interpreting World Music: A Challenge in Theory and Practice." *Popular Music* 16(1): 31–44.

Heidegger, Martin. 1962 [1927]. *Being and Time.* New York: Harper.

Johnson, Mark. 1981. "Introduction: Metaphor in the Philosophical Tradition." In Mark Johnson, ed., *Philosophical Perspectives on Metaphor.* Minneapolis: University of Minnesota Press, pp. 3–47.

Lakoff, George, and Mark Johnson. 1980a. *Metaphors We Live By.* Chicago: University of Chicago Press.

———. 1980b. "Conceptual Metaphor in Everyday Life." *Journal of Philosophy* 77(8): 453–486.

Lausevic, Mirjana. 1998. "A Different Village: International Folk Dance and Balkan Music and Dance in the United States." PhD dissertation, Wesleyan University, Middletown, CT.

Levin, Theodore C. 1996. *The Hundred Thousand Fools of God: Musical Travels in Central Asia (and Queens, New York).* Bloomington: Indiana University Press.

Levy, Mark. 1985. "The Bagpipe in the Rhodope Mountains of Bulgaria." PhD dissertation, University of California, Los Angeles.

Lysloff, René T. A. 2003. "Musical Community on the Internet: An Online Ethnography." *Cultural Anthropology* 18(2).

Manuel, Peter L. 1993. *Cassette Culture: Popular Music and Technology in North India.* Chicago: University of Chicago Press.

May, John, and Nigel Thrift. 2001. "Introduction." In John May and Nigel Thrift, eds., *TimeSpace: Geographies of Temporality*. New York: Routledge, pp. 1–46.

McAllester, David P. 1954. *Enemy Way Music*. Cambridge, MA: Peabody Museum, Harvard University.

Merleau-Ponty, Maurice. 1989 [1945]. *Phenomenology of Perception*. London: Routledge, Humanities Press.

Merriam, Alan. 1964. *The Anthropology of Music*. Evanston, IL: Northwestern University Press.

Monson, Ingrid. 1999. "Riffs, Repetition, and Theories of Globalization." *Ethnomusicology* 43(1): 31–65.

Nettl, Bruno. 1983. *The Study of Ethnomusicology: Twenty-Nine Issues and Concepts*. Urbana: University of Illinois Press.

Neuman, Daniel M. 1980. *The Life of Music in North India: The Organization of an Artistic Tradition*. Detroit: Wayne State University Press.

Ochs, Elinor, and Lisa Capps. 1996. "Narrating the Self." *Annual Review of Anthropology* 25: 19–43.

Peters, Karen A. 1998. "Representations of Macedonia in Contemporary Ethnopop Songs from Southwestern Bulgaria." Paper presented at the Society for Ethnomusicology Midwest Chapter Meeting, Bowling Green, OH.

Rees, Helen. 2000. *Echoes of History: Naxi Music in Modern China*. New York: Oxford University Press.

Rice, Timothy. 1994. *May It Fill Your Soul: Experiencing Bulgarian Music*. Chicago: University of Chicago Press.

———. 1996. "The Dialectic of Economics and Aesthetics in Bulgarian Music." In Mark Slobin, ed., *Retuning Culture: Musical Changes in Central and Eastern Europe*. Durham, NC: Duke University Press, pp. 176–199.

———. 2001. "Reflections on Music and Meaning: Metaphor, Signification, and Control in the Bulgarian Case." *British Journal of Ethnomusicology* 10(1): 19–38.

———. 2002. "Bulgaria or Chalgaria: The Attenuation of Bulgarian Nationalism in a Mass-Mediated Popular Music." *Yearbook for Traditional Music* 34: 25–46.

———. In press. *The Music of Bulgaria*. New York: Oxford University Press.

Richards, I. A. 1981 [1936]. "The Philosophy of Rhetoric." In Mark Johnson, ed., *Philosophical Perspectives on Metaphor*. Minneapolis: University of Minnesota Press, pp. 48–62.

Ricoeur, Paul. 1981 [1978]. "The Metaphorical Process as Cognition, Imagination, and Feeling." In Mark Johnson, ed., *Philosophical Perspectives on Metaphor*. Minneapolis: University of Minnesota Press, pp. 228–247.

Rodel, Angela. 2002. "The Grassroots Globalization of Real Punk: From Subculture to Counterculture." Paper presented at the 47th annual meeting of the Society for Ethnomusicology, Estes Park, CO, October 23–27.

Seeger, Anthony. 1987. *Why Suyá Sing*. Cambridge: Cambridge University Press.

Shelemay, Kay Kaufman. 1998. *Let Jasmine Rain Down: Song and Remembrance among Syrian Jews*. Chicago: University of Chicago Press.

Silverman, Carol. 1982. "Bulgarian Lore and American Folkloristics: The Case of Contemporary Bulgarian Folk Music." In Walter W. Kolar, ed., *Culture and History of the Bulgarian People: Their Bulgarian and American Parallels.* Pittsburgh: Tamburitza Press, pp. 65–78.

———. 1983. "The Politics of Folklore in Bulgaria." *Anthropological Quarterly* 56(2): 55–61.

Slobin, Mark. 1993. *Subcultural Sounds: Micromusics of the West.* Hanover, NH: University Press of New England.

Soja, Edward W. 1989. *Postmodern Geographies: The Reassertion of Space in Critical Social Theory.* London: Verso.

Steinglass, Matt. 2001. "An Unlikely Prodigy in an African New World." *New York Times,* September 2, Section 2.

Stock, Jonathan J. P. 1996. *Musical Creativity in Twentieth-Century China: Abing, His Music, and Its Changing Meaning.* Rochester, NY: University of Rochester Press.

———. 2001. "Toward an Ethnomusicology of the Individual, or Biographical Writing in Ethnomusicology." *The World of Music* 43(1): 5–19.

Stokes, Martin. 1994. *Ethnicity, Identity and Music: The Musical Construction of Place.* New York: Berg.

Sugarman, Jane C. 1997. *Engendering Song: Singing and Subjectivity at Prespa Albanian Weddings.* Chicago: University of Chicago Press.

Taylor, Timothy D. 1997. *Global Pop: World Music, World Markets.* New York: Routledge.

Tenzer, Michael. 2000. *Gamelan Gong Kebyar: The Art of Twentieth-Century Balinese Music.* Chicago: University of Chicago Press.

Titon, Jeff Todd. 1988. *Powerhouse for God: Speech, Chant, and Song in an Appalachian Baptist Church.* Austin: University of Texas Press.

Turino, Thomas. 1993. *Moving Away from Silence: Music of the Peruvian Altiplano and the Experience of Urban Migration.* Chicago: University of Chicago Press.

———. 2000. *Nationalists, Cosmopolitans, and Popular Music in Zimbabwe.* Chicago: University of Chicago Press.

Wachsmann, Klaus. 1982. "The Changeability of Musical Experience." *Ethnomusicology* 26(2): 197–215.

Wallerstein, Immanuel. 1974, 1980, 1989. *The Modern World System,* 3 vols. New York: Academic Press.

Waterman, Christopher Alan. 1990. *Jùjú: A Social History and Ethnography of an African Popular Music.* Chicago: University of Chicago Press.

Witherspoon, Gary. 1977. *Language and Art in the Navajo Universe.* Ann Arbor: University of Michigan Press.

# 5

# Reflections on Music and Identity in *Ethnomusicology*

The title of this chapter is a pun. To provide a systematic limit on a preliminary study of a vast and important topic, the chapter reflects on the treatment of the theme of music and identity in the field of ethnomusicology through the prism of one of its major journals, *Ethnomusicology*. Adding further constraints to the project in the interest of both completeness and brevity, I limit this reflection to articles in the journal with the words *identity* or *identities* in the title. As it turns out, the first such article appeared in 1982, and seventeen of them have appeared in the twenty-five-year period from 1982 to 2006.[1] This survey of the literature provides one picture of how American ethnomusicologists have dealt with the theme of music and identity in the last quarter century.

I assumed at the beginning of this study that themes like music and identity/ies, together with many other comparable themes (music and politics, music and gender, the meaning of music, the teaching and learning of music, etc.), were ways that ethnomusicologists organized their research lives (readings, conferences, edited collections of essays) because of the "gluttonous" nature of our field.[2] Our gluttony consists of defining ethnomusicology as the study (the metaphorical eating) of all music from all parts of the world, a definition that contrasts with the suggestion of some of our founders that we focus primarily on folk, tribal, and Asian art music. Organizing our thinking around a variety of theoretical perspectives (functionalism, structuralism, poststructuralism, semiotics, interpretive anthropology, French sociology, etc.) and general themes is one way to bring some order, like a menu does, to our omnivorous

---

1. There is one "short contribution" ten years before Waterman's: Potvin (1972).

2. This characterization of our field occurs in Nettl (1983).

interests. Focusing on themes forces us, in principle at least, to read broadly, regardless of our particular geographical interest, to uncover general processes at work in music around the world.

The themes around which we build our research have multiplied since Alan Merriam provided the first list of twelve in 1964. Most of the themes he identified have endured in our work to the present, for example, native concepts about music; music as symbolic behavior (the meaning of music); and aesthetics and the interrelationship of the arts.

Conspicuous by its absence from Merriam's list, given the topic of this chapter, is the theme of the relationship between music and identity. This and many other themes that are now commonplace emerged after the publication of Merriam's seminal work: encounters with modernity; individual agency; urban and popular music; gender; migration and diaspora; nationalism; and globalization, to name a few. New themes have continued to pop up in the last decade or so and may soon become commonplace themselves, among them music in relation to war, violence, and conflict; music and medical crises such as the HIV/AIDS epidemic; and the music of affinity groups (as opposed to national or ethnic groups).

The theme of identity and its relationship to musical practice developed relatively recently in American ethnomusicology. Not only was it absent from Merriam's discipline-defining book in 1964, but also it was absent from more recent important summations of the field such as Bruno Nettl's *The Study of Ethnomusicology: 29 Issues and Concepts* published in 1993 and the edited handbook *Ethnomusicology: An Introduction,* published in 1992 (Myers 1992). By 2005, however, I found, in surveying the program of the fiftieth anniversary meeting of the Society for Ethnomusicology, that music and identity was by far the best represented theme at the conference, forming the basis for some 83 of about 500 papers (Rice 2005). Somewhere along the way the relationship between identity and music became a major theme in our field. So what happened? When and why did this theme emerge, and what has been its intellectual payoff? Answering these questions is the topic of this chapter.

## OVERVIEW OF THE LITERATURE

A search of the three major English-language journals devoted to general ethnomusicology (*Ethnomusicology, Yearbook for Traditional Music,* and *Ethnomusicology Forum*) for article titles that employ the term *identity* suggests that the theme emerges and begins to be deployed consistently in the early 1980s. The first article was Christopher Waterman's "'I'm a Leader, Not a Boss': Social Identity and Popular Music in Ibadan, Nigeria," published in

*Ethnomusicology* in 1982. After that, the use of the term *identity* in an article title occurs an average of once a year in those journals up to the present.
A search of the titles of the 100 or so book-length musical ethnographies published in English in the last thirty years reveals that the first book with the word
*identity* in the title was not published until 1991 (Sutton 1992). Looking inside
the books, it is possible to discern the theme of identity and music emerging
earlier, in the 1980s; one of the earliest is Manuel Peña's 1985 study of class
identity among Mexican Americans in Texas. After that, the theme of identity
and music forms an important element of most musical ethnographies published in English up to the present.

There are probably three reasons that the theme of the relation between music
and identity emerges in the 1980s. First, identity as a psychosocial category of
analysis gains strength in the literature of sociology, anthropology, cultural studies, and philosophy beginning sometime in the 1960s; in other words, identity
has a relatively short history in those fields that are foundational for ethnomusicology. Second, American identity politics based on race, ethnicity, and gender
gained ground in American universities and cultural life beginning in the 1970s.
Third, there has been, beginning in the 1990s, an increasing sense in ethnomusicology, often from direct fieldwork experience, that people inhabit a world
that is "fragmented" and "deterritorialized"; that they possess unprecedented
opportunities for geographical, economic, cultural, and social mobility untied
to ostensibly traditional ethnic, national, gender, and class identities and categories; and that life "routes" are becoming as or more important than "roots."[3]

When I began this survey, I assumed two things about ethnomusicologists'
research on the theme of music and identity. First, I assumed that we would
look at the general literature on identity to understand how it is being defined
and discussed more generally in the social sciences and humanities. Second,
I assumed that as we worked on this theme in relation to our particular area of
interest, we would cite and build on the publications of those who had written
on this theme before us. One of the results of my survey is that, sadly for me
at least, neither of those assumptions turns out to be true. In the first instance,
ethnomusicologists who have produced this corpus of work seem to take for
granted identity as a category of social life and of social analysis. They do not,
with very few exceptions, cite more general work on identity in the social sciences and humanities, nor do they define the term. In the second instance, their
particular studies are not contextualized, for the most part, in the ethnomusicological literature on music and identity. I am left to infer that these authors

---

3. For two classic statements of this understanding, see Appadurai (1997) and Clifford (1997),
as well as Rice (2003).

understand implicitly that music and identity is a theme around which ethno-musicologists organize their work, but how previous work might impact their work or how their work might build toward useful generalizations or more insightful treatments of the subject doesn't interest them. They seem content, in other words, to leave such work to overview essays such as this one. What worries me is that their failure to think more clearly about identity as a social category and to understand their own particular ethnographic work in relationship to a growing literature on this theme in ethnomusicology is symptomatic of a general problem with the discipline of ethnomusicology, at least as practiced today in the United States. By not embedding our particular ethnographic studies in these two literatures, we are limiting the potential of our field to grow in intellectual and explanatory power.

Having begun with one form of conclusion, I continue with a closer look at the theme of music and identity as it has manifested itself in *Ethnomusicology*. I am particularly interested in how it unwittingly intersects with the treatment of identity more generally, especially in the field of cultural studies. As it turns out, the discussion of identity generally is riven with splits, distinctions, and contradictions that ethnomusicologists would do well to consider and respond to.

## WHAT IS IDENTITY?

Perhaps predictably, the literature on identity is rather confusing on this point. The term itself may have entered the lexicon through the work in the 1950s of psychologist Erik Erikson, who was concerned with the developmental stages of the individual and who gave us the cliché "identity crisis" (Erikson 1959). If the meaning of identity once implied, in philosophy for example, something identical over time, then Erikson's idea of the stages of life seems to have replaced it with a "logic of temporality" (Grossberg 1996). In later years Erikson himself broadened his work to include "the social context of individuals' development" and "the moral and ethical implications of different forms of social organization for humankind" (Marcia 2002). While all subsequent developments in the study of identity cannot be laid at Erikson's feet, some of the main themes find expression in his work.

### Individual Self-Identity

One such theme is the idea that identity is fundamentally about individual self-identity. It is, in other words, a psychological problem for the individual. This has taken at least two forms in the literature on identity. One is a concern for self-definition or self-understanding that implies questions like who am I? and what is my true nature? The other is a concern for the psychology of belonging to, identification with, and "suturing" to social groups.[4]

Although ethnomusicologists have not tended to define identity, let alone make this distinction, a few can be read to have addressed these issues in their work. For example, one way that music contributes to identity in the sense of self-definition or self-understanding is in situations where people work in unrewarding hum-drum jobs but musical competence provides them with a sense of pride and self-worth. Lawrence Witzleben, for example, documents the activities of nine amateur music clubs in Shanghai with a total membership of about 200 musicians. They specialize in playing a core repertoire of "eight great pieces" in a genre called *jiangnan sizhu* (literally, south of the [Yangtze] river silk and bamboo [string and wind music]). "Through participation in a Jiangnan sizhu music club an individual belongs both to a small community in Shanghai society (those who know and play this music) and to a more exclusive one (the club)" (Witzleben 1987: 256). Witzleben's lack of attention to the psychology of the players, that is, to the psychology of self-understanding and of status, is striking. For example, one of the more interesting possibilities for identity that is not addressed concerns the fact that people join these clubs from all walks of life.

> The environment of the club is one which minimizes demarcations based on education, status or wealth.... Several players with menial jobs are among the Jiangnan sizhu musicians most highly regarded by both amateurs and professionals.... Factory workers are numerous, but there are also retail clerks, engineers, doctors of Chinese medicine and retired farmers. (p. 249)

Witzleben suggests, but does not follow up in detail, the possibility that participation in musical clubs such as these may play an important role in self-understanding in general and in this case in providing a sense of self-worth rather more elevated than the one they get from their paying jobs alone and a source of pride absent from low-status and menial jobs.

An excellent study of self-identity as the psychology of belonging is Christopher Waterman's essay about how Dayo, a Yoruba *jùjú* musician in Ibadan, Nigeria, sutures himself to two social groups: the upper classes for whom his band plays music and the lower-class "band boys" whom he simultaneously

---

4. The evocative term *suturing* is given by Hall (1996).

cultivates and exploits (Waterman 1982). As a semiliterate musician, he works in the low-status occupation of musician, akin to being a beggar, along with other low-status musicians whose loyalty he must cultivate. However, since people with money and wealth demonstrate their prestige through the hiring of the best possible musicians, he, as a very successful musician and band leader, has been able to elevate his status to that of a person with some of the same money, prestige, and honor of his clients. Waterman (1982: 66–67) turns this concern for social position into a question of "self-identity" or, perhaps better, self-identification through belonging by reporting that Dayo believes that he is a leader, not a boss. "A boss commands, I don't command." This self-understanding corresponds to the Yoruba value of "in-group egalitarianism" and the redistribution of wealth, which he expresses in conversations with his "band boys" with the phrase "we're all musicians." However, he is vastly wealthier than his band boys, whom he pays a pittance for each engagement. They remain poor and in some cases homeless, while he drives five cars, wears fine clothes, and owns an impressive sound system, placing him closer to belonging to the upper-class group of his wealthy patrons. Dayo seems to construct a self-identity that at once places him close to the social group of wealthy clients he plays for and at the same time keeps him not so socially distant from his band boys that they give up and leave his group to seek their fortunes elsewhere. As it turns out, both groups reject his constructions of identity, but for his personal self-identity that may not matter.

It seems to me that these two processes, creating a sense of self-understanding or self-worth and creating a sense of belonging to preexisting social groups, might be called authoring the self through music, especially through reflection and discourse on one's own musical practice.[5]

## Group Identity

Much more common these days than studies of individual self-identity are studies of group identity. This line of argument probably flows more from identity politics in various countries than from Erikson's work per se. Identity in most of these cases seems to be about collective self-understanding as represented by various characteristics, activities, and customs, including music. A good example from this corpus is Gordon Thompson's study of the self-understanding or identity of an Indian caste called Cāraṇs (Thompson 1991). This

5. Solomon (2000) provides another good example of people singing into existence their personal sense of belonging to a group, in this case particular small settlements of Indians in the highlands of Bolivia.

caste is a heterogeneous group with a variety of professions. Historically some of them were hereditary singers or reciters of epic praise poetry for the Hindu rulers (*rajputs*) of western India. Cāraṇs were apparently confidants of the rulers and considered themselves on a higher social plane than hereditary musicians, especially Muslim musicians, who never developed this level of intimacy with the rulers. Today, the *rajputs* of India are no longer able to support such a function, and members of the caste are turning to other professions. The current controversy concerns identity in the sense of self-understanding. Does the caste include singers and musicians or not? Those who seek to keep themselves differentiated from and elevated over castes that continue to produce professional musicians deny that there are or ever were professional singers among the Cāraṇs. They argue that they did not sing, but rather recited their poetry. They are particularly troubled by Cāraṇs who today emphasize the musical aspects of their art by singing melodiously and using instrumental accompaniment. This seems to be a case where the very act of making music is at issue for self-understanding of the group. There is no doubt that the group exists and who is in the group. There is, rather, controversy among group members over what characterizes the group, what its essential nature is, and how members of the group should be behaving professionally: "they . . . dispute the status of singing as a characteristic of the caste and . . . disagree, in part because the caste is increasingly heterogeneous" in its modern manifestation (p. 389).

## WHERE DOES SOCIAL IDENTITY COME FROM?

There have been two answers to this question, captured in the words *essentialist* and *constructivist*. The home of the essentialist position is the identity politics of nationalism, on one hand, and of opposition to the powerful from subaltern positions defined by ethnicity, race, class, and gender on the other. The essentialist position understands identity in terms of durable qualities and characteristics of the group that are thought to exist from time immemorial. Music's relationship to these stable identities is usually understood in terms of processes of reflection, symbolization, homology, and expression. The constructivist position, on the other hand, holds that identities are always constructed from the cultural resources available at any given moment. Rather than durable and stable, identities are contingent, fragile, unstable, and changeable. The issue in this view of identity becomes whether, to what extent, and how music making and music listening participate in the construction of various forms of emerging and changing social identities. While the latter position has gained the upper hand in recent work in cultural studies and in ethnomusicology, it has had to contend with the on-the-ground continuing practice of the essentialist position in such arenas as American identity politics and nationalist discourses in post-socialist Eastern Europe and Central Asia. Most of the articles in this corpus deal with situations where new identities are in fact emerging for various political and social reasons, rather than with situations, still rather common in the world, where someone or some social group or some government is positing a durable, essential identity.

The authors of works in this corpus, almost to a person, repeat the mantra that music helps to construct social identities. In this context, then, it is surprising to see how often they fall back into a discussion in which the social identity already exists, and music's role is primarily to symbolize, or reflect, or give performative life to a preexisting identity. For example, whether reflection or construction is at stake is confused in Lara Allen's study of a new hybrid genre called "vocal jive," which developed in the Black townships of South Africa in the 1950s (Allen 2003). As for reflection, we learn that as a popular recorded music, it "expressed a locally-rooted identity reflective of their everyday lives" (p. 237) by employing "local melodies, current township argot, and topical subject matter" (p. 234). But it did it in an international jazz-pop-blues-based style that expressed a hybrid identity also evolving at the time. Later she says that the music helped to "form" an identity:

> The musical eclecticism of vocal jive was politically significant in that its merger of Western and African elements to form a non-tribal, internationally-oriented, urban African cultural identity was at odds with policies of racial segregation promulgated by British colonials and Afrikaner settlers, and consolidated under apartheid. . . . Even in particularly repressive political contexts, commercial popular music can arguably function in a seditious manner. (p. 238)

She argues that

> hybrid styles such as vocal jive embodied the urban, non-tribal, partially Westernized experience and identity of township dwellers, whose existence the government wished to deny. . . . By nurturing the development of hybrid musical styles that expressed an identity rejected by the government, and by allowing dissident lyrics, the recording industry provided the mass of ordinary township people with a powerful means to voice cultural resistance, whether overtly, or more often, in a covert, ambiguous, contingent, fluctuating manner. (p. 243)

In this case, the social identity seems to have come first, and music reflected the hybrid nature of that identity (part African, part urban, part Westernized) through the music's own iconically hybrid form. Of course, a new hybrid identity in urban Africa does not qualify as a durable national or ethnic identity dating back for centuries or even millennia as most essentialist arguments have it. Still this case illustrates how hard it is for constructivist arguments not to fall back on essentialist ones.

Constructed identities become an issue in situations of change or where the weak and the powerful are fighting over issues of identity. Some authors make convincing claims for music participating in the construction of new or imagined identities.[6] Peter Manuel, for example, makes the point that flamenco is associated with three downtrodden social groupings in Spanish society: those living in the region of Andalusia, Gypsies, and people of the lower classes (Manuel 1989). He argues that music is "not merely a passive reflection of broader sociocultural phenomena that shape" it but can play an "important role ... in expressing and, to a considerable extent, helping to shape modern Andalusian identity" (p. 48). Performers of flamenco seem to be constructing a new sense of group self-understanding through their creation of new genres of music that have begun a process of "dignification" and professionalization of the tradition. These changes "enhance the image of Andalusia and its gypsies" and thus form a "particularly important symbol of their [more dignified] identity" (p. 57). This seems to be a constructivist project aimed at expressing a new self-understanding and a new image for others to latch onto. In addition to the dignification of traditional flamenco, two new genres are participating in the formation or construction of identity. One is *flamenco arabe,* the setting of Arab songs to flamenco *cantes* (melodic forms). "*Flamenco arabe* represents a reaffirmation of Andalusia's distinct cultural heritage in the form of a celebration of its Moorish ties. At the same time it may be seen as a willful renunciation of the economic and political domination imposed over the centuries by Madrid" (p. 59). Another genre, *flamenco pop,* responds to the urbanization and migration of proletarian workers to Barcelona and Madrid and is made up of a mixture of various influences including rock and Cuban popular music. The texts "celebrate gypsy values of freedom and hostility to authority" (p. 61) and participate "in the formation of a new urban identity" (p. 62). The genre has "become an important symbol of the new urban Andalusian consciousness. ... Its fusions ... serve to influence and articulate aspects of modern urban social identity" (p. 62). Here it seems clear that new social groups with new social identities are not being formed. Rather what is at stake are new self-understandings, the need for which is created by long-standing social grievances and new economic and social conditions that

6. My favorite example of this line of thinking comes not from this corpus of articles in *Ethnomusicology* but from a musical ethnography by Sugarman (1997).

make life even worse than before. The point is made that the construction of identity as a form of self-understanding through music is accomplished when identities need to be or are being changed. Music helps that process by changing itself or, better, by being changed by the musicians who want to participate in the construction of new identities (self-understandings) and the symbolic presentation or representation of that self-understanding to others so that others' understandings of the group can change as well.

## HOW MANY IDENTITIES DO WE POSSESS?

One claim about identity associated with the constructivist approach is that identity, rather than being unitary, is multiple and fragmented. Instead of a single self with enduring, deep, and abiding qualities, we possess multiple selves (gendered, racialized, ethnicized, nationalized, etc.) whose expression is contingent on particular contexts and specific performances of the self in those contexts. Music as a performance and as a context would seem to provide a particularly fruitful arena for the expression of multiple identities in context. Similarly, music as a complex semiotic form with multiple features (melody, rhythm and meter, timbre, texture, and form) inherent in its very being would seem to provide an ideal sign for symbolizing multiple aspects of identity simultaneously and temporally.[7]

A good example of music's role in the articulation of multiple senses of identity as both belonging and self-understanding is Thomas Turino's study of three forms of social identity in highland Peru, and of music's role in their production (Turino 1984). The three identities are indigenous, or Indian; *criollo*, or Hispanic; and *mestizo*, or mixed between the two identities. By altering their performance of music on a small guitar-like instrument called the *charango*, the residents of these highland communities can express their sense of belonging to one or another of these identities. When, for example, musicians strum block chords on a flat-backed, metal-stringed version of the instrument, they express their sense of belonging and identification with the indigenous population. When, on the other hand, they pluck melodies in parallel thirds on a rounded-back, nylon-stringed version of the instrument, they proclaim their allegiance to upper-class *criollo* values and a hoped-for suturing to that class identity. Finally, their *mestizo* identity is performed iconically when they structure performances, as they sometimes do, to include references to all three identities. Turino gives one example in which the performer began with a typical Indian

7. For a more detailed explication and example of this position, see Rice (2001).

agricultural song; segued into a set of *waynos,* the most important *mestizo* genre; and ended with a *criollo* waltz. Thus, separate or single performances make public declarations of a sense of belonging to one, two, or all three of the multiple identities available to residents of this highland region of Peru.[8]

## HOW IS IDENTITY CREATED?

The notion that identity is constructed leads naturally to questions about who is doing the constructing. To answer this question, some sort of agency is usually posited for individuals; that is, individuals become agents in the construction of their own identities (their sense of belonging to groups, their self-understanding) in the conditions of modernity.[9] In another line of reasoning indebted to Michel Foucault, the self that could or would create an identity is a product of various "regimes" and "discourses" and thus is not a free agent in the creation of identities. As Nikolas Rose puts it, following Foucault, our relation to ourselves is less the result of active agency than "the object of a whole variety of more or less rationalized schemes, which have sought to shape our ways of understanding and enacting our existence as human beings in the name of certain objectives—manliness, femininity, honour, modesty, propriety, civility, discipline, distinction, efficiency, harmony, fulfillment, virtue, pleasure" (Rose 1996: 130). He acknowledges, in fact, that although these regimes exist, "human beings often find themselves resisting the forms of personhood that they are enjoined to adopt" (p. 140). Though he claims that no theory of agency is required to explain this resistance, most writers, myself included, would employ it precisely at this moment. Music can be understood in both ways: as a regime of self-creation (subjectification) and as a tool of resistance to those regimes. In the latter instance, the ideology of creativity often associated with music gives the sense that composers and performers of music have the power, the agency if you will, to model new and alternative forms of behavior not given by the "rationalized schemes" of everyday familial and governmental discourse and discipline.[10] On the other hand, music very often is precisely one of the modalities, to use an intentional pun, or "technologies"

8. Multiple identities are elucidated in three other studies in this corpus but not summarized in the main body of the text: Summit (1993), about the clash of Jewish and American identities; Reed (2005), on the clash of ethnic and religious identities; and Gerstin (1998), on the intersection of national, urban–rural, and individual identities.

9. For an example of this view, see Giddens (1992); for an application of this position to ethnomusicology, see Rice (2003).

10. For one of the most detailed elucidations of this point, see Sugarman (1997).

that conveys to a society its fundamental values in such domains as manliness, femininity, modesty, distinction, and pleasure. These technologies, according to Rose, work on two axes. One he calls "intellectual techniques" like reading, writing, and numeracy, which can transform "mentalities." The second axis consists of "corporealities or body techniques." One thinks of manners and etiquette, for example, which "inculcate the habits and rituals of self-denial, prudence and foresight" (p. 138). Musical practice would seem to be both an intellectual and a corporeal technology. At the intellectual level, its use or non-use of notation and its valorization (or not) of orality and improvisation may create particular kinds of selves and self-understandings that function well within specific social and cultural circumstances. At the corporeal level, many traditions with strong teacher–student relations inculcate specific performa-tive forms of obedience and respect that create not just good music but good people as well.

One article that can be read as mediating these two perspectives is David Harnish's study of shifting identities and their effect on musical practice at a temple festival at Lingsar on the island of Lombak in Indonesia (Harnish 2005). Two religious groups have historically claimed the festival as their own: the Balinese Hindus and the Muslims, called Sasaks. Although "ethnic tensions and contestations" were a feature of the festival, both groups managed to coex-ist. They explained to Harnish, who has been studying the festival on and off for twenty years since 1983, that each element of the festival was necessary and could not be changed. So he was surprised that, when he attended the festival in 2001, much about the musical practice had in fact changed. Some genres of music had disappeared and some new ones had been added. Still the par-ticipants claimed that nothing much had changed. What was going on? "Some forces both within and outside the government" were at work to differenti-ate religious identities more clearly than they had been in the past (p. 3). One Sasak group that had predominated on the island and that was only nominally Muslim ("maintain[ing] indigenous, pre-Islamic customs and shar[ing] a few beliefs with Hinduism and Buddhism") had been superseded in importance by another group that had adopted a much stricter form of Islam coming from Saudi Arabia (p. 5). In response, the Hindu Balinese were more anxious to demonstrate their ties, their sense of belonging, to Balinese culture. These new political and religious beliefs were impacting the performance of music at the festival. So in this case we have a clear case of changes in musical practice reflecting larger social, political, and religious shifts in the self-understanding of Hindu and Muslim groups. Harnish complicates the issue, however, by argu-ing that these outside forces are not enough to explain the musical changes, that individual agency at the local level must also be described: "though the govern-ment and other external forces promoted new actions, individuals negotiated and reinterpreted these actions" (p. 19). With that point in mind, he examines the actions of three "subjects" to illustrate how each interprets and acts out his understanding of processes enveloping the society. They, "through the force of their actions and personal negotiations with ritual history and modernist powers, have helped shape the contemporary reality of the festival" (p. 20). Harnish's study provides a good example of the disarticulation of agency and construction. In this case, agency helps the music to reflect the larger social and cultural conditions, discourses, and "regimes" that seem to be creating new senses of identity in the first place.

## WHO DEFINES AND INSTITUTIONALIZES IDENTITIES?

While some authors seem content to claim agency for all individuals, others raise questions about the link between identity, agency, and power. If identities are constructed, then who are "the agents that do the identifying" (Brubaker and Cooper 2000: 14).[11] Can everyone be an agent or only some people? Are agents the creators of the discourses, or do individuals make choices among the discourses available to them? Are agents an individual self, a clique of politically motivated identity makers, or organs of the state? Does one identify oneself, or is one identified by others? Identity politics is centered in the ground between these extremes of identification. Who has the power to define identities, and do all individuals have the same range of identity choices and the same mobility in making identity choices? "Each society sets limits to the life strategies that can be imagined, and certainly to those which can be practised" (Bauman 1996: 35). As Lawrence Grossberg observes, "some individuals may have the possibility of occupying more than one such [subject] position, . . . some positions may offer specific perspectives on reality that are different from others, [and] some positions come to be more valued than others. . . . The question of identity is one of social power and its articulation to, its anchorage in, the body of the population itself" (Grossberg 1996: 99). In terms of agency, the question becomes: "who gets to make history?" As Grossberg puts it, "agency—the ability to make history, as it were—is not intrinsic to subjects and to selves. Agency is the product of diagrams of mobility and placement which define or map the possibilities of where and how specific vectors of influence can stop and be places. . . . Such places are temporary points of belonging and identification" (p. 102).

---

11. I would like to acknowledge here the salutary impact this article has had, in a general way, on my thinking about identity.

Conceived in the West as an archetypal instance of self-expression, musical choices, whether in the making or the listening, allow individuals acting as agents to identify with groups of their choosing and to escape the bonds of tradition provided by parents, schools, and other governmental apparatuses. In some instances, music can literally give voice to the powerless to label themselves and to express their existence as a group and their "nature" in contexts where the powerful either do not acknowledge their existence or label and identify them in ways they find objectionable. In societies where the powerful control education and propaganda through literacy and the literate media, the orality and performativity of most musical traditions provide the powerless or those seeking power with an important and potentially very public and effective mode of expression. On the other hand, music patronized and controlled by the state through such institutions as cultural ministries and by such commercial institutions as the music industry, advertising, and media play a powerful role in creating and defining groups, in identifying and classifying them, and in specifying who may associate or identify with them and who may not. In these sorts of cases, ethnomusicologists tend to speak about "contestation" and "negotiation" of identities and about different "subject positions" from which contested identities are proposed.

In this corpus, two articles stand out for their documentation of different ways powerful entities establish identities through music.[12]

One is Peter Manuel's study of salsa as a symbol of Puerto Rican national identity despite the fact that *salsa*'s roots are in Cuban dance forms of the 1940s and 1950s (Manuel 1994). In fact, Puerto Ricans and Nuyoricans (Puerto Ricans living in New York City) regard *salsa* "as local in character." He believes this is because *salsa* has been "appropriated and resignified ... as symbols of their own cultural identity" (p. 250), which is cosmopolitan, urban, not European or North American, and linked to Latin American culture. The musical structures, which combine Afro-Latin music with modern, flashy popular music and with a few elements native to Puerto Rico, seem to provide an excellent iconic expression (though he doesn't say so) of that hybrid identity. On the other hand, not everyone agrees. Some argue that the fact of *salsa*'s roots in Cuban music is a fatal flaw in its claim to being a symbol of national identity. They argue instead that other genres native to Puerto Rico should be its symbol of national identity, including (1) *jíbaro* music, a guitar-based music of rural peasants (*jíbaros*); (2) *bomba,* a drum-based vocal music originating among lower-class Blacks; and (3) *plena,* a lower-class and lower-middle-class

---

12. For an interesting study in this corpus of a state apparatus determining a musical expression of identity in the face of widespread opposition, see Daughtry (2003).

recreational music from the town of Ponce that uses the tambourine (*pan-dareta*) prominently plus scraper (*guiro*) and guitar or accordion. According to Manuel, none of these claims by their advocates have been successful because each genre is limited by its origins in lower-class social groups in a context where most Puerto Ricans and Nuyoricans understand themselves as moving up in a cosmopolitan world. These genres are too associated with backwardness rather than with modernization. This is certainly an interesting reversal of the claims of European folklorists that precisely such rural, "backward" genres should be the symbols of an essentialist national identity. In effect, Manuel is arguing that in the absence of government-imposed nationalist cultural policies, mass mediation and popularity are crucial to a particular kind of music working as a symbol of national identity. The key to his argument that *salsa* is the most potent symbol of national identity for Puerto Ricans and Nuyoricans is "its appeal across a broad spectrum of Latino nationalities, age groups, and social classes" (p. 271). *Salsa* "has become identified with a new sense of Latino identity which is at once international, and yet rooted in local community culture" (p. 272). *Salsa*'s symbolic value has emerged in a particular social situation of racial discrimination, a sense of otherness in the United States, and the fact of living in "tight Puerto Rican enclaves" within New York City. It has participated in processes of "helping them to outgrow the cultural inferiority complex of the 1930s–1950s and discover a new pride in their language and Latino musical heritage." It is "not just reiteration and borrowing, but creative appropriation and reformation," or in other words, "the resignification of the borrowed idiom to serve as a symbol of a new social identity" (pp. 272–274). He concludes that "there is little agreement as to what form cultural nationalism should take, just as Puerto Ricans themselves may hold varied forms of social identity" (pp. 276–277). In that context, the popularity of the music in the mass media seems to be the agent that makes *salsa* the music best able to express the identity of contemporary, urbanized Puerto Ricans and Nuyoricans.

The other example of music's role in the contestation of power over the labeling and assignment of identity is Chris Goertzen's study of the small Occaneechi band of Indians in the state of North Carolina (Goertzen 2001). In this case the North Carolina Commission of Indian Affairs, a commission made up of members of Indian tribes in the area, has the power to decide who is an Indian and who is not. They have so far denied the Occaneechi's application for Indian status and identity based on their gut feeling that they are not "really" Indians. On the other hand, the Occaneechi understand themselves to be Indians due to their kinship relationships with recognized tribes, their documented history in the area, a lifestyle that values hunting and fishing in addition to whatever menial jobs they hold, and other Indian values such as sharing and giving away their wealth. As far as music is concerned, the Indians of North Carolina have, for all practical purposes, lost their original musical traditions and have taken up the musical traditions associated with powwows of Indians from the central Plains region of the United States. These powwows were originally cultivated in the 1960s by the larger Indian groups in the region as a way to assert difference during a period when Indian schools were closing and integration with the larger society was being forced on them. Unfortunately the smaller groups, such as the Occaneechi, didn't take up powwow music during this period and so "remained 'hidden in plain sight,' as many North Carolina Indians phrase it" (p. 68). Even though they have started recently to host powwows and musical performances, they can't convince the larger tribes that they are Indians; these larger groups do not seem to accept the powwow as an unambiguous symbol of Indian identity. For the Occaneechi themselves, on the other hand, powwows work in multiple ways. First, they are a way to express enduring local values of community and sharing and to create a sense of belonging to and identifying with a community of Indians. Second, "powwows provide adults with a focus for self-esteem and intellectual engagement that may be lacking in the work week," characterized by "hum-drum jobs" due to low educational levels (p. 70). Finally, the powwows express a particular form of self-understanding: "each local powwow, by representing traditional Indian and rural values and through celebrating the history of given communities, asserts the primacy of spiritual health and community life over material improvement" (p. 70). If the large tribes do not find the performance of powwows a convincing sign of Indian identity, most non-Indians do. "Powwows are the main tool North Carolina Indians have for defining their collective identity to outsiders. . . . Indians use powwows to encourage the surrounding communities to respect both the nature and the boundaries of their communities" (p. 71). So musical practice in relation to identity works for insiders in one way (a sense of belonging and self-understanding), for some outsiders (other Indians) not at all, and for Whites as a symbol of a specific, "different" Indian identity. Until the North Carolina Commission of Indians recognizes their Indian identity, the Occaneechi may partake of the psychological benefits of their own self-understanding, but not of the social and economic benefits that recognition of their identity by the commission would confer.

## WHAT DOES MUSIC CONTRIBUTE TO IDENTITY?

While these questions do not exhaust the theoretical issues at stake in the study of identity and how music studies might contribute to them, I turn in the interest of space to a question that is specific to the ethnomusicological literature on music, namely, what are the particular contributions of music to discussions of social identity?[13] There seem to be four basic positions in the literature. The first is that music gives symbolic shape to a preexisting or emergent identity. That symbolic shape is inherent in the structures of music and usually constitutes an iconic representation of elements of identity. Music's temporality can be an icon of the temporal logic of identity. Moreover, music has the ability to index different aspects of multiple identities through the multiplicity of its formal properties (melody, harmony, rhythm, timbre, etc.). Second, musical performance provides the opportunity for communities sharing an identity to see themselves in action and to imagine others who might share the same style of performance. Third, music may contribute to an identity its "feel" or affective quality.

Christopher Waterman makes this last point in his study of music's role in the construction of pan-Yoruba identity in Nigeria (Waterman 1990). Yoruba as a label for an ethnic group in Nigeria was invented sometime in the early twentieth century from an amalgam of local groups, who were understood to contrast with more culturally distant groups, such as the Hausa and Igbo. In this context, whatever is labeled Yoruba music, and especially its emergent popular forms, is participating, along with politics, education, and language, in a process of construction of a new identity rather than acting as a reflection of a well-established identity. However, although Waterman claims such a constructivist position, the main line of argument flows from a structuralist perspective: "the role of neo-traditional music in enacting and disseminating a hegemonic Yoruba identity is grounded in the iconic representation of social relationships as sonic relationships" and, one might add, performative or visual relationships (p. 372). While his argument begins with the idea of reflection, he turns it into a constructivist argument by claiming that *jùjú* performances "externalize these values and give them palpable form" (p. 376). The latter idea, palpability, seems to be one of the special claims about what music can do in the constructivist project. One gets the sense here that Yoruba identity actually has

---

13. One point common to discussions of identity but omitted here is the idea that identity is always constructed out of difference; that is, one's self-understanding is constituted by the construction of an "other." On the other hand, Robbins (1996) argues that it might be possible to transcend this position by focusing less on cultural identity and more on cultural exchange. This entails on our part not imagining the other as essentially different from us, but as having agency; considering the possibility of openness and change; and putting our selves in their places with some knowledge of how they operate. Music would seem to contribute to both of these two propositions. On the one hand, music gives groups a strong and immediate experience of the specificity of their favored styles of making music and its difference from other groups' styles. On the other hand, in the postmodern era, musicians delight in the opportunities music provides for specific and deeply satisfying forms of dialogue and exchange that counter the discourses of difference perpetrated in the linguistic and political domains by identity makers of various political persuasions. The authors of works in this corpus do not concern themselves much with either point of view.

been constructed elsewhere (in dictionaries of the Yoruba language, in school-
ing, and in political action of various kinds), but music provides the identity with "its interactive ethos or 'feel': intensive, vibrant, buzzing, and fluid"
(p. 376). Since music can't name the identity, this claim may be more persuasive
than the constructivist one. Or minimally one might claim that music participates in a constructivist project by giving it not its name but its "feel" and emotional resonance.

The fourth contribution of music to identity is the claim that music gives to
an identity, especially a subaltern identity, a positive valence. This argument was
made by Manuel for Puerto Rican music, by Allen for South African "vocal jive,"
and by Barbara Krader (1987) for singers in Croatia and Bosnia-Herzegovina.

This topic is clearly an area where theories about the relationship between
music and identity could develop, but theories are not worked out in the ethnographic articles I have cited so far. Such a theory does appear, however, in
an article by Thomas Turino specifically devoted to theory rather than ethnography (Turino 1999). Applying to music the semiotic theories of Charles
Sanders Peirce (1839–1914), an American philosopher, Turino argues that it is
the iconic quality of music as a sign that is one source of its emotional power.
Musical iconicity consists of its structural similarity to other aspects of culture
and shared behaviors, and as such contributes an emotionally satisfying sense
that the identity being constructed through music is "natural." In addition,
music's ability to index common experiences of a community and one's shared
social experience with that community contributes to the emotional power of
music. "Music integrates the affective and identity-forming potentials of both
icons and indices in special ways, and is thus a central resource in events and
propaganda aimed at creating social unity, participation, and purpose" (p. 236).
This theoretical work is, in my opinion, very necessary if the full potential of
organizing our scholarly work around themes is to be realized. The existence of
such work makes its absence from the ethnographic articles in this corpus all
the more striking.

## CONCLUSION

The seventeen articles published since 1982 in *Ethnomusicology* with the word
*identity* in the title are clearly just the tip of an iceberg of ethnomusicological interest in the theme of music's role in creating, constructing, articulating,
negotiating, and reflecting social identities. Each of the sixteen ethnographic
articles provides an interesting window into processes of identity formation
in particular cases from virtually every region of the world: Africa (four),
Latin America (four), Europe (three), North America (two), East Asia (one),

South Asia (one), and Southeast Asia (one); only studies from the Pacific and the Middle East are missing. All kinds of identity, including multiple identities in conflict, are examined: ethnic (five), national (four), regional (three), class (two), religious (three), community (two), tribal (two), caste (one), hybrid (one), and individual (one).

What is missing in all this variety is the desire to create a coherent, interrelated, unified body of work that connects with the larger literature on identity and works out the potentially fascinating cross-cultural theoretical implications and general tendencies at work whenever music is used to create a sense of individual or social identity. I regard this failure to achieve coherence and reference within this corpus as a structural weakness in our work on this theme. If this pattern is true for the other themes around which we ethnomusicologists organize our work, and I fear that it might be, then we have a structural weakness in our discipline that diminishes the efficacy of our research in general and limits the potential of ethnomusicology, at least in its American form, to make a powerful contribution to scholarship on music.

## REFERENCES

Allen, Lara. 2003. "Commerce, Politics, and Musical Hybridity: Vocalizing Black South African Identity during the 1950s." *Ethnomusicology* 47: 228–249.

Appadurai, Arjun. 1997. *Modernity at Large: Cultural Dimensions of Globalization.* Minneapolis: University of Minnesota Press.

Bauman, Zygmunt. 1996. "From Pilgrim to Tourist—or a Short History of Identity." In Stuart Hall and Paul du Gay, eds., *Questions of Cultural Identity.* London: Sage Publications, pp. 18–36.

Brubaker, Rogers, and Frederick Cooper. 2000. "Beyond 'Identity.'" *Theory and Society* 29: 1–47.

Clifford, James. 1997. *Routes: Travel and Translation in the Late Twentieth Century.* Cambridge, MA: Harvard University Press.

Daughtry, J. Martin. 2003. "Russia's New Anthem and the Negotiation of National Identity." *Ethnomusicology* 47: 42–67.

Erikson, Erik. 1959. *Identity and the Life Cycle.* New York: International Universities Press.

Gerstin, Julian. 1998. "Reputation in a Musical Scene: The Everyday Context of Connections between Music, Identity, and Politics." *Ethnomusicology* 42: 385–414.

Giddens, Anthony. 1992. *Modernity and Self-identity: Self and Society in the Late Modern Age.* Stanford, CA: Stanford University Press.

Goertzen, Chris. 2001. "Powwows and Identity on the Piedmont and Coastal Plains of North Carolina." *Ethnomusicology* 45: 58–88.

Grossberg, Lawrence. 1996. "Identity and Cultural Studies—Is That All There Is?" In Stuart Hall and Paul du Gay, eds., *Questions of Cultural Identity.* London: Sage Publications, pp. 87–107.

Hall, Stuart. 1996. "Introduction: Who Needs Identity?" In Stuart Hall and Paul du Gay, eds., *Questions of Cultural Identity*. London: Sage Publications, pp. 1–17.

Harnish, David. 2005. "New Lines, Shifting Identities: Interpreting Change at the Lingsar Festival in Lombok, Indonesia." *Ethnomusicology* 49: 1–24.

Krader, Barbara. 1987. "Slavic Folk Music: Forms of Singing and Self-Identity." *Ethnomusicology* 31: 9–17.

Manuel, Peter. 1989. "Andalusian, Gypsy, and Class Identity in the Contemporary Flamenco Complex." *Ethnomusicology* 33: 47–65.

———. 1994. "Puerto Rican Music and Cultural Identity: Creative Appropriation of Cuban Sources from Danza to Salsa." *Ethnomusicology* 38: 249–280.

Marcia, J. E. 2002. "Erikson, Erik Homburger (1902–94)." In Neil J. Smelser and Paul B. Baltes, eds., *International Encyclopedia of the Social and Behavioral Sciences*. Amsterdam: Elsevier, p. 4737.

Merriam, Alan P. 1964. *The Anthropology of Music*. Evanston, IL: Northwestern University Press.

Myers, Helen, ed. 1992. *Ethnomusicology: An Introduction*. New York: W.W. Norton.

Nettl, Bruno. 1983. *The Study of Ethnomusicology: Twenty-Nine Issues and Concepts*. Urbana: University of Illinois Press.

Peña, Manuel H. 1985. *The Texas-Mexican Conjunto: History of a Working-Class Music*. Austin: University of Texas Press.

Potvin, Gilles. 1972. "The Canadian Broadcasting Corporation and Canadian Folk Cultures: The Preservation of Ethnic Identity." *Ethnomusicology* 16: 512–515.

Reed, Daniel B. 2005. " 'The *Ge* Is in the Church' and 'Our Parents Are Playing Muslim': Performance, Identity, and Resistance among the Dan in Postcolonial Côte d'Ivoire." *Ethnomusicology* 49: 347–357.

Rice, Timothy. 2001. "Reflections on Music and Meaning: Metaphor, Signification, and Control in the Bulgarian Case." *British Journal of Ethnomusicology* 10: 19–38.

———. 2003. "Time, Place, and Metaphor in Musical Experience and Ethnography." *Ethnomusicology* 47: 151–179.

———. 2005. "SEM Soundbyte: What Are We Thinking?" *SEM Newsletter* 39(4): 1.

Robbins, Kevin. 1996. "Interrupting Identities: Turkey/Europe." In Stuart Hall and Paul du Gay, eds., *Questions of Cultural Identity*. London: Sage Publications, pp. 61–86.

Rose, Nikolas. 1996. "Identity, Genealogy, History." In Stuart Hall and Paul du Gay, eds., *Questions of Cultural Identity*. London: Sage Publications, pp. 128–150.

Solomon, Thomas. 2000. "Dueling Landscapes: Singing Places and Identities in Highland Bolivia." *Ethnomusicology* 44: 257–280.

Sugarman, Jane C. 1997. *Engendering Song: Singing and Subjectivity and Prespa Albanian Weddings*. Chicago: University of Chicago Press.

Summit, Jeffrey A. 1993. " 'I'm a Yankee Doodle Dandy?': Identity and Melody at an American Simha at Torah Celebration." *Ethnomusicology* 37: 41–62.

Sutton, R. Anderson. 1992. *Traditions of Gamelan Music in Java: Musical Pluralism and Regional Identity*. Cambridge: Cambridge University Press.

Thompson, Gordon R. 1991. "The Cāraṇs of Gujarat: Caste Identity, Music, and Cultural Change." *Ethnomusicology* 35: 381–391.

Turino, Thomas. 1984. "The Urban-Mestizo Charango Tradition in Southern Peru: A Statement of Shifting Identity." *Ethnomusicology* 28: 253–270.

———. 1999. "Signs of Imagination, Identity, and Experience: A Peircian Semiotic Theory for Music." *Ethnomusicology* 43: 221–255.

Waterman, Christopher A. 1982. "'I'm a Leader, Not a Boss': Social Identity and Popular Music in Ibadan, Nigeria." *Ethnomusicology* 26: 59–71.

———. 1990. "'Our Tradition Is a Very Modern Tradition': Popular Music and the Construction of Pan-Yoruba Identity." *Ethnomusicology* 34: 367–379.

Witzleben, J. Lawrence. 1987. "Jiangnan Sizhu Music Clubs in Shanghai: Context, Concept and Identity." *Ethnomusicology* 31: 240–260.

# 6

# Ethnomusicological Theory

"Ethnomusicological theory," despite its name and despite the fact that it in some ways permeates our field, has yet to take firm root in our disciplinary imagination.[1] Indeed, the phrase appears to be used rarely, in comparison to references to an unmodified "theory" in or for ethnomusicology. Minimally, ethnomusicology today engages with three types of theory: social theory, music theory, and discipline-specific ethnomusicological theory. Unmodified references to theory have tended to obfuscate the nature of ethnomusicological theory and have left ethnomusicologists a bit unsure, and perhaps even insecure, about the relevance and place of theory, however understood, in their work.[2]

1. I cannot resist the use of "our" here and elsewhere in this chapter, because I regard a discipline as, among other things, constituted by conversations among a community of scholars. But I want to be careful to point out that the disciplinary conversations I am speaking about are expressed in English, which, perhaps unfortunately, dominates not only conversations in the United States, the United Kingdom, Canada, Ireland, Australia, New Zealand, and parts of Africa but also in international forums. Meetings of the International Council for Traditional Music (ICTM) illustrate productively the extent to which different national and language traditions, and thus different ethnomusicologies, exist all over the world. The ICTM is an ideal body for creating interdisciplinary conversations among them. Attempts by the US Society for Ethnomusicology to encourage such conversations include its 2005 fiftieth anniversary meeting (see *Ethnomusicology* 2006, 50[2]) and its 2008 annual meeting in Mexico City, which used the slogan "Borderless Ethnomusicologies," simultaneous translations of some sessions, and papers delivered in Spanish to signal the desire of many to broaden the conversation to all corners of the world.

2. This chapter was first presented at the 2009 Fortieth World Conference of the International Council for Traditional Music in Durban, South Africa, and was entitled "What and Where Is Theory in Ethnomusicology?" Subsequently I presented it at the Universities of California in Berkeley, Los Angeles, Riverside, and Santa Barbara, and at Istanbul Technical University. I am grateful to the faculty and students at those universities for the ideas they shared with me in the discussions that followed. Many of the issues they raised helped to reshape the article into its present form. In addition, I want to thank Michael Bakan, Judith Becker, Harris Berger,

Three publications by Mervyn McLean, Ruth Stone, and me illustrate the problem I have in mind. McLean (2006), in his book *Pioneers of Ethnomusicology*, laments that "American ethnomusicology is now awash with theory" (p. 337) "derived mostly from outside disciplines" (p. 259), when, in his view, more solid, straightforward description is what is really needed.[3] On the contrary, my recent review of the literature in the journal *Ethnomusicology* on the theme of music and identity revealed virtually no references to theory from outside the discipline or indeed much in the way of intradisciplinary theorizing (Rice 2007). Viewed from this limited angle, ethnomusicology could hardly be said to be awash in theory. This small survey notwithstanding, it is probably fair to say that American ethnomusicologists today typically cite a wide range of theory from a variety of disciplines.

Against McLean's implication that treading water in theory from other disciplines distracts us from more important tasks, Stone (2008: 225), in her book-length survey *Theory for Ethnomusicology*, argues that "theory is the essential complement to the rich ethnographic detail of ethnographic description." However, she points out that, though "many ethnomusicologists espouse the centrality of theory" to the field, "theoretical discussions are . . . typically brief and cursory in most ethnomusicological accounts" (p. ix). If theory is central to the field, why is it only treated briefly? This is not a logical problem, but an accurate characterization of the discipline's treatment of theory. Without engaging in an extended critique of individual works, I think it is fair to say that ethnomusicologists often reference theory from outside the discipline for the authority and interdisciplinarity it appears to give to their work, but it is rarely the object of sustained argumentation.[4] As Stone (2008: ix) puts it, "A very few ethnomusicologists engage in detailed theoretical discussion. . . . These . . . ethnomusicologists are definitely in the minority."

J. Martin Daughtry, Juniper Hill, Steven Loza, Daniel Neuman, Sherry Ortner, Helen Rees, Suzel Reily, Anthony Seeger, Jane Sugarman, Timothy Taylor, Michael Tenzer, Louise Wrazen, and two anonymous referees, whose comments and suggestions on previous drafts helped me reconsider and develop my ideas, and eventually to retitle the paper.

3. In this narrative, McLean, a distinguished ethnomusicologist from New Zealand, is a stand-in for others who argue against the importation of social theory into the discipline of ethnomusicology. Such arguments rarely appear in print and, in my experience, are more typically voiced in interpersonal and casual communications. He is an excellent ethnomusicological theorist in the sense proposed here (e.g., McLean 1979, 1986).

4. The practical, if tawdry, function of brief and cursory references to social theory for the purpose of establishing intellectual authority was brought home to me when, some years ago, I applied for a small grant to do some very basic, pedestrian, but necessary follow-up field research in Bulgaria for a project I was working on. My application was honest in its depiction of the rather prosaic nature of the research task, even as the broader topic was, I thought, worthy of investigation. The application was denied. The next year I infused it with some not irrelevant,

What is this theory that McLean, Stone, and I are referring to? For the most part, it is theory from the social sciences and humanities that goes by various names: for example, social theory, cultural studies, critical theory, literary theory, linguistic theory, psychological theory, postcolonial theory, feminist theory, and philosophical theory (or simply philosophy). In these discursive domains, theory is associated both with ideas (deconstruction, hermeneutics, structuralism, feminism, embodiment, etc.) and with the names of "theorists": earlier writings with Theodor Adorno, Émile Durkheim, Claude Lévi-Strauss, Karl Marx, and Max Weber, for instance, and more recently with Arjun Appadurai, Homi Babha, Pierre Bourdieu, Judith Butler, Néstor García Canclini, Jacques Derrida, Michel Foucault, Clifford Geertz, bell hooks, Jacques Lacan, Raymond Williams, and others.[5]

These theorists, and their theories, make bold claims about the social and cultural world, claims that have reoriented or changed much thinking about society and culture and that have implications for many fields of study. For the sake of simplicity I will call all these "social theory," regardless of their source in particular intellectual traditions. Social theories facilitate the "blurring of boundaries" between disciplines (Geertz 1973) because, while they may originate in anthropology, history, linguistics, literary studies, philosophy, psychology, or sociology, scholars in many disciplines have found their insights useful for a wide range of projects. Not always constrained, as scientific theories are, by the demands of formal methodologies for their demonstration, they nonetheless make novel and engaging claims about such fundamental human matters as how meaning is created and interpreted, how culture is inculcated and sustained, the nature of the self and subject, how power is exercised and resisted, and relationships between the mind and body, the public and the private, and the material and ideal worlds.

Although social theories may not demand to be proven through experimentation, they nonetheless guide, inform, and illuminate empirical, on-the-ground, often qualitative investigations that can be judged by the fit they

but not really necessary, references to social theory, and I was given the award. Clearly scholars in other fields who review grant applications in the United States think ethnomusicologists should be participating with them in, and contributing to, a broad, interdisciplinary discussion of themes and issues of common interest.

5. I am aware that this list, with a few exceptions, may appear to reinscribe a system that has been called White or high or Eurocentric theory, a system that has been critiqued by many scholars, including ethnomusicologists (see, e.g., Loza 2006). In doing so, I describe ethnomusicology's past, not my and others' hopes for its future. No ethnomusicologist would object to Loza's call for a broader, more inclusive vision of social theory, with special consideration of theories created in the particular culture or culture area that an ethnomusicologist studies. But to implement that vision, each of us has to not only champion (and perhaps translate, as others have the French theorists) our favorite neglected social theorists but also use their theories for the writing of what

propose between the theory and the data encountered in the study.[6] Examples of this sort of productive theorization include Pierre Bourdieu's (1977) claim that nonverbal practice is as important in the transmission of culture as verbalized statements, and Michel Foucault's (1978) notion that some aspects of human life taken as "natural," such as sex, have been constructed through discourse tied to powerful institutions. These insights, generated in specific cultural, social, and disciplinary milieux, are then taken by scholars in other fields as potentially applicable to their own studies. Social theories are (1) interdisciplinary in the sense that they exceed their disciplinary roots; (2) suggestive of new points of view, and so requiring application to particular cases but not proof per se; (3) generative of interpretations rather than scientific explanations; (4) critical of common-sense notions of what appears "natural" about human life; (5) open-ended and unbounded, in the sense that new ones come on the scene rather frequently; and (6) sometimes resisted for their discomfiting challenge to complete mastery of a discipline and for coming from outside the discipline or the culture to which they are applied.

The disagreement between McLean, on the one hand, and Stone and me, on the other, on the centrality of social theory to ethnomusicology speaks to differing notions of an inside and an outside to the field. McLean and others who resist social theory seem to view ethnomusicology, or their particular area of study, or indeed their culture, as bounded. Social theory then appears to be an intrusion that needs to be resisted. Those who advocate for its relevance and centrality seem to view ethnomusicology as unbounded in terms of its intellectual sources; they have accepted Geertz's notion of blurred boundaries between and among disciplines, and are anxious to participate in a common, shared, interdisciplinary conversation about the nature of human artistic, biological, cultural, and social life by contributing to it studies of music's importance and role in making those lives what they are.[7] For

---

I call "ethnomusicological theory." Merely to advocate for the relevance of social theory from outside the Eurocentric canon may unwittingly reproduce the brief and cursory arguments from authority that characterize much of ethnomusicology's treatment of even that canon.

6. I use "empirical" in the broad sense advocated by Tyler Bickford (2010) to refer to any research, such as ethnographic fieldwork, based on observation and experience, rather than in the narrow sense of research based on experimentation.

7. What I am calling the common conversation raises critical issues of inclusion and exclusion (Jackson 2006). Deborah Wong (2004: 304) has also pointed to the distance that can exist between these conversations and the struggles of intellectuals and musicians (themselves intellectuals) from the communities we study to be heard and to contribute to "political action, social responsibility, and intellectual thought." In a related vein, Harris Berger (personal communication) suggested "a distinction . . . between theoretical work that seeks only to produce general insights into social life and those forms of theory that . . . go further to engage in social criticism or pursue an activist agenda."

such scholars, social theory is within the field of ethnomusicology as they understand it.[8]

No matter whether one views the field as bounded or unbounded, however, the idea that ethnomusicology is a derivative discipline, dependent on borrowing theory from anthropology and other fields, and rather weak in generating its own theories, seems to persist. This view is difficult to demonstrate with citations since it surfaces mainly in discussions at conferences and in seminar rooms, but there may be a kind of inferiority complex about the discipline's relation to theory and our collective ability to theorize about music. One of the goals of this chapter is to help us move beyond these feelings by understanding more clearly the theorizing we already do and, in the process, help us develop a more robust theoretical tradition.[9]

The first step in this process is for us to cease using the word *theory* in its unmodified form. In particular, ethnomusicological theory needs to be defined more clearly and treated to sustained consideration. If we are better able to recognize ethnomusicological theory when we see it and if we engage with it and with social theory, we should be able to generate more intellectual power in the discipline and contribute more cogently to the general, interdisciplinary conversations now animating the humanities and social sciences. It is my hope that attending to ethnomusicological theory will make it possible for every ethnomusicologist to engage in detailed and focused considerations of it and to regard such theorizing not as a borrowed imposition (welcome or unwelcome) on the field, but as a desirable, indeed necessary, part of each ethnomusicologist's contribution to it.

## THEORY IN THE HISTORY OF ETHNOMUSICOLOGY

Perhaps striking by its absence from my list of types of theory is scientific theory; this is because I believe that most ethnomusicologists no longer regularly employ it. In the early years of ethnomusicology, from 1950 to about 1980 (and before 1950, if we count comparative musicology), ethnomusicologists worked

---

8. Conversations with Anthony Seeger and Timothy Taylor helped me articulate this point.

9. Many of the principal overviews of our field (Kunst 1959; Nettl 1964; Hood 1971; Myers 1992) have contributed to the confusion about the nature of ethnomusicological theory by privileging method over theory to an extraordinary extent, leaving theory certainly underdiscussed, if not largely undiscussed. Even what these authors call theory is often simply a theme or an issue around which some of our work has crystallized (e.g., gender and music, urban music, teaching and learning of music) without much reference to the theories we have developed ourselves or borrowed from other disciplines to help us understand these processes. Merriam (1964), Nettl (1983), and Stone (2008) are exceptions.

within the domains of scientific and music theory. Since the late 1970s, however, these forms of theory have been to a large extent supplanted by social theory, although to be sure, both scientific theory and music theory continue to have their advocates (see, e.g., Becker 2004, 2009, and Bakan 2009 for the former; Tenzer 2006 for the latter; and Arom 1985 for both).[10] In the earlier period, some of the most influential figures in the field believed that ethnomusicologists worked within a scientific frame and that ethnomusicology was a science, indeed a comparative science. Jaap Kunst (1959: 1) referred to ethnomusicology as "our science." Alan Merriam (1964: 25) wrote, "The ethnomusicologist is, in effect, sciencing about music." Bruno Nettl (1983: 11) defined ethnomusicology as "the science of music history." Mantle Hood (1971) created "hardness scales" that would allow ethnomusicologists to compare reliably and objectively music from around the world along many dimensions of musical sound. Around 1980, however, there was an "interpretive turn" in ethnomusicology away from science, a turn that responded to the attack by critical theory and continental philosophy on positivism in the social sciences. Today, we rarely write about hypotheses generated within a scientific theory; instead, we are concerned with the crisis of representation, multiple views of truth from different social and historical positions, interpretations of meaning, plumbing reflexively the depths of individual experience, and so on. This "paradigm shift," when it goes unnoticed, is probably one source of confusion about ethnomusicological theory.

McLean, one of Merriam's acolytes, wrote that "as a discipline, ethnomusicology is more concerned with science than with art. Appreciation of exotic forms of music, their intrinsic worth, and even a desire to promote them may play a small part, but it is not essential. . . . [Science] provides the necessary frame of mind for scholarship" (McLean 2006: 21). He criticizes the field of ethnomusicology for an unproductive shift "from the descriptive to the theoretical, from the 'what' and 'where' to the 'how' and 'why'" (p. 331). McLean fails to notice the paradigm shift from scientific to social theory, or, if he notices it, he decries it. Furthermore, he errs in his understanding of science. While description of the what and where is fundamental to science, it gains its power over human thought because of its well-tested theories about the how and why of the physical world. If ethnomusicology were truly based on science, as he claims, then we would all, with keen methodological precision, be observing, testing, and

---

10. I am grateful to Michael Tenzer for reminding me that Simha Arom's work is relevant here. In a personal communication, Tenzer wrote, "He has been adamant about using rigorous methodology to generate scientific, social, and music theory inductively. In this way he systematically rules out possibilities one by one to confirm conclusions that are explicitly validated by the music-makers."

experimenting within theories about the hows and whys of musical behavior and practices. If we ever did that, it would have been, with a few exceptions, in the past, not the present (see Becker 2009 and Bakan 2009 for the prospect of a "scientific (re)turn" in ethnomusicology). As we think about ethnomusicological theory, it is important to keep in mind this shift around 1980 from scientific theory and method toward hermeneutics and social theory, a shift marked by, indeed causing, a concomitant decline in publications devoted solely to the methods of music analysis, transcription, and fieldwork.

Stone's (2008) welcome review of "theory for ethnomusicology" is also not clear on the distinction between scientific and social theory. With a few exceptions, she focuses on ethnomusicologists' use of social theory, although she doesn't call it that. Although these theories are interpretive rather than scientific in their orientation and claims, she describes them using the rhetorical apparatus of scientific theories (methods, methodology, explanatory power) and claims they all display to varying degrees a "scientific attitude and approach" (p. 220). On the contrary, it is useful to distinguish scientific from social theory, because each leads to different demands and expectations in terms of methods and procedures, on the one hand, and fact or truth claims, on the other. Scientific theories make claims that can be tested and verified through experimentation and observation; after repeated confirmation in observational and experimental settings, scientists regard the theory as a "fact," at least until future observations undermine it. Social theories, on the other hand and as Stone points out, provide us with "orientations" and "assumptions" that guide particular studies and help us ask interesting "research questions." A social theory "illuminates" some matters while obscuring others. Rather than producing facts, it invites us to consider alternative interpretations. As the philosopher Paul Ricoeur (1981: 193) put it, "Between absolute knowledge and hermeneutics it is necessary to choose."[11]

## WHAT IS ETHNOMUSICOLOGICAL THEORY?

Ethnomusicological theory involves the writing of descriptions, classifications, comparisons, interpretations, and generalizations about music (and possibly sound) in general, about particular musical traditions, about music in a set of

---

11. This shorthand characterization of differences between scientific and social theory flies over many subtleties. One of the more interesting is the conflict in science between foundationism, associated with Karl Popper's injunction to attempt to falsify theories rather than to prove them through repeated observation, and naturalism, associated with Thomas Kuhn's view that "falsification applies to logic and not to empirical studies" and does not comport with the way

related communities, or about music in relation to cognitive, artistic, experiential, social, cultural, political, and economic issues, themes, and processes. Ethnomusicological theory may have its roots in scientific, social, or music theory, but it is not fundamentally about borrowing ideas from other disciplines, though it may entail doing so as a starting point. It may also have its roots in our own and our predecessors' field observations. In other words, it may arise entirely from within the field of ethnomusicology with little or no reference to social theory. No matter its roots, however, ethnomusicological theory is integral and indispensable to the field and not optional window dressing.[12]

One of the reasons we may not have a clear idea of the nature of ethnomusicological theory is that it too often remains hidden from view in our work. Part of the purpose of laying out the terrain of ethnomusicological theory in this chapter is to enable the writing of explicit ethnomusicological theories by all of us in all our work. Theory should not be an "an important mark of a distinguished ethnomusicologist" (Stone 2008: ix), but a taken-for-granted part of every ethnomusicologist's intellectual toolkit. Ethnomusicological theory in some form is always implicit in our particular research and is inescapable, but it contributes more effectively to the advancement of the field when made explicit. As Stone (2008: xii) puts it, "Theory underlies ethnomusicological inquiry and even implicit theories have a bearing on the analyses that result from our fieldwork.... Theory should ultimately make ideas transparent and strengthen the quality of the intellectual conversation."

Writing ethnomusicological theory involves, at its minimum and as Stone suggests, conversations among ethnomusicologists. Such theorizing, in essence, takes one of the following forms (explicitly or implicitly): (1) I have read your work, I find it relevant to my own, and this is how I'm going to apply it; (2) I have read your work, I find it limited in certain ways, and its insights could be expanded if

science is actually practiced (Proctor and Capaldi 2006). I am grateful to William I. Newman, UCLA professor of earth and space science, physics and astronomy, and mathematics, for our discussions of "fact" and "truth" in science and for referring me to this source, which contains a very useful review of the philosophy of science, especially as it applies to qualitative studies in psychology and, by extension perhaps, to musical-ethnographic studies.

12. The label "ethnomusicological theory" does not imply that "ethnomusicology" is, for all time, an adequate or appropriate name for our discipline. Some are seriously troubled by the label. A discussion that I hosted at the 2005 annual meeting of the Society for Ethnomusicology ended in a contradiction: some would like to change the name of our discipline, but not at this moment when the relatively recent widespread understanding and adoption of the term *ethnomusicology* in the academy in the United States has given us a brand identity and thus a practical advantage in the marketplace of ideas and academic jobs. Those readers unhappy with the locution "ethnomusicological theory" can get to the idea I am driving at by calling it "anthropology-of-music theory," "world-music theory," "cultural-musicology theory," or something similar.

some new ideas or observations that I provide were taken into consideration; or (3) I have read your work (and everybody else's who has written on this topic) and I think there is a significant gap in these studies that I propose to fill by taking a new approach. It is through conversations of this sort (i.e., theorizing in this manner) that we build the intellectual capacity of ethnomusicology to make powerful, provocative, memorable, and insightful statements about the particular musical traditions we study and about music in general. When we neglect to have these conversations, the intellectual richness of the field is compromised. Without explicit ethnomusicological theory developed in conversations among ourselves, the field is in danger of being little more than the sum of a succession of idiographic reports from here and there, a kind of academic journalism of fleeting interest, but of little or no long-term consequence.

## THE FIELD OF ETHNOMUSICOLOGICAL THEORY

What ethnomusicological theory has been for the last thirty years can perhaps best be understood by considering that it exists within a "field of ethnomusicological theory" (Figure 6.1).[13] Ethnomusicology today is, at its core, a discipline based on field research in one or more local environments, and so the center of the field of ethnomusicological theory is occupied by what I take to be the center of gravity of ethnomusicological research: local, idiographic, ethnographic (or historical), community-based, thematically focused studies.[14] It is from these local, particular studies that we have built and presumably will continue to build the discipline, and it is the relationship between these studies and ethnomusicological theory that is elucidated here. The right side of Figure 6.1 proposes that ethnomusicological theory exists in three conceptual locations: within local studies, beyond local studies, and beyond the bounds of our discipline, where it may contribute to more general social and scientific theories, to area studies, or to subjects such as media studies, gender

13. I use the "field" metaphor in its common sense of a field of study, a fertile ground for intellectual inquiry. Having laid it out in this way, it probably could be analyzed as a "field of cultural production" (Bourdieu 1993), that is, a social space with agents, rules, hierarchies, orthodox/heterodox opinions, and doxic practices. That would be fascinating, but I have not undertaken that project here.

14. Historical research has increasingly become important in our field, and yet, I would argue, its core principles have arisen from synchronic, ethnographic research. This core practice then seeps into the kind of history we write. That is, historical studies tend to be community based and thematically focused. Someday it may become more difficult to make this argument confidently, but one of the signs of the ascendance of historical study in ethnomusicology will be graduate curricula with courses on historical, as well as on fieldwork, methods.

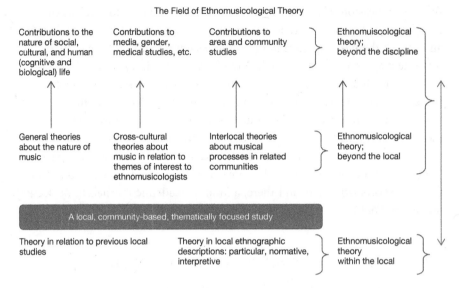

The Field of Ethnomusicological Theory

| Contributions to the nature of social, cultural, and human (cognitive and biological) life | Contributions to media, gender, medical studies, etc. | Contributions to area and community studies | Ethnomuiscological theory; beyond the discipline |

| General theories about the nature of music | Cross-cultural theories about music in relation to themes of interest to ethnomusicologists | Interlocal theories about musical processes in related communities | Ethnomusicological theory; beyond the local |

A local, community-based, thematically focused study

| Theory in relation to previous local studies | Theory in local ethnographic descriptions: particular, normative, interpretive | Ethnomusicological theory within the local |

**Figure 6.1** The field of ethnomusicological theory.

studies, education, cognition, medicine, and so forth.[15] The arrows indicate the movement that occurs within this theoretical field. Ethnomusicological theory within the local may, and in my view should, contribute to ethnomusicological theory beyond the local level and vice versa: ethnomusicological theory beyond the local will almost inevitably inform, either implicitly or explicitly, local studies and the theorizing we do in them.

Figure 6.1 of the field of ethnomusicological theory does not suggest an obvious narrative order; it certainly should not be "read" from top left to bottom right. The figure is meant to be taken in as a whole, though it is difficult to do so at first sight. Writing, however, requires the imposition of narrative order. The various locations in the field are taken up in this order, beginning with the conceptual center of the field—local, idiographic studies—and ending with general theories about the nature of human life:

1. Local, idiographic studies
2. General theories about the nature of music

15. Although I situate ethnomusicological theory within a general field of social, cultural, cognitive, and biological theory, music theory, in everything from terminology to detailed musical analyses and explanations, remains an important method in developing ethnomusicological theory. Music theory tries to explain how music is structured and, in the most engaging work for humanists and social scientists, to uncover the cognitive, psychological, biological, and creative processes that bring those structures into existence and allow them to be perceived and acted on.

3. Ethnomusicological theory within local ethnographic studies
4. Theory in relation to previous local studies
5. Interlocal theory about musical processes in related communities and their contribution to community and area studies
6. Cross-cultural theories about music in relation to the many themes of interest to ethnomusicologists and their contribution beyond the discipline to general studies of those themes
7. General theories about the nature of social, cultural, and human (cognitive and biological) life

## LOCAL, IDIOGRAPHIC STUDIES

Our local, idiographic studies can be understood to have, minimally, two dimensions: first, they are based in some form of society or community; second, they tackle one or more of the themes or issues around which research in ethnomusicology has historically crystallized.

Ethnomusicology, as a kind of social science, tends to focus on communities of people as the starting point for study; this contrasts with an emphasis in some other music disciplines on the individual, the musical work, the repertoire, or the genre as the starting point. For example, even when we focus on individuals, as many have done, we tend to examine them in relation to a community: Virginia Danielson's (1997) study of Umm Kulthūm in relation to nationalism in Egypt; Steven Loza's (1999) study of Tito Puente in relation to a musical genre popular in the Latino community; the autobiography of Navajo healer Frank Mitchell (1978), constructed in conversation with Charlotte Frisbie and David McAllester; and so forth.[16] Stone (2008: 20) lists communities alongside other "study objects," such as individuals, song, repertories, events, musical processes like improvisation, and musical genres, but I prefer to argue that ethnomusicologists tend to embed each of these study objects within an overarching concept of community or society.[17]

---

16. I may seem to be arguing against myself here. In Rice (2003), I tried to define the parameters of "subject-centered" musical ethnography. But the self or subject referred to in that paper is a thoroughly social self as it emerges from and reattaches itself to an emergent array of social units and communities.

17. In this chapter I argue at a number of points with Ruth Stone's account of "theory for ethnomusicology." I do so with the greatest respect, because hers is arguably the first serious, extended attempt in a quarter of a century to take on ethnomusicological theory in a systematic way. The most important previous discussions are by Alan Merriam (1964) and Bruno Nettl (1983). I do so in the spirit of the kind of friendly, but productive, disciplinary conversations we both advocate. Her arguments are, to echo Claude Lévi-Strauss, good to think with.

Four types of community are fundamental to the organization of our community-based studies: (1) communities defined geographically, such as nations, regions, cities, towns, and villages; (2) communities defined by ethnic, racial, religious, and kinship (family) groups; (3) communities formed around a shared style, affinity, taste, or practice such as punk rock, surfing, motorcycle racing, or Barbie Dolls (see Slobin 1993 for affinity groups and Caudron 2006); and (4) communities organized as, or within, institutions, such as musical ensembles, schools and conservatories, recording and broadcast companies, places of worship, the military, prisons, and clubs and bars. When ethnomusicological theory is written within local community studies, that theory can in turn contribute to broader, beyond-the-local theorizing about music in the same or similar communities.

The second dimension of local, idiographic studies is populated by the major themes around which ethnomusicologists organize their work, themes such as music and identity, the teaching and learning of music, the politics of music, gender and music, and many more. By my count ethnomusicologists currently deal with more than forty different themes.[18] Alan Merriam created the first comprehensive list of such themes (twelve of them) in his 1964 book, *The Anthropology of Music*. Most are to one degree or another still with us, including native concepts about music, the social behavior of musicians, the meaning of music, and music learning. In the 1970s, event analysis; urban and popular music; individual musicians; emotion, euphoria, and trance as responses to music; and a number of others emerged. In the 1980s, gender, the history of music, individual agency, identity, and media and technology came along. In the 1990s, politics and power, diaspora, and globalization made the list. In the first decade of this century, tourism; music in relation to war, violence, and conflict; and the use of music in relation to illness and the HIV/AIDS epidemic became prominent.

Stone (2008) points out that some scholars refer to these themes as theory and perhaps for that reason she includes consideration of a number of them in her survey of theory for ethnomusicology. She calls gender, ethnicity, and identity "theoretical orientations" and "issues," and acknowledges that they are "of a somewhat different order than other [social] theories we have previously considered" (p. 145). Indeed, they are of a different order; they are not theories at all. It is important to distinguish these themes from the social theory that is the principal focus of her book and that forms the general intellectual environment in which most ethnomusicologists work today. Each of these themes or problematics may have social theory associated with it (e.g., Stuart Hall 1996

---

18. The Society for Ethnomusicology website (http://webdb.iu.edu/sem/scripts/home.cfm) lists more than ninety "subjects and theoretical categories." The International Council for Traditional Music website (http://www.ictmusic.org/) lists ten study groups devoted to themes, six devoted to communities (areas of the world), and two that combine both.

on identity, Jean Piaget and Bärbel Inhelder 1969 on learning theory, and Arjun Appadurai 1996 on globalization), but identity, learning, and globalization are not theories. They are themes to which social theory can be applied and that generate discipline-specific ethnomusicological theories to illuminate the issues particular to each local study.

These two dimensions, community and themes, inform all our local studies. With this in mind, we can now examine how theory enters these studies. The first and most obvious way is through general theories that ethnomusicologists have created about the nature of music.

## GENERAL THEORIES ABOUT THE NATURE OF MUSIC

Ethnomusicology has made extraordinarily important contributions to under-standing the nature of music through the writing of ethnomusicological theory beyond the local. Its principal and most important intervention has been a sustained argument over more than a half century against the notion, purveyed in most Western scholarship, that music is only or primarily an art form made for its own sake, mystically transcendent in its effects, and with little or no "social or civic significance."[19] By employing social theory from other fields and con-necting it to what ethnomusicologists have learned about the nature of music as a human behavior and practice in hundreds, perhaps thousands, of partic-ular studies, we have created a far different and, I dare say, richer picture of the nature of music and its significance for human life than that created, until recently, by historical musicologists studying Western art music. Among other things, ethnomusicologists have taught us that it demeans music to regard it only, or perhaps even primarily, as an art.

One form of ethnomusicological theory consists of metaphors about the essential nature of music (Rice 2003). Against the metaphorical claim that music is an art, a theory buttressed by reference to certain streams in the Western philosophical tradition, ethnomusicologists have proposed many other com-peting metaphors to capture their understanding of the nature of music:

- Music is a form of entertainment, a theory that probably originates in Western common sense, but then has been transformed into a theory embedded within structural–functionalist social theory (Merriam 1964).

---

19. The phrase "social or civic significance" comes from F. E. Sparshott's delightful article on the aesthetics of music in the 1980 edition of the *New Grove Dictionary of Music and Musicians*. He continues laconically, "When an art claims autonomy, it may be a sign that it accepts a periph-eral place in the culture of its day" (Sparshott 1980: 123).

- Music is a system of signs capable of bearing meaning, from philosophical semiotics and linguistic semiology (Turino 1999; Nattiez 1990).
- Music is a social behavior and thus its structures may be homologous to or iconic of other social structures and behaviors, from Marx, Weber, and Lévi-Straussian structuralism among others (Lomax 1968; A. Seeger 1980).
- Music is a nonverbal practice that can, outside verbal discourse, create gendered individuals and other socially constructed subjectivities, from Bourdieu's practice theory (Sugarman 1997).
- Music is a text that can be read for meaning, from Ricoeur's phenomenological hermeneutics and Geertz's interpretive anthropology (Roseman 1991).

Making metaphors is not the only way ethnomusicologists write general theory about the nature of music. Sometimes ethnomusicological theory tells us what music does or how it came to be the way it appears to be. Here are some examples:

- Music's particular form and effects depend on its means of production, from Marxism (Manuel 1993).
- "Large-scale economic and political structures articulate with and broadly condition the localized microprocesses of musical performance" (Waterman 1990a: 3), a claim perhaps influenced by Marxist thought and by Immanuel Wallerstein's (2004) world-system theory.
- Music, when performed, creates community, from Durkheim, Bourdieu, Giddens, and others (Askew 2002).
- Musical structures reflect cultural and social structures, from Lévi-Straussian structuralism and others (Becker and Becker 1981).
- Musical performances construct and produce social structures and cultural values, from Durkheim, Bourdieu, and others (A. Seeger 1987).
- "Jazz (and ... music generally) ... [is] always already directed toward power relationships" (Wong 2004: 318–319), from Amiri Baraka, Harold Cruse, Cornel West, and others, and the musicians with whom the author worked.

Ethnomusicologists do not need to apologize, as they sometimes do, for borrowing social theory to help them make these general claims about the nature of music. By applying social theories in a careful way, grounded in detailed ethnographic and historical research, ethnomusicologists engage in discipline-specific ethnomusicological theory of potentially great importance. Certainly our colleagues in other disciplines are doing pretty much the same thing: borrowing social theories that may come from outside their original disciplinary home to help them ask new questions and see the objects of their studies in novel and fruitful ways.

Sometimes ethnomusicologists make claims about the nature of music that seem to be discipline specific and not obviously indebted to a particular social theory. An example is Benjamin Brinner's (1995) extensive theorization of musical competence in his book on Javanese gamelan musicians. In it, he makes the general claim that "excitement may be one of the more widespread goals of musical interaction" (p. 206). The interaction may be "positive or negative in nature, a goal to be achieved or failure to be averted" (p. 207). This is not the most important theoretical work he does in this book, but for those interested in interaction between and among musicians in particular cases, this might be an interesting general theory about the nature of music to be examined and applied to other particular cases. In any case, it is an example of ethnomusicological theory, which, to build our discipline, it would be a good idea to watch for.

Obviously there is no shortage of ethnomusicological theory about the general nature of music. The principal weaknesses in this part of the field of ethnomusicological theory may be the unasked and unanswered questions that arise from a consideration of these theories. For example, how do we understand our ethnomusicological theories about the nature of music? Are they taken as "facts" in the way, for example, biological scientists take the theory of evolution as a fact demonstrated by repeated observations over a century or more?[20] Are they theories that are still in need of demonstration through application to more local, particular contexts, or do we take them as assumptions no longer in need of demonstration? Do they need to be fleshed out and critiqued? What issues do they raise? Are they worth bothering with? Have they been superseded and are no longer relevant? We might answer these questions differently for each of the ethnomusicological theories mentioned previously. Ethnomusicological theory is weak not in the existence of theories of this type, which are legion, but in our critical examination of them. We have not engaged in rich enough conversations with these ethnomusicological theories, either from the perspective of our particular, local studies or by putting them in conversation with one

20. Evolutionary biologist Ernst Mayr (2001: 264) writes: "It is very questionable whether the term 'evolutionary theory' should be used any longer. That evolution occurred and takes place all the time is a fact so overwhelmingly established that it has become irrational to call it a theory. . . . Scientific arguments about [common descent, speciation, and natural selection] . . . do not in any way affect the basic conclusion that evolution as such is a fact."

another. More theoretical conversations about each of them and their implications for the discipline and for our local, particular studies would surely put
ethnomusicological theory about the general nature of music on more stable
ground and give us more confidence in the power and importance of our own
theorizing.

## ETHNOMUSICOLOGICAL THEORY WITHIN LOCAL ETHNOGRAPHIC STUDIES

Ethnomusicological theory about the nature of music is created at the intersection of our local musical studies with social theory and ethnomusicological
theory beyond the local. The issue, which remains ambiguous in Stone's (2008)
account, is whether we regard theory and ethnographic descriptions as distinct
from theory and "complementary" to it or whether we believe that theory ines-
capably suffuses description and that description without theory is impossible.
In my view, ethnomusicological theory, whether widely shared or idiosyncratic
to the investigator, inevitably guides and frames the production of what Stone
(2008: 225) calls "the rich ethnographic detail of ethnographic description." This
view is expressed in Figure 6.1 by placing ethnographic descriptions within the
field of ethnomusicological theory. I will illustrate the way ethnomusicological
theory suffuses ethnographic description with examples from my own work.[21]

Ethnomusicological description comes in three forms: particular, normative,
and interpretive.[22] Each of these descriptions engages explicitly or implicitly

---

21. The division between those who separate description from theory and those who prefer to
understand description as embedded in theory is well known in sociology. Robert Emerson
(1988: 96) writes: "Grounded theorists tend to view data and theory as distinct phenomena: theory . . . may suggest where to collect data and what kinds of data to collect, but [theory]
is not seen as inherent in the very notion of data in the first place. Field data, however, are never
theoretically 'pure,' but are always products of prior interpretive and conceptual decisions made
by the fieldworker." I am grateful to UCLA sociology professor Gail Kligman for referring me to
this source, which raises many issues of potential interest to ethnomusicologists.

22. An excellent example of the productive mix of particular, normative, and interpretive
description to create a richly theoretical local ethnography is Jane Sugarman's (1997) account
of singing at weddings among Albanians from the Lake Prespa region of the central Balkans.
Beginning each chapter with a particular description before passing on to normative descriptions of how men and women sing at these community social events, she is able, combining
her ethnographic observations with ideas from social theorists Pierre Bourdieu and Michel
Foucault, to arrive at an interpretation of how singing, and the community's evaluations of
particular performances, "penetrated to the bedrock of the community's social ideology. . . .
[Their singing] techniques contribute to the community's ongoing formulation of its notions
of society and morality" (pp. 21–22), including patriarchy, gender, personhood, male honor,

with ethnomusicological theory.[23] The theoretical nature of description can be hidden from view when not made explicit. Explicit use of theory, often in the form of self-reflection, opens up the possibility of theoretical conversations, which are at the core of how effective theorizing works.[24]

Particular musical descriptions are attempts to characterize the nature of a single item, for example, a musical performance, a musical work, a musical instrument, a musical event, and so on. For my doctoral dissertation I worked on what Bulgarian scholars called "two-voiced singing," a style that attracted me, I have to admit, for its strangeness compared to Western norms, especially of harmony (Rice 1977). Using Western music theory, the theoretical framework I brought with me into the field, I could describe one aspect of a particular song in this tradition like this: this song was performed in two parts; one woman sang the melody, and two women performed an accompanying part that alternated between the tonal center and a pitch one step below it, creating a rich texture of frequently sounding harmonic seconds.

The research problem I set myself was to try to understand (not to explain) how nonliterate or barely literate Bulgarian village singers thought about and understood their own tradition. To gain these understandings, I turned to a social theory, in this case, an approach in cultural anthropology called cognitive anthropology, which is concerned with how people in a culture perceive, organize, and think about the world and how they express that cognition and knowledge in language. This approach, widely used by ethnomusicologists in the late 1970s and early 1980s, gave us the emic–etic dichotomy, which is now a largely taken-for-granted part of the ethnomusicologist's theoretical toolkit (Zemp 1979; Rice 1980; Feld 1981; Koskoff 1982; Sakata 1983). Using interview techniques suggested by this theory of culture, I learned that singers had their own ways of describing these parts, and I could write a particular description based on "native" or "emic" theory. Interviews with singers

female modesty, reciprocity, hierarchy, and equality. This is ethnomusicological theorizing of a high order about musical and social processes in a particular culture with significant implications for those wishing to engage in a conversation about how music helps to construct social ideology in another culture or cross-culturally.

23. As Harris Berger and Juniper Hill reminded me in personal communications, in arguing for the theoretical underpinnings of particular, normative, and interpretive descriptions, I am eliding distinctions that some may still wish to draw between local-level "descriptions" and "interpretations," on the one hand, and "theory" about general or cross-cultural processes in human life, on the other. These two views are not contradictory and can be held together by those who wish to do so.

24. Stone (1982, 2008) provides excellent examples of laying out one's assumptions (theories) explicitly before beginning a local ethnographic study.

revealed that they do not appear to have a native concept of melody; one singer said that she was "crying out," not "singing a melody." The two other singers said they "followed" the woman who "cried out." This verb pointed both to their position behind the woman crying out and to how they followed her lead rhythmically. Using social theory, I was able to move beyond Western music theory into the musical culture of these singers, a culture that was, according to the tenets of the theory, in their minds and expressed in language.

Normative descriptions apply not to single items but to a collection of items: how musical performances characteristically are organized, how a musical instrument is typically made, the musical style of a collection of pieces or performances, and so on. Bulgarian scholars (e.g., Kaufman 1968) had created a normative label for an important tradition of singing in southwest Bulgaria: "two-voiced singing" (*dvuglasno peene*). The notion that this label represented anything other than a relatively straightforward, accurate, normative description never occurred to me until I ran into an exception during my fieldwork (Rice 1988, 2004). In one village the singer who cried out ascended one step, while the singers who followed descended one step, creating the interval of a third, a type of "voice leading" not normative for this style. Even worse, while my transcription of the two voices showed a third, I was hearing a second. I was deeply confused. Eventually, some singers in a nearby village told me that they didn't just sing in two voices, as the normative description of the style suggested. They sang in three voices: one singer "cries out" (*izvikva*); one of them "follows straight" (*pravo buchi*, literally, "roars"), that is, sings a single pitch on the tonal center; and the other one "follows crookedly" (*krivo buchi*), moving between the tonal center and the note below (Figure 6.2). The singing from these two villages contradicted the normative description of two-voiced singing and taught me that normative descriptions always are theories about the regularities of a collection of musical works or practices. Most of the time repeated observation allows us to take normative description for granted as "facts," but their facticity becomes complicated and problematic when observation proves them to be false or incomplete in some way.

My findings provided an opportunity to enter into a theoretical conversation with Bulgarian scholars who had studied this tradition. When I showed them this example, they used their theory of the style to describe it as a haphazard, insignificant variation from its norms; this particular instance was not enough to dislodge their musical theory of the style. The singers' own words, which I took to be an expression of their musical culture, contradicted Bulgarian scholars' explanation and theory: this performance clearly was not a haphazard, accidental variation on a norm, but a fully conscious, well-understood practice,

**Figure 6.2** Bulgarian three-voiced song.

expressed in language. This is an example of how a social theory, namely, that culture involves the cognitive, mental organization of phenomena expressed in language, can help in the creation of a new ethnomusicological theory of the musical culture that structures a musical practice.[25]

Interpretive musical descriptions, which Clifford Geertz (1973) called "thick descriptions," involve the reading of musical practices for their social and cultural meaning, and more recently for the sorts of power relationships they express or challenge. The language-elicitation techniques of cognitive

25. As Juniper Hill reminded me, Lila Abu-Lughod's (1991) article "Writing against Culture" speaks forcefully of how certain generalizing practices associated with the culture concept exercise power over others. Abu-Lughod advocates writing "ethnographies of the particular" and argues that "generalization, the characteristic mode of operation and writing of the social sciences, can no longer be regarded as neutral" (pp. 149–150). She is not, however, speaking against all forms of beyond-the-local theorizing, just in favor of better forms of writing to convey it, specifically writing devoted to the particulars of people's "everyday lives" and actions (p. 155). It is a subtle argument with many twists and turns between particularity and generality, and well worth reading in counterpoint to the writing of ethnomusicological theory.

anthropology allowed me some insights into the meanings of musical practices. I discovered that Bulgarian villagers did not seem to have a cover term for what I called "music," an indication among other things that taking for granted a term can conceal a whole world of ethnomusicological theory (see, e.g., Nzewi 1997 on "rhythm" and the symbolic violence it may do to African musical concepts). Instead, they split up what I had taken to be their musical practices into many domains: song/sings/singer (*pesen/pee/pevitsa*); play-thing (tune)/plays/player (*svirnya/sviri/svirach*); drum/drums/drummer (*tŭpan/tupa/tŭpandzhia*); and so forth. Viewing their musical practices from the inside or in their terms allowed me to understand for the first time the social meanings embedded in their practices: singing and song were the domain primarily of women, men were the players of musical instruments with few exceptions, and drummers came principally from the Rom minority. I began to interpret or read these practices as gendered and as marking ethnic boundaries, that is, as having social and cultural meaning (Rice 1980).[26]

A particular social theory like cognitive anthropology helped me to understand Bulgarian music in new and productive ways, but each social theory has its limitations. It provides one perspective among many that could be applied helpfully to the description of a musical culture. I ran into the limitations of cognitive anthropology when I tried to learn to play the Bulgarian bagpipe (Rice 1994). Using Western music theory, I could describe rather easily the scalar, melodic, rhythmic, and metrical structures of the dance music played on the instrument. But two aspects of the style eluded me. One was the rhythm of nonmetrical "slow songs" (*bavni pesni*). To this day I have never written a particular or normative description of the rhythm of these songs, nor am I confident that my transcriptions of particular slow songs have any explanatory power whatsoever; they certainly do not capture an insider, emic, culturally informed view of this practice. My evasion of such a description illustrates how description is driven by theory, or, more to the point in this case, how description is avoided because of the lack of a theory or framework to guide it.

The other problematic aspect of the style was the dense ornamentation on the instrument. In this case, deploying the techniques of cognitive anthropology was unhelpful. My principal teacher lacked a vocabulary to describe many of the structural features of his performances, including the ornamentation. The problem for

---

26. Questions like this one about the nature and boundaries of the music concept have been with us at least since Merriam (1964). But clearly whether we ask this question, and how we answer it, can guide the structure of our research and the questions we ask. In that way they constitute an ethnomusicological theory. Attempts to broaden our field of inquiry to "sound" illustrate the theoretical burden of our concepts of music and the boundaries we impose between it and other sounds in our environment (see, e.g., Feld 1982, 2009, and Erlmann 2004).

me was that I didn't just want to understand his cognition; I wanted to be able to play the ornamentation as he did. Eventually I learned to do so and in the process gained new understandings of the tradition that I could express in words but that he could not. At that moment I realized that cognitive anthropology was a relatively blunt instrument for understanding musical culture. Cognitive anthropology depends on language to study cognition, whereas much of music cognition within culture is language-free (see C. Seeger 1977 for the "linguocentric predicament" and the "musicological juncture"). So whereas much ethnomusicological writing at the time emphasized the difference between etic or outsider analyses and emic or insider understandings, I was forced from musical experience to theorize a new ethnomusicological space between those poles, a space neither completely inside nor completely outside, but a space in which, through self-reflection, I could claim to think about Bulgarian music in a way that yielded adequate performances within the style (Rice 1995).

This theory of a space between emic and etic represents an ethnomusicological challenge, or at least an alternative, to a basic tenet of cognitive anthropology: important aspects of musical culture are not expressed in words by natives, but are knowable and can be expressed accurately in words and performed by outsiders who move within natives' cultural horizons. If culture is to be understood as cognitive knowledge of the phenomena in a world, then it appears that music culture may be fundamentally different from at least some other aspects of culture, such as the residence rules about where a couple goes to live after they get married. To my knowledge, my theoretical intervention, which I expressed many years ago and which might be part of an ethnomusicological theory of the nature of music culture, has never been taken up by other scholars and become part of an ethnomusicological conversation.[27] I don't feel myself alone in this. It seems to me that too much ethnomusicological theory goes unrecognized, undiscussed, and unanswered. We have not yet built a strong tradition of theoretical conversations about our ideas of what music is, what it does, and how it comes into being.

Learning to play dance melodies on the bagpipe opened up a conversation with my teachers that I could not previously participate in and that created the possibility for further interpretive descriptions. Once I had acquired what my teacher called "bagpiper's fingers," we could converse in finger motions: moving his hands in the air or on the instrument, he could now say to me, "do it this way" or "don't do it that way," and, watching his fingers with the practice-based

---

27. Meki Nzewi (1997) discovered this space between emic and etic coming from the opposite direction I did, moving from the inside to the outside of the African music tradition. He even gave the space a name, "emetic," with apparently no pun intended. I am grateful to Jacqueline Cogdell DjeDje for suggesting this source.

knowledge of my own bagpiper's fingers, I could understand what he meant. We were working in what Pierre Bourdieu (1977) calls the domain of practice.

It turned out that these tiny ornaments, which were now the object of detailed consideration in our lessons, were the bearer of social and cultural meaning. My principal teacher was a middle-aged former villager, but when I studied with him he was a very prominent, urban professional musician (Rice 1994). His manner of ornamentation featured frequent use of complex mordents (moving from the melody note up one tone and back again). When his nephew, a prominent bagpiper of the next generation, taught me to play a few tunes, his ornamentation featured many more inverted mordents (moving from the melody note down one tone and back) than did his uncle's. When I played what I had learned from the nephew for the uncle, the latter demanded that I play these tunes with mordents, claiming that playing inverted mordents in certain parts of the melody was aesthetically "empty." Playing inverted mordents was clearly incapable of, as some Bulgarians put it, "filling his soul," perhaps because it was no longer an index of his past life in his native village. On the other hand, his nephew told me that playing inverted mordents was more complex (even though the same number or even fewer notes were actually played) and indicative of a more modern, progressive, and pan-Bulgarian (rather than regional) approach to playing the bagpipe in tune, as it were, with modern times.

This local ethnographic example illustrates the general ethnomusicological theory, borrowed from interpretive anthropology, that musical practices and gestures can bear, and be read for, their social and cultural meaning. Does it have any implications for that theory? For example, are there any limitations on what aspects of musical style or practice can bear meaning? I think it is fascinating to realize that meaning in this case is borne in some of the smallest details of musical style, in contrast to those who have shown such a connection at grosser levels of performance practice, for example, Alan Lomax's cantometrics (1968) and Daniel Neuman's (1980) demonstration of the relationship between social status and the amount of solo performance time in a concert of North Indian classical music. We will learn more about this in the next local study I consider.

## THEORY IN RELATION TO PREVIOUS LOCAL STUDIES

Central Javanese gamelan music is practiced by a community in a region on the island of Java within the nation of Indonesia. This type of music has presented analysts with fascinating problems when it comes to trying to pin down very precisely the nature of modality, called *pathet* in this tradition. R. Anderson Sutton (1998: 637) outlines the history of these theoretical conversations, beginning with Jaap Kunst's *De toonkunst van Java* (Music in Java) (1934) and continuing with

Mantle Hood's 1954 study of "the nuclear theme [played on the single-octave metallophone *saron*] as a determinant of *pathet*." Judith Becker (1972) expands the analysis to include a multioctave treatment of the *pathet* concept. Vincent McDermott and Sumarsam (1975) look at the quasi-improvisatory "elaborating parts" played on the metallophone called *gendèr* for their role in defining *pathet*. Susan Walton (1987) adds vocal music into the mix. Despite the fact that this theoretical thread is generated more by music theory than by social theory, I still find it significant as ethnomusicological theory for a number of reasons. First of all, it is theoretical. That is, the work in this thread is trying to figure out the "what" of *pathet*, which is apparently a complex, not a simple, matter. What is it? How is it defined? How are particular *pathets* brought to performative life? How can we recognize a particular *pathet* when we hear it? These are discipline-specific theoretical questions at what Ruth Stone (2008) calls the jeweler's eye view; they go beyond particular description to posit a normative idea about an important concept in Javanese music. Answering these questions surely gets at some important things about the culture of Javanese gamelan music. Second, they build on each other. One of the most important features of ethnomusicological theory is that new work responds to previous work to create a more sophisticated, fine-grained understanding of musical practice, whether local or broadly comparative. For those interested in Javanese music, I can only imagine that they find this sort of theoretical conversation exciting and engaging and, as a consequence, are perhaps challenged to take the next step in theorizing *pathet*.

In 1998, Marc Perlman did just that in an article on "the social meaning of modal practice" in this music. He contributes to the conversation about *pathet* by adding some social theory into the music theory mix. Citing studies of music in many other parts of the world, he begins with the general ethnomusicological theory that "musical elements and practices are remarkably versatile carriers of social meaning" (Perlman 1998: 45). The *gendèr* player must balance between a performance governed by the idea of the particular *pathet* and one governed by melodic considerations. If the performance "privileges" *pathet*, then Perlman reads it as signifying a mainstream, central, courtly, and male style. If the performance privileges a closer adherence to the melody, then it signifies two marginal positions in society: "the peripheral (geographically marginal) and the female" (p. 46).

As ethnomusicological theory, this article does three important things. First, it builds on and expands the theory of *pathet* developed in previous studies— the progress of the discipline of ethnomusicology depends on new studies extending and challenging older studies.[28] Second, it adds another theory, the

28. In a personal communication, Judith Becker pointed out that Sarah Weiss has taken the argument even further in her book *Listening to an Earlier Java* (2006).

general ethnomusicological theory that music is a sign system capable of carrying meaning, to flesh out and extend our understanding of *pathet*. It claims that *pathet* is not only a device for structuring music but also a signifier of the players' social position. Third, Perlman's theorizing in this case moves the study of *pathet* from the jeweler's eye view, that is, a parochial study of a feature of Javanese music, to a position beyond the local. He contributes to and provides an ethnographic example of a general ethnomusicological theory, the theory that music can bear social meaning even in the fine details of musical performance. Perlman (1998) concludes with the theoretical claim that "the more detailed our technical analyses, the more opportunities we will have to show how sounds and context are subtly intertwined" (p. 68). This claim or theory has broad implications for the entire field of ethnomusicology by transcending its source in a particular local community study and contributing beyond the local to the general ethnomusicological theory that he employed in the first place.

## INTERLOCAL THEORY ABOUT MUSICAL PROCESSES IN RELATED COMMUNITIES

Returning to ethnomusicological theory beyond local musical ethnographies, comparing musical processes in related communities should yield ethnomusicological theory about, for example, the cultural work different musical genres do: within a geographically bounded culture; in a particular ethnic, racial, religious, or kinship group; in nations within a particular area of the world; or in a set of historically or socially related institutions, such as prisons in the United States.[29] Such interlocal ethnomusicological theorizing has the potential to inform future local musical studies of the region, group, genre, or institution. Probably the best stimulant for such ethnomusicological theory is shared musical, historical, and social experience within and among these communities: for example, African American history and experience and the "origins" or "Africanisms" debate about the African roots of various genres of music performed by African Americans (Maultsby and Burnim 2001); punk rock around

29. To fit clearly in the category of community-based studies in the field of ethnomusicological theory, institutions probably need to be directly comparable on the basis of imputed shared experience, for example, music in US schools and conservatories of music (compare, e.g., Kingsbury 1988 and Nettl 1995). When an interlocal study of musical institutions expands to include, say, conservatories in Finland (Hill 2005), Uzbekistan (Merchant Henson 2006), and Kazakhstan (Rancier 2009), then such comparisons may take on more of the character of a theme-based study.

the world; *maqam* as a structural principle in the Middle East and its exten-sions; and problems of musical notation in East Asia.

The music performed in Bulgaria today clearly shares a history with that of many other nations and could be understood and theorized from many beyond-the-local perspectives: in relation to music of other nations in the Balkans, in the former Soviet "bloc," in Europe, or in the former Ottoman Empire; the music of its Rom minority in relation to Rom minority music in many other countries, as an example of transnational music making, or as minority music within a nation-state; and many others. The shared experience of communism in central, eastern, and southeastern Europe and its fall between 1989 and 1991 has generated a plethora of local studies of music's role in and response to the transition from totalitarianism to democracy and from a command to a market economy and in ameliorating or exacerbating tensions around the EU-nification of Europe. Along the way some useful interlocal ethnomusicological theorizing has emerged about this region of the world. Edited volumes, in this case by Mark Slobin (1996) and Donna Buchanan (2007a), seem to be ideal media for initiating such community-based interlocal conversations.

In the introduction to his edited collection *Retuning Culture: Musical Changes in Central and Eastern Europe*, Slobin (1996) makes a number of trenchant theoretical suggestions. He points out that, after the revolutions of 1989–1991, music played a vital role in new forms of public ritual (song contests, parades, stadium rallies) that contributed to the formation of new communities and political alliances (p. 7). He claims that "music is layered into consciousness in three strata: current, recent, and long-term—all of which occur simultaneously in the present" (p. 11). Individuals calling on different memories, different parts of their memory, or their "collective memory" give to music competing inter-pretations, some of which are able "to sustain nonnational forms of identity," even as communist and some postcommunist governments tried, and continue to try, to erase them (p. 8). He argues that the local studies in his volume can be understood from three perspectives, or in relation to what I would call themes (modernity, identity, and continuity), and he makes a few comparisons in each of them. Finally, writing about communist regimes' desire to control and order virtually every aspect of life, from practical action to ideation, he writes that "it is impossible to cleanse the spontaneous from music. Music's social and cultural role is always that of shape-shifter" (Slobin 2008: 4), even under the pressure of totalitarianism. Each of these suggestions has a slightly different theoretical burden, but they are good examples of ethnomusicological theory that could inspire further beyond-the-local theorizing along these lines and that could inform the questions asked in future local ethnographic studies.

In the preface to her edited collection *Balkan Popular Culture and the Ottoman Ecumene: Music, Image, and Regional Political Discourse*, Buchanan

(2007b) reports that the project was inspired by the comments of a scholar of Slavic literature and culture who wrote that "he did not discern 'a deep Balkan cultural identity shared by the cultures of these highly disparate nations'" (p. xviii, quoting Wachtel 1998: 7). Buchanan, on the contrary, wondered how this claim comported with the "remarkable, intraregional confluences of style in the instrumental music, song, and dance of local ethnopop artists" (p. xviii), similarities that might augur a "Balkan cosmopolitanism." The articles in the volume take up this point, including two of her own contributions. One is about a nineteenth-century Turkish popular song, "Üsküdara gider iden" (On the Way to Üsküdar), which is also found in the "national" repertoire of many nations and ethnic groups that emerged from the Ottoman Empire (Buchanan 2007c). The other is about contemporary Bulgarian ethnopop music (*chalga*), which, because of its shared features with similar forms in the region (*muzică orientală* in Romania, *turbofolk* in Serbia, "commercial folk music" in Albania), may be an "illustration of an emergent Balkan cosmopolitanism" (Buchanan 2007d: 260).

What her articles and the others reveal, however, is that, while all these genres are compiled, often by Romani musicians, from a mix of ostensibly Ottoman, local-traditional, and modern-Western musical elements and are perhaps cosmopolitan in that sense, the meanings associated with each genre are rather different: for example, ethnonationalism in Serbia, but a potential embrace of multiculturalism in Bulgaria. Jane Sugarman (2007), in a section of her article in the collection called "A Common 'Balkan' Music?," claims that ethnopop music performed by Albanians in Kosovo and Macedonia may not participate in the creation of an emergent Balkan identity, but rather it works out local issues of identity (p. 300). Pointing out that Muslim groups in the Balkans (Roma, Albanians, Bosnians, Pomaks, Torbesi, Turks) may have a different attitude to the Ottoman legacy sounded in these songs than do Christian groups (Slobin's notions of memory strata and collective memory might be useful here), she writes:

What these performances often share is a continuity of practice that dates back to an era when a Muslim identity overrode a national one. For most of these groups, the period since 1990 has involved a protracted effort, often a bloody one, to gain legitimacy or even an acknowledgement of one's existence. I thus see their similar musical performances as assertions of cultural distinctiveness addressed in large part to neighbors who simultaneously stigmatize them and appropriate their identities. (Sugarman 2007: 302–303)

Productive ethnomusicological theory about musical processes in interlocal community-based studies can only occur when someone, in this case Buchanan, makes a theoretical proposal and someone else, in this case Sugarman, takes it seriously and engages in conversation with it. This exchange certainly doesn't settle the matter; rather, it suggests its complexity and the value of further ethnomusicological theorizing along these lines.

Both Slobin and Buchanan, in these edited collections and in their introductions to them, are creating ethnomusicological theory that has implications beyond our discipline, in this case in area studies. Slobin's notion that music is in some ways uncontrollable, even by totalitarian states, suggests that music may contribute something unique to the social, cultural, and political processes that have animated this part of the world for many years. Studying musical practice, Buchanan suggests, might give ethnomusicologists a special, perhaps even privileged, window through which to understand what may be a move in this new era from Balkanization to "a potential Balkan cosmopolitanism" (Buchanan 2007b: xx). If European-area-studies specialists ignore these ethnomusicological theories, their analyses are surely the weaker for it.[30] But on the other hand, to be influential, the implications of such ethnomusicological theories need to be refined and supported by yet more subtle interlocal, intradisciplinary conversations.

## CROSS-CULTURAL THEORIES ABOUT THEMES AND ISSUES

Since we all organize our local studies around one or more of the many themes that have interested ethnomusicologists since its inception, such themes ought to be especially fruitful for the writing of ethnomusicological theory beyond the local or at what Stone (2008) calls the bird's-eye or satellite view. We often organize conference sessions around themes, and the ICTM sponsors many theme-based study groups, as if we believed that cross-cultural theoretical conversations, rather than simply the sharing of stories, were possible, desirable, and important. Perhaps the most ubiquitous theme in our field today concerns the relationship between music and identity (Rice 2007). Authors of journal articles and book chapters on this theme provide a number of potentially

---

30. Turning a blind eye (or deaf ear) to music may be endemic to area and community studies. Edwin Seroussi (2009) offers such a critique of Jewish studies in his ironically titled essay "Music: The 'Jew' of Jewish Studies." Seroussi acts strategically by, like Daniel, taking the argument into the lion's den, publishing his critique in a journal of Jewish studies. Tellingly, he begins by summarizing for nonexperts some of ethnomusicology's principal insights about music's central and special role in human life and ipso facto its relevance for Jewish life and Jewish studies. This is a strategy more of us should employ if we hope to contribute to theory beyond our discipline.

fruitful examples of ethnomusicological theory, each illustrating a different source of theory.[31] Here are three examples.

Christopher Waterman's (1990a) "social history and ethnography" of Yoruba popular music contains an idea that might be fruitful for an ethnomusicological theory of how music and social identity are related. He points out that the identity label "Yoruba" was invented in Nigeria sometime in the early twentieth century, and Yoruba identity is continually being constructed in the language-based discourses of politics, journalism, and education. Music's contribution to Yoruba identity formation seems to be different from those couched in linguistic terms. Waterman (1990b: 376) argues that "an effective performance of jùjú . . . predicates not only the structure of the ideal society, but also its interactive ethos or 'feel': intensive, vibrant, buzzing, and fluid." This idea seems to be based on the anthropological idea that culture "allow[s] people to see, feel, imagine [and] understand" things in particular ways (Ortner 2006: 14). His application of that idea to his particular study is an example of ethnomusicological theory within the local. But this theory might be applicable to many other cases. Ethnomusicology could extend its theoretical reach if authors made explicit the potential ramifications beyond the local of their ethnographic studies and if readers recognized such implications, whether implicit or explicit, and took them seriously.

Martin Stokes (1994) borrows from the work of social anthropologist Fredrik Barth (1969) to make a general argument for music's role in ethnic, class, and gender identity formation, not as a representative or constituent part of an "essence," but through "the construction, maintenance and negotiation of boundaries" (p. 6). Barth's social theory has been broadly influential in a number of disciplines concerned with questions of social identity, and Stokes uses it to create an ethnomusicological theory of music's role in the formation of social identity. Making Barth's theory particular to music and quoting Simon Frith (1987: 149), Stokes (1994) suggests that music might play a role different from other cultural practices in boundary formation: "What music (pop) can do is put into play a sense of identity that may or may not fit the way we are placed by other social facts" (p. 24). Music, Stokes points out, can also be an especially effective, if highly coded, "means by which people recognise identities and places, and the boundaries which separate them" (p. 5), and a playing field on which the powerful and powerless struggle for control of how and where

---

31. In addition to journal articles and book chapters, the last decade has seen a remarkable efflorescence of beyond-the-local, theme-based, single-authored books and collections of essays. Here, for example, are ten from the last ten years: Judith Becker (2004), Berger (2009), Greene and Porcello (2005), Lysloff and Gay (2003), Moisala and Diamond (2000), Qureshi (2002), Ritter and Daughtry (2007), Slobin (2008), Turino (2008), and Weintraub and Yung (2009). These books can undoubtedly be mined for both ethnomusicological theories and conversations about them, but I leave that as an exercise for the reader.

the boundaries are marked and defined. Such a beyond-the-local ethnomusico-logical theory has great potential to guide the design of our local, ethnographic studies and to illuminate the particular, normative, and interpretive descriptions we eventually write.

Folklorist Giovanna Del Negro and ethnomusicologist Harris Berger (2004: 156), drawing on communications theory, the ethnography of performance, and the folklorist Richard Bauman's (1989) notion of the performance of self, suggest that musical performances in some contexts can be used not to connect the self to a larger social entity with an ethnic, national, gender, or class identity, but to construct the self as an aesthetic object, an object of enjoyment for an audience watching a performance of self. Musicians and singers, they argue, in certain contexts may be "artists of identity," in addition to whatever artistic skills they possess. This is an ethnomusicological theory about music and identity pregnant with possibilities for local musical ethnographies, for thinking comparatively about music's role in constructing the self as a subject, and for the understanding of other selves in our world.

All these ethnomusicological theories (that music is an important practice for negotiating boundaries between ethnic groups, that music provides an ethnic identity with its feel, that musical performance is a way to construct an aestheticized self-identity) are potentially important contributions to the discipline. However, their brief and cursory citation will leave ethnomusicology still undertheorized unless we engage in conversation with them and put them into conversation with each other. We have, in other words, plenty of ethnomusicological theorizing about music's contribution to individual and social identity, but we need noisier and more frequent theoretical conversations that flesh them out, critique them, and move them toward more sophisticated, fine-grained explanations and understandings of music's importance in human life. If repeated observation under different circumstances and convincing, subtle argumentation support these theories, then they may become part of theories of identity beyond our discipline.[32]

## GENERAL THEORIES ABOUT THE NATURE OF HUMAN LIFE

The best chance for ethnomusicology to contribute to theories of the nature of human cultural, social, and biological life lies in our ethnomusicological

---

32. In a conversation in 2010 with a professor from the Department of Women's Studies at UCLA, she professed herself completely puzzled by the idea that music (or sound for that matter) might be relevant to gender or feminist theory.

theories of the general nature of music and in the theories we develop through consideration of the many themes that interest us. Although we may worry that we have not made such contributions, I think that some of our theorizing has that potential. Here are two examples.

In Anthony Seeger's (1987) study of the Suyá Indians of the Amazon basin, he makes explicit his intent to contribute to social theory in the very first sentence of the preface: "This is a book about singing in a native South American community . . . and the role of music in social processes" (p. xiii). He argues that musical performance is not a reflection or result of the material and physical world in which the Suyá live. Rather, "each performance re-creates, re-establishes, or alters the significance of . . . the persons, times, places, and audiences involved" (p. 65). Two instances illustrate this point. The Suyá year is divided into rainy and dry seasons, but he argues that these seasons are established not by changes in the weather, but by changes in the ceremonies performed and the songs that are sung. "Seasonal songs did not simply follow the vagaries of rainfall and drought, but rather established the changing season. When the new season's song had begun, it really was that season—whether or not the rains suddenly stopped or began to fall once again" (p. 70). Singing had a similar effect on the age-grade status of individuals. Age-grade changes were not the inevitable result of the ticking of one's biological clock, but were sung into being.

> Each time a person sang he or she reaffirmed (or established for the first time) a certain age status. A young boy might learn a long shout song for the first time. An adult man might begin not to force his voice as high as before. An older man might begin to clown before he had more than a single grandchild, or an old woman might retain the sober demeanor characteristic of a younger woman. Every ceremony was the opportunity to reaffirm not only what one was (a male and a member of certain groups) but what one believed one was or wanted to be. (A. Seeger 1987: 78)

This ethnomusicological theory of what music does in human societies has important implications for our local studies. Just as important, it challenges social scientists to rethink their understanding of how societies understand themselves and of music's contribution to that understanding. Social scientists ignore our insights into the role of music in human life at their peril, but whether they do so or not is their problem, not ours.[33] Our job remains,

---

33. Martin Stokes (1994: 1) comments on this problem in a somewhat ironic tone, writing, "In accordance with the highly pervasive fiction of an earlier musicology, music is still . . . considered [by anthropologists] a domain of a special, almost extra-social, autonomous experience. What ethnomusicologists deal with in the societies they study is—anthropologists are

however, to make our ethnomusicological theory as convincing and as strongly argued as possible.

Thomas Turino (1999) takes up, implicitly, the possibility raised by Waterman that the significance of music for identity has to do with the feelings it generates and expresses. He does so by considering a social theory rather than by writing a local ethnography. Working with the semiotic theory of the American philosopher Charles S. Peirce, he argues that music is such a powerful sign of identity because it is a sign of "direct feeling and experience," unmediated by language (p. 250). "Music involves signs of feeling and experience rather than the types of mediational signs that are about something else," for example, language signs (p. 224). Peirce's work represents the sort of social theory (in the broad sense in which I am using that term) that has transcended its disciplinary roots in philosophy to influence thinkers in a number of fields, including the social sciences. Turino has used it to create an ethnomusicological theory. His argument may be understood as in conversation with the claim that musical practice can be considered a text (symbol) with meaning. Turino, following Peirce, seems to be arguing that, while music may be read for meaning as language can be, it is after all a different kind of sign system from language signs. Music does something else for humankind besides create meaning, something just as or even more important:

> When people shift to symbolic thinking and discourse [as in language] to communicate about deep feelings and experiences, the feeling and reality of those experiences disappear and we are *not* satisfied. This is because we have moved to a more highly mediated, generalized mode of discourse, away from signs of direct feeling and experience. Symbols . . . fall short in the realm of feeling and experience. That is why we need music. (Turino 1999: 250, emphasis in original)

This argument about what music may contribute to human existence is an example of ethnomusicological theory with important implications for our understanding of human being in the world. Whether it should be treated as a fact, an assumption, or a claim in need of further demonstration in local studies might be the locus of an important intradisciplinary conversation about the nature of music.

Turino returns us to what may be a set of root questions that ethnomusicology should be capable of addressing based on our broad-ranging ethnographic and historical studies. What does music do for humankind? Is music unique in

residually inclined to assume—either the diversionary or the arcane. By definition they cannot be dealing with the kinds of events and processes that make up the predominantly verbal and visual 'real life' of which social reality is assumed to consist."

this regard, or, if not unique, how is it positioned in relation to other human behaviors? Suzel Reily (personal communication) wondered whether questions like these might constitute a "common project," if one were still desirable in our postmodern age. Acknowledging her debt to her teacher John Blacking, she wrote, "Ultimately, I think our goal still is to determine how musical humans are: how did humans become musical beings, why are they musical beings, and how do they use this capacity in the world?" Our collective engagement with these questions, including a conversation with Turino's ideas along this line, might help ethnomusicological theory escape from its disciplinary frame to make a significant contribution to the social and life sciences.

## CONCLUSION

It is my hope that this explication of the field of ethnomusicological theory will aid in the emergence of a richer intellectual landscape in our field, especially if we keep in mind the following points.

First, the field of ethnomusicological theory covers every aspect of the research enterprise from our local ethnographic descriptions to our general claims about the nature of music. Ethnomusicological theory is inescapable.

Second, ethnomusicological theory everywhere in this field can be understood as conversations among ethnomusicologists about a question that arises from particular community-based studies; from our interest in a common theme, such as music and identity; or from our interest in general questions about the nature of music and the many roles it plays in human life. We have generated a significant number of ethnomusicological theories over the years, but when we neglect to have conversations with each other about them, our theoretical claims remain thin and insufficiently subtle, textured, and grounded in observation, and the intellectual richness of our field is compromised.

Third, if ethnomusicological theory pervades our field from local, particular descriptions to ambitious claims about the nature of music and its importance in social and cultural life, and if ethnomusicological theory is about conversations between and among ourselves that serve to advance our theoretical claims, then ethnomusicologists must ask themselves this question: In this particular study, with whom do I want to engage in a theoretical conversation?

- Do I want to have it with myself by examining critically the assumptions (ethnomusicological theories) I bring with me to my research project?
- Do I want to have it principally with those in the community I am studying and writing about?

- Do I want to have it with those who have previously studied the community I am studying?
- Do I want to have it with those interested in the same themes and issues that I am interested in?
- Do I want to have it with those who have made general claims about the nature of music?
- Do I want to have it with nonethnomusicologists who study communities similar to the one I am studying?
- Do I want to have it with scholars outside the discipline who work on themes that interest me?
- Do I want to have it with other humanists and social and life scientists concerned with the nature of human social, cultural, and biological life?

We cannot demand that we all answer these questions in the same way, but we can demand that we all ask and answer them for each of our local studies. Doing so explicitly will ensure the intellectual growth of our discipline.

Fourth, ethnomusicological theory sometimes depends on insights borrowed from social theory, but often it is generated from within our field, in the context of our particular, local studies. It is important to recognize, acknowledge, and take seriously the theory we have written even as some champion the insights about music gained from the social theories we read.

Fifth, ethnomusicological theory is easier to find, criticize, and develop when (1) authors make it explicit in their work; (2) they tell us how their idiographic study fits into the literature on similar communities; (3) they tell us how the themes that are central to their study have been treated in the past by other authors writing on those themes in other communities; or (4) they propose, for us all to consider, a general theory that arises from their particular local study about the nature of music.

Sixth, if we hope to contribute to social theory and not just borrow from it, then intradisciplinary conversations about our own theories need to be more frequent, explicit, and pointed. We also need to take them more vigorously than we seem to do now into the conversational arenas beyond our field where they might be influential: journals and conferences of academic societies devoted to community studies, thematic studies, or the humanities and social and life sciences.

Seventh, it is through ethnomusicological theory that we engage with each other's work and create and build the discipline of ethnomusicology. We will not build our discipline solely through our idiographic studies, as rich, detailed, and fascinating as they may be. We will not build our discipline solely through our methods, as precise, refined, culturally sensitive, and replicable as they may be. We will not build our discipline solely through reading and appropriating social theory. To build our discipline, we must, in addition to all this, write ethnomusicological theory within and beyond our local studies and within the general field of the human sciences.

# REFERENCES

Abu-Lughod, Lila. 1991. "Writing against Culture." In Richard G. Fox, ed., *Recapturing Anthropology: Working in the Present.* Santa Fe, NM: School of American Research Press, pp. 137–162.

Appadurai, Arjun. 1996. *Modernity at Large: Cultural Dimensions of Globalization.* Minneapolis: University of Minnesota Press.

Arom, Simha. 1985. *Polyphonies et polyrhythmies instrumentals d'Afrique centrale: Structure et méthodologie.* Paris: SELAF.

Askew, Kelly M. 2002. *Performing the Nation: Swahili Music and Cultural Politics in Tanzania.* Chicago: University of Chicago Press.

Bakan, Michael B. 2009. "Measuring Happiness in the Twenty-First Century: Ethnomusicology, Evidence-Based Research, and the New Science of Autism." *Ethnomusicology* 53(3): 510–518.

Barth, Fredrik. 1969. *Ethnic Groups and Boundaries: The Social Organization of Difference.* Bergen, Norway: Universitets Forlaget.

Bauman, Richard. 1989. "Performance." In Erik Barnouw, ed., *The International Encyclopedia of Communications.* Oxford: Oxford University Press, pp. 262–266.

Becker, Judith. 1972. "Traditional Music in Modern Java." PhD dissertation, University of Michigan, Ann Arbor.

———. 2004. *Deep Listeners: Music, Emotion, and Trancing.* Bloomington: Indiana University Press.

———. 2009. "Ethnomusicology and Empiricism in the Twenty-First Century." *Ethnomusicology* 53(3): 478–501.

Becker, Judith, and A. L. Becker. 1981. "A Musical Icon: Power and Meaning in Javanese Gamelan Music." In Wendy Steiner, ed., *The Sign in Music and Literature.* Austin: University of Texas Press, pp. 203–215.

Berger, Harris. 2009. *Stance: Ideas about Emotion, Style, and Meaning for the Study of Expressive Culture.* Middletown, CT: Wesleyan University Press.

Bickford, Tyler. 2010. "Call and Response—Revisited (Ethnomusicology and Empiricism)." *Ethnomusicology* 54(2): 345–246.

Bourdieu, Pierre. 1977. *Outline of a Theory of Practice,* translated by Richard Nice. Cambridge: Cambridge University Press.

———. 1993. *The Field of Cultural Production: Essays on Art and Literature,* edited by Randall Johnson. New York: Columbia University Press.

Brinner, Benjamin. 1995. *Knowing Music, Making Music: Javanese Gamelan and the Theory of Musical Competence.* Chicago: University of Chicago Press.

Buchanan, Donna A., ed. 2007a. *Balkan Popular Culture and the Ottoman Ecumene: Music, Image, and Regional Political Discourse.* Lanham, MD: Scarecrow Press.

———. 2007b. "Preface and Acknowledgements." In Donna A. Buchanan, ed., *Balkan Popular Culture and the Ottoman Ecumene: Music, Image, and Regional Political Discourse*. Lanham, MD: Scarecrow Press, pp. xvii–xxviii.

———. 2007c. "'Oh, Those Turks!': Music, Politics, and Interculturality in the Balkans and Beyond." In Donna A. Buchanan, ed., *Balkan Popular Culture and the Ottoman Ecumene: Music, Image, and Regional Political Discourse*. Lanham, MD: Scarecrow Press, pp. 3–54.

———. 2007d. "Bulgarian Ethnopop along the Old *Via Militaris*: Ottomanism, Orientalism, or Balkan Cosmopolitanism." In Donna A. Buchanan, ed., *Balkan Popular Culture and the Ottoman Ecumene: Music, Image, and Regional Political Discourse*. Lanham, MD: Scarecrow Press, pp. 225–267.

Caudron, Shari. 2006. *Who Are You People? A Personal Journey into the Heart of Fanatical Passion in America*. Fort Lee, NJ: Barricade Books.

Danielson, Virginia. 1997. *The Voice of Egypt: Umm Kulthūm, Arabic Song, and Egyptian Society in the Twentieth Century*. Chicago: University of Chicago Press.

Del Negro, Giovanna P., and Harris M. Berger. 2004. *Identity and Everyday Life: Essays in the Study of Folklore, Music, and Popular Culture*. Middletown, CT: Wesleyan University Press.

Emerson, Robert M. 1988. *Contemporary Field Research: A Collection of Readings*. Prospects Heights, IL: Waveland Press.

Erlmann, Veit, ed. 2004. *Hearing Cultures: Essays on Sound, Listening, and Modernity*. New York: Berg.

Feld, Steven. 1981. "'Flow Like a Waterfall': The Metaphors of Kaluli Musical Theory." *Yearbook for Traditional Music* 13: 22–47.

———. 1982. *Sounds and Sentiment: Birds, Weeping, Poetics, and Song in Kaluli Expression*. Philadelphia: University of Pennsylvania Press.

———. 2009. "Acoustemologies." Charles Seeger Lecture. Annual Meeting of the Society for Ethnomusicology, Mexico City, November 20, 2009.

Foucault, Michel. 1978. *The History of Sexuality*. New York: Pantheon Books.

Frith, Simon. 1987. "Towards an Aesthetic of Popular Music." In Richard Leppert and Susan McClary, eds., *Music and Society: The Politics of Composition, Performance and Reception*. Cambridge: Cambridge University Press, pp. 133–150.

Geertz, Clifford. 1973. *The Interpretation of Cultures*. New York: Basic Books.

Greene, Paul D., and Thomas Porcello, eds. 2005. *Wired for Sound: Engineering Technologies in Sonic Cultures*. Middletown, CT: Wesleyan University Press.

Hall, Stuart. 1996. "Introduction: Who Needs Identity?" In Stuart Hall and Paul du Gay, eds., *Questions of Cultural Identity*. London: Sage Publications, pp. 1–17.

Hill, Juniper. 2005. "From Ancient to Avant-Garde to Global: Creative Processes and Institutionalization of Finnish Contemporary Folk Music." PhD dissertation, University of California, Los Angeles.

Hood, Mantle. 1954. *The Nuclear Theme as a Determinant of Patet in Javanese Music*. Groningen: J. B. Wolters.

———. 1971. *The Ethnomusicologist*. New York: McGraw-Hill.

Jackson, Travis. 2006. "Rearticulating Ethnomusicology: Privilege, Ambivalence, and Twelve Years in SEM." *Ethnomusicology* 50(2): 280–286.

Kaufman, Nikolai. 1968. *Bŭlgarska mnogoglasna narodna pesen* [Bulgarian many-voiced folk song]. Sofia: Bulgarian Academy of Sciences.

Kingsbury, Henry. 1988. *Music, Talent, and Performance: A Conservatory Cultural System*. Philadelphia: Temple University Press.

Koskoff, Ellen. 1982. "The Music-Network: A Model of Organization of Musical Concepts." *Ethnomusicology* 26(3): 353–370.

Kunst, Jaap. 1934. *De toonkunst van Java*. 's-Gravenhage: M. Nijhoff. (3rd enlarged ed., *Music in Java*, ed. Ernst Heins, 1973.)

———. 1959. *Ethnomusicology: A Study of Its Nature, Its Problems, Methods and Representative Personalities to Which Is Added a Bibliography*. The Hague: M. Nijhoff. (3rd enlarged ed. of *Musicologica*, 1950.)

Lomax, Alan. 1968. *Folk Song Style and Culture*. Washington, DC: American Association for the Advancement of Science.

Loza, Steven. 1999. *Tito Puente and the Making of Latin Music*. Urbana: University of Illinois Press.

———. 2006. "Challenges to the Euroamericentric Ethnomusicological Canon: Alternatives for Graduate Readings, Theory, and Method." *Ethnomusicology* 50(2): 360–371.

Lysloff, T. A. René, and Leslie C. Gay Jr., eds. 2003. *Technoculture and Music*. Middletown, CT: Wesleyan University Press.

Manuel, Peter. 1993. *Cassette Culture: Popular Music and Technology in North India*. Chicago: University of Chicago Press.

Maultsby, Portia K., and Melonee V. Burnim. 2001. "Overview [of African American Musics]." With contributions by Susan Oehler. In Ellen Koskoff, ed., *The Garland Encyclopedia of World Music, Volume 3: The United States and Canada*. New York: Garland Publishing, pp. 572–591.

Mayr, Ernst. 2001. *What Evolution Is*. New York: Basic Books.

McDermott, Vincent, and Sumarsam. 1975. "Central Javanese Music: The Paṭet of Lara Sléndro and the Gendèr Barung." *Ethnomusicology* 19(2): 233–244.

McLean, Mervyn. 1979. "Towards the Differentiation of Music Areas in Oceania." *Anthropos* 74: 717–736.

———. 1986. "Towards a Typology of Musical Change: Missionaries and Adjustive Response in Oceania." *The World of Music* 28(1): 29–43.

———. 2006. *Pioneers of Ethnomusicology*. Coral Springs, FL: Llumina Press.

Merchant Henson, Tanya. 2006. "Constructing Musical Tradition in Uzbek Institutions." PhD dissertation, University of California, Los Angeles.

Merriam, Alan P. 1964. *The Anthropology of Music*. Evanston, IL: Northwestern University Press.

Mitchell, Frank. 1978. *Navajo Blessingway Singer: The Autobiography of Frank Mitchell, 1881–1967*, edited by Charlotte J. Frisbie and David P. McAllester. Tucson: University of Arizona Press.

Moisala, Pirrko, and Beverley Diamond, eds. 2000. *Music and Gender*. Chicago: University of Chicago Press.

Myers, Helen, ed. 1992. *Ethnomusicology, Volume 1: An Introduction*. The Norton/Grove Handbooks in Music. New York: W. W. Norton.

Nattiez, Jean-Jacques. 1990. *Music and Discourse: Toward a Semiology of Music*. Princeton, NJ: Princeton University Press.

Nettl, Bruno. 1964. *Theory and Method in Ethnomusicology*. New York: Free Press of Glencoe.

———. 1983. *The Study of Ethnomusicology: Twenty-Nine Issues and Concepts*. Urbana: University of Illinois Press.

———. 1995. *Heartland Excursions: Ethnomusicological Reflections on Schools of Music*. Urbana: University of Illinois Press.

Neuman, Daniel M. 1980. *The Life of Music in North India: The Organization of an Artistic Tradition*. Detroit, MI: Wayne State University Press. (Republished by the University of Chicago Press, 1990.)

Nzewi, Meki. 1997. *African Music: Theoretical Concept and Creative Continuum*. Olderhausen, Germany: Institut für Didaktik Populärer Musik.

Ortner, Sherry B. 2006. *Anthropology and Social Theory: Culture, Power, and the Acting Subject*. Durham, NC: Duke University Press.

Perlman, Marc. 1998. "The Social Meaning of Modal Practices: Status, Gender, History, and Pathet in Central Javanese Music." *Ethnomusicology* 42(1): 45–80.

Piaget, Jean, and Bärbel Inhelder. 1969. *The Psychology of the Child*, translated by Helen Weaver. New York: Basic Books.

Proctor, Robert W., and E. J. Capaldi. 2006. *Why Science Matters: Understanding the Methods of Psychological Research*. Malden, MA: Blackwell Publishing.

Qureshi, Regula. 2002. *Music and Marx: Ideas, Practice, Politics*. New York: Routledge.

Rancier, Megan. 2009. "The Kazakh Qyl-qobyz: Biography of an Instrument, Story of a Nation." PhD dissertation, University of California, Los Angeles.

Rice, Timothy. 1977. "Polyphony in Bulgarian Folk Music." PhD dissertation, University of Washington, Seattle.

———. 1980. "Aspects of Bulgarian Musical Thought." *Yearbook of the International Folk Music Council* 12: 43–67.

———. 1988. "Understanding Three-Part Singing in Bulgaria: The Interplay of Concept and Experience." *Selected Reports in Ethnomusicology* 7: 43–57.

———. 1994. *May It Fill Your Soul: Experiencing Bulgarian Music*. Chicago: University of Chicago Press.

———. 1995. "Understanding and Producing the Variability of Oral Tradition: Learning from a Bulgarian Bagpiper." *Journal of American Folklore* 108(429): 266–276.

———. 2003. "Time, Place, and Metaphor in Musical Experience and Ethnography." *Ethnomusicology* 47(2): 151–179.

———. 2004. *Music in Bulgaria: Experiencing Music, Expressing Culture*. New York: Oxford University Press.

———. 2007. "Reflections on Music and Identity in Ethnomusicology." *Muzikologija* [Musicology] (Belgrade) 7: 17–38.

Ricoeur, Paul. 1981. *Hermeneutics and the Human Sciences*, edited and translated by John B. Thompson. Cambridge: Cambridge University Press.

Ritter, Jonathan, and J. Martin Daughtry, eds. 2007. *Music in the Post-9/11 World*. New York: Routledge.

Roseman, Marina. 1991. *Healing Sounds from the Rainforest: Temiar Music and Medicine*. Berkeley: University of California Press.

Sakata, Lorraine. 1983. *Music in the Mind: The Concepts of Music and Musician in Afghanistan*. Kent, OH: Kent State University Press. (Republished by the Smithsonian Institution Press, Washington, DC, 2002.)

Seeger, Anthony. 1980. "Sing for Your Sister: The Structure and Performance of Suyá Akia." In Norma McLeod and Marcia Herndon, eds., *The Ethnography of Musical Performance*. Norwood, PA: Norwood Editions, pp. 7–43.

——. 1987. *Why Suyá Sing: A Musical Anthropology of an Amazonian People*. Cambridge: Cambridge University Press. (Republished by the University of Illinois Press, 2004.)

Seeger, Charles. 1977. *Studies in Musicology, 1935–1973*. Berkeley: University of California Press.

Seroussi, Edwin. 2009. "Music: The 'Jew' of Jewish Studies." *Jewish Studies: Yearbook of the World Union of Jewish Studies* 46: 3–84.

Slobin, Mark. 1993. *Subcultural Sounds: Micromusics of the West*. Hanover, NH: Wesleyan University Press.

——. 1996. "Introduction." In Mark Slobin, ed., *Retuning Culture: Musical Changes in Central and Eastern Europe*. Durham, NC: Duke University Press, pp. 1–13.

——, ed. 2008. *Global Soundtracks: Worlds of Film Music*. Middletown, CT: Wesleyan University Press.

Sparshott, F. E. 1980. "Aesthetics of Music." In Stanley Sadie, ed., *The New Grove Dictionary of Music and Musicians*, vol. 1. New York: Macmillan, pp. 120–133.

Stokes, Martin. 1994. "Introduction: Ethnicity, Identity and Music." In Martin Stokes, ed., *Ethnicity, Identity, and Music: The Musical Construction of Place*. New York: Berg, pp. 1–27.

Stone, Ruth. 1982. *Let the Inside Be Sweet: The Interpretation of Music Event Among the Kpelle of Liberia*. Bloomington: Indiana University Press.

——. 2008. *Theory for Ethnomusicology*. Upper Saddle River, NJ: Pearson/Prentice Hall.

Sugarman, Jane C. 1997. *Engendering Song: Singing and Subjectivity at Prespa Albanian Weddings*. Chicago: University of Chicago Press.

——. 2007. "'The Criminals of Albanian Music': Albanian Commercial Folk Music and Issues of Identity Since 1990," in Donna A. Buchanan, ed., *Balkan Popular Culture and the Ottoman Ecumene: Music, Image, and Regional Political Discourse*. Lanham, MD: Scarecrow Press, 269–307.

Sutton, R. Anderson. 1998. "Java." In Terry E. Miller and Sean Williams, eds., *The Garland Encyclopedia of World Music, Volume 8: Southeast Asia*. New York: Garland Publishing, pp. 630–728.

Tenzer, Michael. 2006. *Analytical Studies in World Music*. New York: Oxford University Press.

Turino, Thomas. 1999. "Signs of Imagination, Identity, and Experience: A Peircean Semiotic Theory for Music." *Ethnomusicology* 43(2): 221–255.

——. 2008. *Music as Social Life: The Politics of Participation*. Chicago: University of Chicago Press.

Wachtel, Andrew. 1998. "Thoughts on Teaching South Slavic Cultures." *NewsNet/ American Association for the Advancement of Slavic Studies* 38(1): 7–8.

Wallerstein, Immanuel. 2004. *World-Systems Analysis: An Introduction*. Durham, NC: Duke University Press.

Walton, Susan. 1987. *Mode in Javanese Music.* Athens, OH: Ohio University Center for International Studies.

Waterman, Christopher A. 1990a. *Jùjú: A Social History and Ethnography of an African Popular Music.* Chicago: University of Chicago Press.

———. 1990b. "'Our Tradition Is a Very Modern Tradition': Popular Music and the Construction of Pan-Yoruba Identity." *Ethnomusicology* 34(3): 367–379.

Weintraub, Andrew N., and Bell Yung, eds. 2009. *Music and Cultural Rights.* Urbana: University of Illinois Press.

Weiss, Sarah. 2006. *Listening to an Earlier Java: Aesthetics, Gender, and the Music of Wayang in Central Java.* Leiden: KTILV Press.

Wong, Deborah. 2004. *Speak It Louder: Asian Americans Making Music.* New York: Routledge.

Zemp, Hugo. 1979. "Aspects of 'Are'are Musical Theory." *Ethnomusicology* 23(1): 5–48.

# The Individual in Musical Ethnography

## (WITH JESSE D. RUSKIN) ■

The individual musician occupies a seemingly paradoxical position in ethno-musicology. On one hand, the name of the discipline, whose roots include the Greek word for nation, race, or tribe (*ethnos*), suggests that it will focus on the study of groups of people, not on individuals. In fact, ethnomusicologists have tended to follow the path implied by the discipline's name by studying the role, meaning, and practice of music within social groups and communities defined by geography (the music of Japan), ethnic or kinship group (African American music), institutions (music in the national conservatory of Uzbekistan), or genre-affinity groups (performers and fans of flamenco). These communities are assumed to share social behaviors and cultural concepts with respect to music, and the object is to understand how musical performance, composition, creativity, and musical works themselves are expressions of and contribute to these shared behaviors and concepts; music, in other words, is viewed as part of a social and cultural system.

On the other hand, at least four factors pull ethnomusicologists toward the study of individual musicians. First, when conducting fieldwork, they work with and rely on individual musicians who are sometimes—but not always—among the most exceptional individuals in a given musical community. Second, as communities under the pressures of globalization and political instability fragment and "deterritorialize," as Arjun Appardurai (1990, 1991) put it, eth-nomusicologists have been drawn to the study of individual musicians who are trying to make sense of collapsing worlds, create new individual identities, and knit themselves into emerging or newly encountered social formations. Third, ethnomusicologists belong to a subculture that values the exceptional and valorizes individual achievement. Fourth, interventions in theory and method over the last quarter century have led ethnomusicologists to highlight individual agency and difference, and acknowledge their own roles in the musical communities they study.

Given these paradoxical forces—long-standing notions of the coherence of social life and culturally shared experience versus dynamic, unstable political realities, the practical exigencies of fieldwork, and new developments in social theory—we were curious about how ethnomusicologists have tried to reconcile the competing poles of the social and the individual in their musical ethnographic work and in their assessments of the field.

One of the seminal interventions in this respect was Kenneth Gourlay's 1978 devastating critique of the pretense of objectivity and scientific omniscience that had characterized ethnomusicological reports up to that point, and his suggestion that the "research process" involved a dialogue between historically and socially positioned individuals (p. 22). In the same year, Charlotte Frisbie and David McAllester brought a single musician and his voice to the foreground of their narrative and shifted authorial credit away from themselves to their primary informant Frank Mitchell (Mitchell 1978). In 1984, the *Worlds of Music* textbook featured an individual in each of its chapters about a particular region of the world (Titon 1984). In 1987, Rice suggested that ethnomusicologists had a long history of foregrounding individual musical creativity, as well as the historical construction and the social maintenance of music, which he claimed were the principal "formative processes" of human music making.

In 2001, Jonathan Stock, responding to Gourlay, Frisbie and McAllester, and Rice, among others, proposed an "ethnomusicology of the individual" in the wake of what he saw as a recent rise in biographical and historical writing in ethnomusicology (see, e.g., Rees 2009). He argued that this "literary trend" was motivated by three factors: the recognition of individuality and exceptionality within the musical communities that ethnomusicologists study, the reflexive turn and critique of representation in the social sciences, and reconceptualizations of culture that account for individual variation and agency.

For some ethnomusicologists, however, the developments of late modernity drove their interest in the theoretical and methodological significance of individual musicians. Mark Slobin, in *Subcultural Sounds: Micromusics of the West* (1993), followed anthropologist Arjun Appadurai (1990, 1991) in imagining an ethnomusicology that accounts for the deterritorialization of culture and the fragmentation of experience in late modernity. He suggested that individuals might profitably become the new locus of ethnomusicological research, since, as he put it, "we are all individual music cultures" (Slobin 1993: ix). Following Slobin, Rice (2003) proposed a model for a "subject-centered musical ethnography."

These and other calls for an ethnomusicology of the individual appear to have the quality of an oxymoron. But despite a focus on communities suggested by the discipline's name, ethnomusicologists have a long tradition of placing individuals prominently in their conception of the field. This article examines how they do this in practice, in their writing of particular case studies. While such scholarly reporting occurs in many forms and genres, we focus on the book-length musical ethnography.

For this study we define a musical ethnography as a book that (1) asks and answers questions about the meaning and function of music in culture and society and (2) is based on fieldwork as an indispensable research method. (Of course, such books may also include other methods such as extensive musical analysis and the use of historical sources.) In the last thirty-five years, book-length musical ethnographies have come to rival journal articles as the most important form for reporting the results of ethnomusicological research. Bruno Nettl (2005: 234) described musical ethnographies as the "meat-and-potatoes book of our field." In our view, the large and fast-growing corpus of book-length musical ethnographies is the fruit of the successful marriage of ethnomusicology's parent disciplines, anthropology and musicology. This rapprochement began to appear in books written during the second half of the 1970s by a new generation of ethnomusicologists trained in schools and departments of music but strongly influenced by the first generation of anthropologically trained ethnomusicologists and in particular by Alan Merriam's (1964) *The Anthropology of Music.*

To understand the position of the individual in musical ethnography, we examined a large sample of the musical ethnographies published between 1976 and 2002. We chose 1976 as the start of the period because we believe that Mark Slobin's *Music in the Culture of Northern Afghanistan,* published in that year, was the first musical ethnography written by a person trained primarily as an ethnomusicologist and not as an anthropologist. We ended the survey period when our sample reached more than 100 books and we saw that certain patterns had been well established. We believe that a review of work published in the ten years between 2003 and 2012 would not significantly alter our conclusions. (The books in our sample are listed at the end of this chapter.)

To be included in our sample, books had to be based in some measure on fieldwork methods; deal with problems suggested by an anthropological approach to music study; and be written by scholars who self-identify as ethnomusicologists, or who engaged in conversations with ethnomusicologists as evidenced by their citations and references. If there was any doubt about whether a book should be included in the sample, we privileged the author's characterization of the work. So, for example, Virginia Danielson's (1997) study of the popular Egyptian singer Umm Kulthūm, while at one level a biography of a deceased individual, was included because the author foregrounded fieldwork and cultural analysis. The vast majority of the books in our sample were published in the United States and other Anglophone countries, but we did include a few English-language works published elsewhere that came to our attention (e.g., Moisala 1991; Weisethaunet 1998; Pejcheva and Dimov 2002). While we do not view ethnomusicology as exclusively an English-language enterprise, it was not practical for us to include a fair sampling of the important work being published in dozens of other languages (e.g., Coppet and Zemp 1978; Allgayer-Kaufmann 1987).

In this chapter we use the word *individual* in as neutral a sense as possible—that is, as a single human being as opposed to a group of human beings. In doing so, we avoid taking a position on any of the many philosophical debates about the nature of the individual and its relationship to a world, although the authors of some of the studies we cite may do so either implicitly or explicitly. For the same reason, we prefer *individual* to some other possible words we might have used such as *person*, which seems to be tied to legal discourse, and *subject*, which seems to imply something about individual experience, ideation, and agency that may not be true of all the works in our corpus, though it is certainly true of some of them.

To locate and define the study of the individual in our sample of musical ethnographies, we address five themes: (1) the importance of individuals in musical ethnographies, (2) the types of individuals discussed and analyzed, (3) the theoretical purposes served by these treatments of individuals, (4) the nature of ethnomusicologists' encounters with individuals, and (5) the narrative strategies employed when individuals are included in musical ethnographies.

## THE IMPORTANCE OF INDIVIDUALS IN MUSICAL ETHNOGRAPHIES

To understand how important individuals are to the narrative structures of musical ethnographies, we placed each book into one of four categories: (1) individuals largely absent from the narrative, (2) individuals present in the narrative to a limited extent, (3) individuals central to the narrative, and (4) single individual as sole subject (biography). We considered individuals largely absent when the author seemed primarily concerned with normative description over individual experience and where individuals were not named or, if they were named, were secondary to generalization about the group (e.g., Chenoweth 1979; Besmer 1983). Only fourteen books in our sample fell into this category. By contrast, individuals were present to a limited extent in just under half of the sample. We placed books in the "present" category when individuals were named and described briefly in passing, often to provide specificity to a broader cultural treatment or to support or complicate a larger argument (Neuman 1990 [1980]); when individuals were named and quoted as sources of information but were neither the primary anchors of the narrative nor the primary objects of analysis (Schechter 1992); when individuals drove the narrative in places but were not the main point of the narrative as a whole (Reily 2002); or when characters were drawn through brief biographies in sectional or chapter-length profiles (Berliner 1978). Most of the remainder of the sample (i.e., nearly half) occupied the "central" category, in which individuals anchored the narrative throughout the book. In such cases, they were treated as the primary objects of analysis, or the primary lenses through which to look at broader topics (Keyes 2002); there was extensive use of attributed quotation (Vander 1988); the book contained detailed biographies or profiles integral to the work as a whole (Bakan 1999); or the researcher's interaction with particular individuals was featured prominently (Hagedorn 2001). Finally, only ten books were placed in the "biography" category, indicating a narrative centered on the life and work of a particular musician, musical family, or ensemble. Six of them named an individual in the title (Mitchell 1978; Porter 1995; Stock 1996; Danielson 1997; Loza 1999; Vélez 2000), one named a band (Hayward 1998), and three did not name their subjects in the title (Rice 1994; Quigley 1995; Groemer 1999). Of these ten, three are about the stars of popular music (Danielson 1997; Hayward 1998; Loza 1999), and the remaining seven focus on individuals who would qualify as "traditional" musicians.

Using this method, we reached three principal conclusions. First, ethnomusicologists attended significantly to individuals throughout the period from 1976 to 2002. Second, the small number of books devoted mainly to a single named individual supports our earlier claim that ethnomusicologists treat individuals more often as members of communities than as autonomous actors. Third, books that focus solely on communities without considering individuals represent a very small portion of the sample.

Viewing the sample temporally yielded two slightly contradictory trends. On the one hand, individuals have been centrally important to the musical ethnographies in our sample from its beginnings in the late 1970s (Berliner 1978; Mitchell 1978). On the other hand, books that ignore individuals completely occupy a prominent part of our corpus only during the early years up to about

1990. Such studies disappear after 1995. Since then, individuals play at least a peripheral role in every musical ethnography. Also, beginning in the mid-1990s, publications focused on a single individual begin to appear. In short, the survey shows that individual-centered studies have increased over the past two decades. This trend occurred early, however, and the place of individuals in musical ethnographies remains a mostly invariant characteristic of books published from the mid-1980s onward.

## WHAT KINDS OF INDIVIDUALS DO ETHNOMUSICOLOGISTS STUDY?

Having established that ethnomusicologists frequently feature individuals in their musical ethnographies while rarely making them the exclusive focus, we then asked ourselves about the types of individuals ethnomusicologists study. Are they the compositional titans and stylistic innovators constructed in studies of the history of Western art music, the stars of popular music studies, average musicians who represent a widespread cultural practice, or nonmusicians of various types (listeners, fans, producers, and the like)?

Ethnomusicologists have claimed, for example, that since music is a communicative art, audiences and the act of listening should be legitimate objects of study for a social science interested in music. In conversations, they once debated whether it was more valuable to study (or study under) the most exceptional musicians in a given community or its most typical practitioners. Some felt that the focus should be on learning the best music from the greatest artists, whereas others, such as the anthropologist John Blacking, felt it more important to form a picture of the "average" musician (see, e.g., Baily 2001: 88). Regardless of whom they worked with, all acknowledged that close involvement with individual musicians is an essential part of the ethnomusicological method and integral to its theoretical insights as well (Nettl 1984: 173).

The debate over what type of individual to work with seems to have faded with the increasing recognition that the two categories are not exclusive, but exist in a dialectical relationship. The exceptional individual does not necessarily stand outside or against the consensus of culture; rather, "the personal, the idiosyncratic, and the exceptional ... [are] very much part of the collective, the typical, and the ordinary" (Stock 1996: 2). Just as shared tradition thrives on individual innovation, as Colin Quigley's (1995) study of Canadian fiddler Émile Benoit suggests, so too does individual innovation often find its greatest expressive potential in shared tradition, as Virginia Danielson's (1997) study of the popular Egyptian singer Umm Kulthūm vividly illustrates.

Furthermore, the question of exceptionality may also be a question of scale. From a distance, an individual such as Émile Benoit may appear as typical, but a deeper understanding of his musical style and role in the community reveals his exceptionality. With these complexities in mind, our analysis shifts toward the types of individuals treated in our sample of musical ethnographies.

Broadly speaking, we suggest that ethnomusicologists write about four types of individual in their musical ethnographies: (1) innovators in a tradition; (2) key figures who occupy important roles in a musical culture; (3) ordinary or typical individuals; and (4) normally anonymous audience members and others who play a role in music production, dissemination, and reception. Although ethnomusicologists have pointed out that, theoretically and as a matter of principle, they could study average musicians and even nonmusicians, the vast majority of musical ethnographies in our survey focus on innovators and other key figures who play some important role in their musical culture.

## Innovators

The authors of about a quarter of these musical ethnographies examine the contributions of innovators within a musical tradition. Innovators tend to play prominent roles in musical ethnographies that take a historical approach, focus on popular music, or feature the encounter between tradition and modernity. As in historical musicology, ethnomusicologists tend to view innovators as agents who move the history of a style down the temporal road. In studies of popular music, where the fame of named individuals and stars and their contributions to the history of a genre are some of the hallmarks of this research domain, innovators often are featured in the narrative. Furthermore, the encounter of a tradition with modernity is frequently personified in these musical ethnographies by an individual who articulates and acts on this key moment in the history of a tradition.

An early example of all three tendencies is Manuel Peña's (1985) *The Texas-Mexican Conjunto: History of a Working-Class Music*. Peña's basic purpose was to mount a Marxist analysis of the economic and social conditions that cause a musical genre to emerge and develop. Using historical and ethnographic methods, he documented the individual innovators (such as Narcisco Martinez, Valerio Longoria, and Tony de la Rosa) of *conjunto* music within the contexts of twentieth-century Mexican American migration, urbanization, class differentiation, and identity formation. Peña's study is fairly typical of the approach to innovative individuals in ethnomusicology. Ethnomusicologists are not allergic to the innovators so lionized by historical musicology, but they figure prominently in only about a quarter of this corpus. When ethnomusicologists do treat innovators, they tend to look not at lives and works, but rather at the unusually effective or creative ways in which these musicians responded to their changing social and historical circumstances.

## Key Figures

The second category of individual in musical ethnography is what we call the "key figure." Over half of the books in our corpus focus on such individuals, who are considered to be "key" in two senses: they play some crucial musical role in the culture—such as being extremely popular, occupying an important position, or being an outstanding representative of the style—and they play an important role in the narrative as a particular example of a general point the author wishes to make. Rice's *May It Fill Your Soul: Experiencing Bulgarian Music* (1994), for example, chronicles the history of Bulgarian traditional music from the 1920s to 1989 by focusing on the musical experience of two key figures: Kostadin Varimezov and his wife, Todora. Kostadin occupied an important position in the official musical culture of Bulgaria during its communist period (1944–1989) as the solo bagpipe player in the orchestra of traditional Bulgarian instruments at the national radio station. His wife, Todora, was a key figure in the sense that she possessed an exceptionally large repertoire of traditional songs learned in the precommunist period. By focusing on Kostadin's transformation from a musically illiterate village player to a literate professional musician, Rice was able to humanize the more general story he wished to tell about Bulgarian musical culture in two distinct historical periods. Neither Kostadin nor Todora was an innovator in the tradition, but Rice shows how their deep knowledge of tradition made possible the innovations of others at the moment Bulgarian tradition encountered modernity.

## Average Musicians

The third category of individual, used in only a small number of musical ethnographies, consists of average or ordinary musicians who must, we suppose, be an important part of every musical tradition. They are chosen not because of their special mastery of—or position in—a tradition but to help the author tell an interesting story. One example of such a study is Harris Berger's *Metal, Rock, and Jazz: Perception and the Phenomenology of Musical Experience* (1999). This book examines how musicians performing in these three genres attend cognitively to music during performance to create a powerful musical groove. In this book, understanding individual musical experience is the point. So, any individual will do, including local and regional journeyman musicians crucial to the vitality of these styles but with little or no apparent artistic or historical significance in the wider world.

## Nonmusicians

The fourth category of individual is nonmusicians, in effect the audience for music. Ethnomusicologists have long argued that, in principle, listeners should be considered musicians, and that they deserve to be studied as seriously as performers and composers are. For example, Danish anthropologist Marc Schade-Poulsen's *Men and Popular Music in Algeria: The Social Significance of Raï* (1999) examines this Algerian urban popular music through its audience. He elicited the biographies of seven "young men in the city" (pp. 75–96) who listened to but did not perform *raï*. He wanted to make the point that there is not a single, unified view of raï, a controversial genre for both traditionalists and Islamic fundamentalists because of its association with discos, parties, and "obscene" cabarets. These individual stories served as particular instances of "the generalizations [the author was] making about social life among youth in Algeria" (p. 76). Since we placed only two books in the sample featuring this type of individual (see also Muller 1999), we conclude that it is safe to say that ethnomusicologists rarely follow this principle.

## WHAT THEORETICAL PURPOSE DOES THE STUDY OF INDIVIDUALS SERVE?

How individuals are treated in musical ethnographies depends to a large extent, we believe, on the author's view of culture. In one view, evident in roughly one-third of the books in the corpus, the author tends toward a "classic" concept of culture in which individuals' ideas and actions are seen as molded by a larger whole (Ortner 2006: 12). From this perspective, culture is constituted of shared ideas and behaviors and the point of the narrative is to explicate the general principles at work in a musical culture. The second view, true of about two-thirds of the books, draws on a host of more recent critical interventions in the social sciences in which the differences between and among individual actors and agents in a society or community are seen as crucial to the reproduction and transformation of its musical culture.[1]

## Studies Based on the Theory That Cultures Are Constituted of Shared Ideas

In the category of works that rest on the theory of shared culture, only a small number either marginalize or ignore individuals altogether to tell a general story. The majority of books focus on general cultural principles but use individuals in the narrative in one of two ways: (1) as specific examples to illustrate and give a human face to the social and cultural principles at stake in the book or (2) to acknowledge individuals as the primary sources of the ethnomusicologist's knowledge, in many cases without giving them life through an extensive biography or anecdotes about their life in the musical culture. Daniel Neuman's *The Life of Music in North India: The Organization of an Artistic Tradition* (1990 [1980]), for example, provides a brief account of a competent but otherwise unremarkable *tabla* player named Yusuf Ali, who concertized in the West with distinguished melodic-solo artists. Western audiences' enthusiastic reception of Ali as a musical equal of the melodic artists helped to transform tabla players' musical, economic, and social status in India. They began to demand more money and more performance time to display their creativity. Neuman tells us about Yusuf Ali not because he is in any sense exceptional but because he illustrates and humanizes the larger point Neuman wishes to make about the homology between musical and social organization in India.

In ethnomusicological fieldwork, individuals are the principal sources of cultural understanding and teachers of musical knowledge and, in some sense, are equivalent to historical musicologists' manuscript sources. One example is Finnish ethnomusicologist Pirkko Moisala's *Cultural Cognition in Music: Continuity and Change in the Gurung Music of Nepal* (1991). Her main goal was to understand music cognition, and so she spent a lot of time with the two most prominent musical specialists in the village, from whom she elicited verbalizations about music. Although she introduces them briefly as characters with lives (pp. 87–90), they are mainly useful to her narrative when she

---

1. See Ortner (1984, 2006) for valuable syntheses of these trends in the social sciences. The emergence of alternative theoretical foundations in ethnomusicology echoes developments in the social sciences during the 1970s and '80s, as outlined by Ortner, when critical theories of gender, race, class, and power dovetailed with a turn toward more historical and practice-oriented approaches to the study of cultures and societies. In a similar vein, see Abu-Lughod's 1991 essay "Writing against Culture" for a valuable critique of the classic concept of culture.

is describing their performances and documenting what they told her about their thought processes. Ethnomusicologists' naming of individuals as sources of information and reporting on the particular musicians who teach them typically flow from their research methodology rather than from their research goals. Such naming and reporting is sometimes the only reason that individuals appear in these musical ethnographies (compare, however, Browner 2002, who has other reasons for naming individuals).

## Studies Concerned with Difference in Culture

The second category is based on a different theoretical foundation. The view of culture as shared among people living in well-defined social groups has been challenged by critical theorists in the social sciences who have argued that societies are not happily homogenous but fragmented along lines of gender, social class, and ethnicity, and that, as a result, cultural ideas and expressions will be similarly fragmented. According to this theoretical perspective, the contestation of musical meaning by individuals and cultural subgroups must be as true as any claims about common, shared meanings and understandings. This is not to say that the shared aspects of culture cease to matter, only that they are refracted through individual personality, social differentiation, and relations of power. In ethnomusicology, this relatively recent development in social theory has taken at least four forms: (1) valorizing individuality, individual skill differences, individual identity, and individual experience among musicians in a culture; (2) reporting on the differences and tensions that exist between and among individuals operating from different social and historical positions within a society; (3) viewing individuals as agents who operationalize, put into motion, give meaning to, and change social, cultural, and musical systems; and (4) foregrounding the experiences of ethnomusicologists and their encounters with individuals during fieldwork.

The valorization of individual difference and individual identity comes rather easily to ethnomusicologists, trained as most of them are in Western traditions that value individuality in general and various forms of musical distinction in particular. In this category are books that focus on differences in knowledge and skill levels, individual musical experience, differences of interpretation, and questions of individual identity. Benjamin Brinner's *Knowing Music, Making Music: Javanese Gamelan and the Theory of Musical Competence and Interaction* (1995) provides a rich example of individual difference in musical competence. In it, he develops a general theory of musical competence and a particular theory of Javanese musical competence. One of the more interesting features of his theory concerns the "individualized" nature of musical knowledge. This individualized knowledge is then deployed within communities of individuals interacting in particular musical contexts (see also Monson 1996; Vélez 2000).

A second approach to registering fragmentation in musical cultures is to claim that culture is defined as much by contestation between and among people operating from different social positions such as age, class, occupation, education, and urban-versus-rural residence as it is by shared understandings and practices. Ethnomusicologists are increasingly addressing the differences of musical interpretation and experience that result from such social stratification. For example, in one part of Raúl Romero's *Debating the Past: Music, Memory, and Identity in the Andes* (2001), he takes individuals as tokens for three competing social positions—traditionalist, modernist, and radical—within the world of contemporary *orquesta típica*, an ensemble of *quena* flute, violin, and harp that originates with the pre-Hispanic Wanka people of the Mantaro Valley of Peru. The traditionalist position is represented by an artist/intellectual who once resided in Europe and who decries modernization and seeks to preserve ancient practices. The modernist position is represented by a clarinet player and music teacher who believes that modern instruments such as the clarinet and the saxophone help to make traditional music sound better, and who claims that the modern is more useful for creating identity than the traditional. The radical position is represented by younger musicians aged fifteen to twenty-five who are experimenting with replacing the harp with the electric bass and the violin with the synthesizer.

In the third approach, scholars view musical individuals as agents who give meaning to—and change—social, cultural, and musical systems in specific instances. Influenced by practice theory and related theories of agency (Ortner 2006: 131–134), this position serves as an antidote to an earlier ethnomusicological theory that music and musicians merely reflect or participate in larger cultural and social systems and processes. This approach is also characteristic of all musical ethnographies that attempt to account for the history of a tradition. One of the clearest examples in our corpus of musical ethnographies is Virginia Danielson's *"The Voice of Egypt": Umm Kulthūm, Arabic Song, and Egyptian Society in the Twentieth Century* (1997). A star of the tradition is at the center of this study and is construed by Danielson as an agent: "One wants to account for the impact of exceptional performers . . . on the culture of their societies without losing track of them as participants affected by their societies" (pp. 15–16). She claims that Umm Kulthūm helped to "constitute" cultural and social life, "advance an ideology of Egyptianess," and create a cultural and artistic world that was simultaneously Arab, Western, and cosmopolitan—and in line with the nationalist politics of the period.

The notion of agency is not restricted, however, to historical studies in which ethnomusicologists, like historical musicologists, treat individuals as the agents of stylistic change. Even in more synchronic studies, many ethnomusicologists work on the assumption that individual musicians are agents of social and cultural practices and that music is not merely a passive reflection of preexisting social and cultural structures. For example, Jane Sugarman's *Engendering Song: Singing and Subjectivity at Prespa Albanian Weddings* (1997) provides richly detailed descriptions of how people at social gatherings in this conservative Muslim community choose whether to sing, what songs to sing, and the manner in which they will sing them. In a tour de force of cultural analysis, Sugarman demonstrates how such seemingly mundane choices create this community's sense of social identity, its sense of social organization around notions of patrilineality and gender, and its sense of "honor and moral order" (pp. 182–197).

A fourth reason for placing individuals at the center of musical ethnographies is the reflexive turn in ethnomusicology, a direction that Gourlay (1978) anticipated with his call to place the encounter of the ethnomusicologist with musicians in the field at the center of their narratives about musical cultures. As they engage in self-reflection about field encounters and as they write themselves into their narratives, they naturally write about the people they meet, not just about abstract features of music, culture, performances, or social structure. In thematic terms, these approaches to reflexivity include recognizing the dialogic achievement of knowledge in fieldwork; problematizing the researcher's social, political, or economic position; and using the self as a source of knowledge, especially in contexts of music learning. Anthony Seeger, for example, places his book *Why Suyá Sing* (1987) within the trend toward reflexive anthropology. Music making, for Seeger, is an important part of the "delicate" economy of knowledge that constitutes fieldwork. Seeger recounts that it wasn't until he and his wife began singing that the Suyá recognized their full value to the community (pp. 19–21). The inclusion of this encounter in Seeger's narrative is doubly useful: it illuminates the complex negotiations involved in fieldwork and reveals something of the Suyá's value system. At a more general level, Seeger suggests that the ethics of reflexive anthropology are rooted in an intersubjective and dialogical approach to field research, one that sees people not as abstract objects, but as thinking subjects with whom ethnomusicologists share knowledge. A particular strength of this book, however, is Seeger's success in registering his own presence without making it a focal point of the entire narrative.

## The Author's Encounter with the Individual

We use the term *encounter* to imply a relationship between researcher and subject that shapes the possibilities of research and the narrative that emerges from it. Accordingly, we placed each book into one of three categories based on the nature of the authors' encounters with the individuals they study: direct encounter, indirect encounter, or both direct and indirect encounter. Direct encounter refers to face-to-face interaction between ethnographer and subject, engaging the usual modes of fieldwork, including interviews and participant observation, as well as the collection of oral histories and the compilation of biographies (Keil 1979; Cooke 1986; Blau et al. 2002) and autobiographies (Mitchell 1978; Groemer 1999; Simonett 2001). Indirect encounter, in contrast, implies a degree of separation between the researcher and the individual subject. It may involve such historical research materials as correspondence, existing biographies, musical scores, recordings, and other secondary sources. And it may also make use of fieldwork methods in developing a picture of the social and ideological world in which the individual lives or lived (see Walser 1993, Stock 1996, and Danielson 1997 for examples of this methodologically hybrid indirect approach). Of the musical ethnographies in which individuals play a central role, our survey shows that over half use only direct methods, whereas a small number use only indirect methods (Becker 1980). A significant number use some combination of direct and indirect methods (Loza 1999).

Although ethnomusicologists often generalize about music and culture from encounters with a limited number of individuals (Shelemay 1997), few musical ethnographies contain detailed reflections on the nature of these relationships and how they impact the research method, theoretical orientation, and narrative presentation. Individual-centered ethnographies, however, tend to deal with these issues more explicitly. Michael Bakan, in *Music of Death and New Creation: Experiences in the World of Balinese Gamelan Beleganjur* (1999), acknowledges the way in which his relationship with two Balinese composers, Asnawa and Sukarata, shaped his narrative. Asnawa serves more as a source of information, evident in the fact that he is frequently cited as a reference in the first three chapters. Sukarata, in contrast, is a focus of the study in the second half of the book, where Bakan recounts his experience studying drumming with him. Bakan discusses how his initial encounters with these composers shaped his theoretical orientation toward the individual and thus his approach to writing their biographies. For instance, his initial misreading of Asnawa's social status, which caused a significant miscommunication between the two, led him to investigate more thoroughly the composer's views of his own social position, as well as other people's views of Asnawa's status. In so doing, Bakan was able to construct a more nuanced picture of the individual as situated within a multifaceted social field. These composers, he discovers, define themselves and their artistic worlds, just as those worlds define them.

## Narrative Strategies

Ethnomusicologists narrativize their encounters with individuals in many ways, with biographical writing being just one (Stock 2001). We extend Stock's argument by situating biography within a fuller typology of narrative strategies used in individual-centered musical ethnography. Our goal in this section is to show how ethnomusicologists have applied a range of narrative techniques, including but not limited to biographical writing, to the problem of situating the individual in musical ethnography. In doing so, we are suggesting a definition of biography that is simultaneously narrower and broader—that is, a more precise placement of what we call "biographical writing" within the ethnomusicology of the individual, and a broader definition of "musical biography" that includes a range of foci and rhetorical techniques.[2]

Focusing on the vast majority of books in this sample that represent individuals centrally or strongly, we have identified five narrative techniques commonly used to write the individual into musical ethnographies: biography, assisted autobiography, dialogue, polyvocality, and analysis of musical texts and performances. In practice, of course, these five techniques often overlap, but they are abstracted here for the sake of clarity. In providing examples of each from the literature, we illustrate not only their particular rhetorical aspects but also the implications of each for theorizing the paradoxical position of the individual in ethnomusicology.

## Biography

The first narrative strategy is biography—defined narrowly here as a monologic account of an individual's life and work, constructed from either historical research, fieldwork, or some combination of the two. Biographical writing takes at least three forms: book-length treatments of a single individual or family (Rice 1994; Porter 1995); formal and encapsulated biography, which may include isolated sections or chapters devoted to individuals (Berliner 1978; Keil 1979); and the character-driven narrative, in which biographies of many individuals are integrated into the storyline (Lortat-Jacob 1995; Berger 1999). Biographical writing, when approached from an ethnomusicological perspective, necessarily engages the researcher in a host of social, cultural, historical, and personal issues. In writing her book on

2. The latter point was inspired by a personal conversation with A. J. Racy, who suggested that for musical biography to be truly ethnomusicological, it must incorporate a range of texts and perspectives—personal, historical, ethnographic, and musical.

Egyptian icon Umm Kulthūm, for example, Virginia Danielson was drawn not only to the life story and musical texts of this individual but also to "larger questions about Egyptian and Arab culture and society" (Danielson 1997: 3). As one of her consultants put it, "Egyptians not only like her voice, we respect *her*. . . . We look at her, we see fifty years of Egypt's history. She is not only a singer" (p. 4, emphasis in original). The iconic performer, Danielson concludes, must be understood as shaped by the society (e.g., its institutions, aesthetics, and imaginative proclivities) that she in turn helped to reshape in innovative ways.

Chapter-length biographies, or those confined to a particular section of the book, such as those found in Paul Berliner's (1978) and Charles Keil's (1979) pioneering ethnographies, appear different in orientation from the book-length biography in that their primary goal is to add some color and specificity to a broadly drawn narrative of a musical culture (see also Capwell 1986). In other cases, biographical chapters or sections are integral to the construction of the narrative as a whole, and general arguments are advanced through these particulars (Kippen 1988; Turino 2000; Florine 2001).

Yet another approach to biography is the character-driven narrative, in which individual personalities move the storyline along just as they might in a work of fiction. Bernard Lortat-Jacob's *Sardinian Chronicles* (1995) is a classic example of this approach. The dissolution of concepts of culture and field, as well as abstract ideas such as "tradition" and "identity," are exemplified here in narrative form as a series of particular encounters between the author and the individuals whose music he is studying. Certain aesthetic preferences, repertory choices, types of musical experience, recognizable expressive and emotive qualities, and parameters of acceptable musical and social interaction are observable. But any totalizing vision of Sardinian "culture" or the research "field" is eschewed.

## Assisted Autobiography

The second narrative strategy is "assisted autobiography" (Erdman 1997), in which individual recollections or oral autobiographies are recorded, transcribed, or reprinted by the author in extended form with little or no alteration, restructuring, or interpretive interruptions. Following Jeff Titon (1980) and Veit Erlmann (1996), we differentiate assisted autobiography or assisted life story from anthropological biography or life history primarily by the extensiveness and continuity of the quotations and by the emphasis on accurately presenting the individual's voice. Titon notes that a distinguishing feature of life story is the fact that it is first and foremost a *story*, a fiction that "affirms the identity of the storyteller in the act of telling. The life story tells who one thinks one is and how one thinks one came to be that way" (Titon 1980: 290). Likewise, in assisted autobiography, the telling is just as important as the facts.

Perhaps the most extended work of assisted autobiography in this corpus is Frisbie and McAllester's oral history, *Blessingway Singer: The Autobiography of Frank Mitchell* (Mitchell 1978), in which Mitchell himself is credited as author. The book consists primarily of Mitchell's own words, culled from extensive interviews conducted by Frisbie and McAllester. The book is much more than an autobiography, however. In footnotes, the editors give us a considerable amount of contextual information derived from historical and field research, including Mitchell's own correspondence and his comments to other researchers. The "assisted" in assisted autobiography points to the multiple layers of editorial choice and interpretation that are involved in capturing and textualizing an individual's "voice."

## Dialogue

The third narrative technique is dialogue, a postmodern ethnographic technique used to decenter ethnographic authority by situating knowledge and historicizing the field encounter (Clifford and Marcus 1986; Marcus and Fischer 1986). This concept is a reaction to totalizing representations, such as the "ethnographic present," that render cultures as closed systems that stand outside of history. It is an approach that seeks to replace the "truth" claimed by an omniscient ethnographer with the "partial truths" generated in the research encounter. In musical ethnography, this takes the form of actual or constructed dialogue between ethnomusicologist and research consultant, and dialogue among research subjects that reveals the tone and content of local discourses about music. Such narratives are written in many ways, including with the use of extended interview transcripts, either standing alone or juxtaposed with an interpretative monologue by the author (Loza 1999; Browner 2002)—this latter technique is referred to as an "ethnographic pair" by Tara Browner (2002), who builds on the work of Mary Louise Pratt (1986) and James Clifford (1988). This approach facilitates the possibility of multiple interpretations by placing the author's monologic narrative directly alongside that of the subject's own words. Another strategy is to write "situated dialogue," distinguishable from interview transcripts by its more literary presentation and its placing of particular speakers within specific contexts. This may involve direct quotation (Levin 1996; Myers 1998) or the author's verbatim recollection of a certain conversation (Herbst 1997).

Another dialogic technique is implicit dialogue or "dialogue in monologic form" (Rice 1994: 9–12), a monologue intended to evoke, though not necessarily reproduce verbatim, the specificity of the fieldwork conversations that inspired it. This is an approach that Michelle Kisliuk (1998) considers carefully. She argues that because "there is no definable border between the 'field' and the space of writing," ethnographic writing is inevitably shaped by the field experience and vice versa. To capture this "immediacy and particularity," she adopts a dialogic approach in which "the ethnographer weaves a narrative based on the *conversations* within which she is engaged" (p. 14, emphasis in original). The problem of "voice" and representation cannot be solved, she argues, by placing "reams of direct quotes" into the text. What is required is sensitivity to the always shifting power relations involved in the research encounter, something she suggests is best done through this evocative dialogic approach.

## Polyvocality

The fourth narrative technique used in individual-centered musical ethnography is "polyvocality" (Clifford and Marcus 1986: 15). A well-worn idea in anthropological literary criticism, we define it for our purposes as a strategy for incorporating multiple voices into a narrative. It is distinguishable from biography and dialogue in that voices may not be anchored to particular life histories nor presented in the context of specific conversations or interviews. The emphasis is on individual voice, experience, knowledge, and worldview, any of which may or may not contain biographical information. Polyvocality in its realist form incorporates these multiple voices into an overarching monologic narrative (Monson 1996; Averill 1997). Mark Slobin (1989), in his ethnography of the American Jewish cantorate, chooses this strategy thoughtfully. He writes that he was interested in a "bottom-up" approach, a presentation of the "story" of the *hazzanim* as a "counterpoint of overlapping, sometimes dissonant voices" (p. xi). He approaches the book as a "source-book"—an oral history of sorts that allows readers room to hear his informants' voices, "enter their world," and form their own interpretations (p. xii). He chose not to contextualize or identify the voices beyond general characteristics (e.g., male, female), because he felt that, in the absence of clearly defined patterns of relationships, it would confuse rather than clarify matters to provide biographical details on all of the speakers, and be too cumbersome to do so with such a large sample.

If realist polyvocality is a strategy for incorporating multiple voices into an otherwise monologic narrative, surrealist polyvocality treats the play and polyphony of voices as constitutive of the narrative itself.[3] This type of experimental technique is rather rare in musical ethnography (see, e.g., Herbst 1997 and Myers 1998). Edward Herbst's *Voices in Bali* (1997) is one of the few books using this strategy, and he explicitly rationalizes the use of layered dialogue as an effective way of capturing the author's research process. The originality of his approach lies in its explicit attention to shifts in voice and perspective, the "ongoing continuum between inner experience and outer forms" (p. xx), often marked in the narrative by changes in textual formatting and layout. What is important for Herbst is not only the incorporation of a variety of voices but also a reflexive attention to shifts in the ethnographer's own voice or perspective. The ethnographer, too, speaks with multiple voices—the scholarly voice, the experiential voice, and the conversational voice, among others.

## Analysis of Texts and Performances

The fifth narrative technique we wish to posit is the analysis of musical texts and observations of performances to paint a picture of an individual's life, work, and milieu, with or without explicit reference to biography or autobiography. David Coplan's (1994) study of South Africa's Basotho migrant "word music," or *sefela*, demonstrates how the deep study of texts and performances can reveal the personal aspects of cultural forms, as well as the inclination of individual artists to present their experience in social terms. Coplan's description of *sefela* captures this paradox neatly: "sefela is a poetic autobiography composed in social context, a personal odyssey of common travails and travels" (p. 88). He invokes Raymond Williams's concept of the "structure of feeling" to describe this imaginative process whereby individual artists articulate their own experiences as a finely balanced assessment of the real and ideal, of "social reality and social aspiration" (pp. 28–29).

This process is what Jeff Titon (1988), in reference to the very different performative tradition of charismatic preaching, refers to as "allegoresis"—the interpretation of life events in terms of broad cultural patterns, belief systems, or community values. This process of allegoresis allows individual memory, through public performance, to become a means of articulating shared beliefs, values, and meanings in the remembered events of everyday life. Titon writes that the pastor Brother John "weld[ed] the church members into one through

---

3. See Clifford (1981: 563–564) on "surrealist ethnography"; see Marcus and Fischer (1986: 45–76) for a discussion of realist, dialogic, and surrealist approaches to ethnographic writing; and see Tyler (1986) on the poetic and polyphonic character of what he calls "postmodern ethnography."

personal narrative, passing tradition through individual experience to forge communal truth" (p. 461). These reflections, along with many others in our corpus (e.g., Qureshi 1986, Shelemay 1998), demonstrate ways in which musical texts and performance analysis can be used to shed light on the seemingly paradoxical position of the individual in ethnomusicology. Musical texts, in these cases, are placed in dialogue with ethnographic observations to advance theoretical discussion of the relationship between individual, culture, society, and history.

Our aims in presenting this typology are both analytic and synthetic. On one hand, we parse ethnomusicological biography into its particular representational techniques and provide examples of the rationales that ethnomusicologists give for each. On the other hand, we treat biographical writing as but one narrative approach among several used to center the individual in musical ethnography. As part of a more broadly conceived ethnomusicology of the individual, we suggest that biography and ethnography are intertwined. Neither one represents a distinct set of research methods, nor an entirely different narrative focus. At the methodological level, the dividing line is unclear, since each may incorporate a combination of methods, including fieldwork and the study of documentary evidence. Nor is the division clear at the level of narrative. The notions of biographical writing as exclusively focused on the personal or unique and of ethnographic writing as denoting the cultural or general do not apply to the ethnomusicology of the individual. The two categories begin to blur as ethnomusicologists direct biography toward culture and society, and channel ethnography into the life experiences and perspectives of individuals.

## CONCLUSIONS

In our survey of over 100 book-length musical ethnographies published by ethnomusicologists (and a few fellow travelers) between 1976 and 2002, we found that the study of individuals is now a norm in the discipline even as ethnomusicologists retain an interest in broadly shared musical, cultural, and social processes within communities. It seems that Slobin's (1993) and Stock's (2001) calls for an ethnomusicology of the individual and Rice's (2003) proposal for a subject-centered musical ethnography are being answered within an overarching concern for music as a constituent element of shared culture. No matter how attentive they are to particular musicians in their writing, ethnomusicologists are always at pains to understand those individuals as embedded in or manipulating culturally shared ideas and practices.

The maintenance of a musical culture, however, is far from being a fully shared and coordinated community effort; it is often "intensely personal and idiosyncratic" in its workings, the result of specific relationships between particular teachers and students (Shelemay 1997: 199). Kay Kaufman Shelemay has remarked that during field research, abstract concepts such as "culture" and "field" inevitably dissolve into "a stream of individuals" with whom the researcher becomes entangled (p. 201). Culture, she suggests, can no longer be thought of as located in a spatial "field" or place where ethnomusicologists study. Rather, culture and field are better thought of as constituted in and through the relationships of individuals. Bruno Nettl (1984) has gone so far as to suggest that the discipline of ethnomusicology is largely defined by these idiosyncratic relationships between master teachers and their ethnomusicologist students. He suggests that the musicians with whom ethnomusicologists study are more than just teachers of individual researchers; they are also "teachers of the field," the primary sources of insight into the relationship between music and culture. It seems clear that while ethnomusicology shares with anthropology an interest in the general and comparable features of culture and society, ethnomusicologists possess an acute awareness, perhaps resulting from the ethnographic method or from the same cultural tropes employed by historical musicologists, of the significance of individuals—including themselves—both to their field research and to the cultures they represent. Still, we aver that the converse of Shelemay's formulation is also true. Ethnomusicologists' engagement with individuals, an inevitable and necessary consequence of information gathering during fieldwork, leads them into new entanglements with society and culture. Ethnomusicology's ongoing engagement with individuals has revealed the intensely personal aspects of culture and the fundamentally social aspects of the individual.

This paradoxical situation is evident in our sample of musical ethnographies. In spite of their long-standing and continuing focus on the social life of music and musicians, ethnomusicologists throughout our survey period have included individuals prominently in their books. This corpus, in fact, displays an interesting "curve": at either end of the sample, books that ignore individuals entirely and those that focus the entire narrative on a single individual, family, or ensemble represent only a small part of the corpus. The vast majority of books fall in the middle, using individuals in some important way for various narrative and theoretical purposes.

We found that the type of individual musician included in these books depends on the author's research goals. Studies of the history of traditions, including the encounter with modernity (about one-quarter of the corpus), focus on innovators who made stylistic breakthroughs that dealt with new, emerging cultural, social, political, and economic realities. Fully half of the books deal with key figures, knowledgeable and articulate musicians who occupy respected positions within a tradition, and who help the author make general points about the musical culture. The remaining quarter deal with average musicians and nonmusicians, or they ignore individual musicians altogether. These are narratives animated by themes and issues that trump the particular qualities of innovative or key musicians.

Since fieldwork is the central method used by ethnomusicologists to gather knowledge about musical cultures, it is not surprising that nearly two-thirds of the books feature face-to-face, direct encounters with the individuals featured in the writing. But given what seems to be an increasing concern with the writing of musical histories in ethnomusicology, it is understandable that in about a third of these musical ethnographies the authors complement their fieldwork by researching individuals through printed, archival, and recorded sources.

This study illustrates that the apparent paradox of the individual in ethnomusicology represents not an irresolvable problem, but rather a challenge that has spurred a variety of methodological, theoretical, and narrative solutions. The inclusion of individual musicians may result from ethnomusicologists' attempts to reconcile the particulars of fieldwork with cultural generalization. Individuals may also be included because ethnomusicologists, in their field studies, have been exposed to concepts of selfhood that undercut Western notions of individual autonomy and free agency. The attention to individuals in ethnomusicology also reflects a broader shift in the social sciences toward theories of agency, practice, power, and historical change. Theories of culture that account for modernity and globalization are impetuses as well. The notion that musical cultures are fragmented and deterritorialized seems to drive the now common—indeed, practically unavoidable—ethnomusicological study of individuals. No matter the reason, our survey of musical ethnographies points to how ethnomusicologists seek to understand the cultures and communities they study by paying careful and respectful attention to the individual musicians they encounter in their research.

## REFERENCES

Abu-Lughod, Lila. 1991. "Writing against Culture." In Richard G. Fox, ed., *Recapturing Anthropology: Working in the Present*. Santa Fe, NM: School of American Research Press, pp. 137–162.

Allgayer-Kaufmann, Regine. 1987. *O aboio: Der Gesang der Vaqueiros im Nordosten Brasiliens*. Hamburg: Karl Dieter Wagner.

Appadurai, Arjun. 1990. "Disjuncture and Difference in the Global Cultural Economy." *Public Culture* 2(2): 1–24.

———. 1991. "Global Ethnoscapes: Notes and Queries for a Transnational Anthropology." In Richard G. Fox, ed., *Recapturing Anthropology: Working in the Present*. Santa Fe, NM: School of American Research Press, pp. 191–210.

Averill, Gage. 1997. *A Day for the Hunter, a Day for the Prey: Popular Music and Power in Haiti*. Chicago: University of Chicago Press.

Baily, John. 2001. "Learning to Perform as a Research Technique in Ethnomusicology." *British Journal of Ethnomusicology* 10(2): 85–98.

Bakan, Michael B. 1999. *Music of Death and New Creation: Experiences in the World of Balinese Gamelan Beleganjur*. Chicago: University of Chicago Press.

Becker, Judith. 1980. *Traditional Music in Modern Java: Gamelan in a Changing Society*. Honolulu: University of Hawaii Press.

Berger, Harris M. 1999. *Metal, Rock and Jazz: Perception and the Phenomenology of Musical Experience*. Middletown, CT: Wesleyan University Press.

Berliner, Paul F. 1978. *The Soul of Mbira: Music and Traditions of the Shona People of Zimbabwe*. Berkeley: University of California Press.

Besmer, Fremont. 1983. *Horses, Musicians, and Gods: The Hausa Cult of Possession-Trance*. South Hadley, MA: Bergin and Garvey.

Blau, Dick, Charles Keil, Angeliki Keil, and Steven Feld. 2002. *Bright Balkan Morning: Romani Lives and the Power of Music in Greek Macedonia*. Middletown, CT: Wesleyan University Press.

Brinner, Benjamin. 1995. *Knowing Music, Making Music: Javanese Gamelan and the Theory of Musical Competence and Interaction*. Chicago: University of Chicago Press.

Browner, Tara. 2002. *Heartbeat of the People: Music and Dance of the Northern Pow-Wow*. Urbana: University of Illinois Press.

Capwell, Charles. 1986. *The Music of the Bauls of Bengal*. Kent, OH: Kent State University Press.

Chenoweth, Vida. 1979. *The Usarufas and Their Music*. Dallas: SIL Museum of Anthropology.

Clifford, James. 1981. "On Ethnographic Surrealism." *Comparative Studies in Society and History* 23(4): 539–564.

———. 1988. *The Predicament of Culture: Twentieth Century Ethnography, Literature, and Art*. Cambridge, MA: Harvard University Press.

Clifford, James, and George E. Marcus. 1986. *Writing Culture: The Poetics and Politics of Ethnography*. Berkeley: University of California Press.

Cooke, Peter. 1986. *The Fiddle Tradition of the Shetland Isles*. Cambridge: Cambridge University Press.

Coplan, David B. 1994. *In the Time of Cannibals: The Word Music of South Africa's Basotho Migrants*. Chicago: University of Chicago Press.

Coppet, Daniel de, and Hugo Zemp. 1978. *'Aré'aré: un peuple mélanésien et sa musique*. Paris: Éditions du Seuil.

Danielson, Virginia. 1997. *"The Voice of Egypt": Umm Kulthūm, Arabic Song, and Egyptian Society in the Twentieth Century*. Chicago: University of Chicago Press.

Erdman, Joan, with Zohra Segal. 1997. *Stages: The Art and Adventures of Zohra Segal*. New Delhi: Kali for Women.

Erlmann, Veit. 1996. *Nightsong: Performance, Power, and Practice in South Africa*. Chicago: University of Chicago Press.

Florine, Jane L. 2001. *Cuarteto Music and Dancing from Argentina: In Search of the Tunga-Tunga in Córdoba*. Gainesville: University Press of Florida.

Gourlay, Kenneth A. 1978. "Toward a Reassessment of the Ethnomusicologist's Role in Research." *Ethnomusicology* 22(1): 1–35.

Groemer, Gerald. 1999. *The Spirit of Tsugaru: Blind Musicians, Tsugaru-Jamisen, and the Folk Music of Northern Japan.* With the Autobiography of Takahashi Chikuzan. Warren, MI: Harmonie Park Press.

Hagedorn, Katherine J. 2001. *Divine Utterance: The Performance of Afro-Cuban Santería.* Washington, DC: Smithsonian Institution Press.

Hayward, Philip. 1998. *Music at the Borders: Not Drowning, Waving and Their Engagement with Papua New Guinean Culture (1986–96).* London: J. Libbey.

Herbst, Edward. 1997. *Voices in Bali: Energies and Perceptions in Vocal Music and Dance Theatre.* Middletown, CT: Wesleyan University Press.

Keil, Charles. 1979. *Tiv Song: The Sociology of Art in a Classless Society.* Chicago: University of Chicago Press.

Keyes, Cheryl L. 2002. *Rap Music and Street Consciousness.* Urbana: University of Illinois Press.

Kippen, James. 1988. *The Tabla of Lucknow: A Cultural Analysis of a Musical Tradition.* Cambridge: Cambridge University Press.

Kisliuk, Michelle. 1998. *Seize the Dance: BaAka Musical Life and the Ethnography of Performance.* New York and Oxford: Oxford University Press.

Levin, Theodore. 1996. *The Hundred Thousand Fools of God: Musical Travels in Central Asia (and Queens, New York).* Bloomington: Indiana University Press.

Lortat-Jacob, Bernard. 1995. *Sardinian Chronicles.* Chicago: University of Chicago Press.

Loza, Steven. 1999. *Tito Puente and the Making of Latin Music.* Urbana: University of Illinois Press.

Marcus, George E., and Michael M. J. Fischer. 1986. *Anthropology as Cultural Critique: An Experimental Moment in the Human Sciences.* Chicago: University of Chicago Press.

Merriam, Alan P. 1964. *The Anthropology of Music.* Evanston, IL: Northwestern University Press.

Mitchell, Frank. 1978. *Blessingway Singer: The Autobiography of Frank Mitchell, 1881– 1967,* edited by Charlotte Frisbie and David McAllester. Tucson: University of Arizona Press.

Moisala, Pirkko. 1991. *Cultural Cognition in Music: Continuity and Change in the Gurung Music of Nepal.* Jyväskylä, Finland: Gummerus Kirjapaino Oy.

Monson, Ingrid T. 1996. *Saying Something: Jazz Improvisation and Interaction.* Chicago: University of Illinois Press.

Muller, Carol Ann. 1999. *Rituals of Fertility and the Sacrifice of Desire: Nazarite Women's Performance in South Africa.* Chicago: University of Chicago Press.

Myers, Helen. 1998. *Music of Hindu Trinidad: Songs from the Indian Diaspora.* Chicago and London: University of Chicago Press.

Nettl, Bruno. 1984. "In Honor of Our Principal Teachers." *Ethnomusicology* 28(2): 173–185.

———. 2005. *The Study of Ethnomusicology: Thirty-One Issues and Concepts.* Urbana: University of Illinois Press.

Neuman, Daniel M. 1990 [1980]. *The Life of Music in North India: The Organization of an Artistic Tradition.* Chicago: University of Chicago Press.

Ortner, Sherry B. 1984. "Theory in Anthropology Since the Sixties." *Comparative Studies in Society and History* 26(1): 126–166.

———. 2006. *Anthropology and Social Theory: Culture, Power, and the Acting Subject.* Durham, NC: Duke University Press.

Pejcheva, Lozanka, and Ventsislav Dimov. 2002. *The Zurna Tradition of Southwest Bulgaria.* Sofia: Bulgarian Musicology Researches.

Peña, Manuel H. 1985. *The Texas-Mexican Conjunto: History of a Working-Class Music.* Austin: University of Texas Press.

Porter, James. 1995. *Jeannie Robertson: Emergent Singer, Transformative Voice.* Knoxville: University of Tennessee Press.

Pratt, Mary Louise. 1986. "Fieldwork in Common Places." In James Clifford and George E. Marcus, eds., *Writing Culture: The Poetics and Politics of Ethnography.* Berkeley: University of California Press, pp. 27–50.

Quigley, Colin. 1995. *Music from the Heart: Compositions of a Folk Fiddler.* Athens: University of Georgia Press.

Qureshi, Regula Burckhardt. 1986. *Sufi Music of India and Pakistan: Sound, Context and Meaning in Qawwali.* Chicago: University of Chicago Press.

Rees, Helen, ed. 2009. *Lives in Chinese Music.* Urbana: University of Illinois Press.

Reily, Suzel. 2002. *Voices of the Magi: Enchanted Journeys in Southeast Brazil.* Chicago: University of Chicago Press.

Rice, Timothy. 1987. "Towards a Remodeling of Ethnomusicology." *Ethnomusicology* 31(3): 469–488.

———. 1994. *May It Fill Your Soul: Experiencing Bulgarian Music.* Chicago: University of Chicago Press.

———. 2003. "Time, Place, and Metaphor in Musical Experience and Ethnography." *Ethnomusicology* 47(2): 151–179.

Romero, Raúl R. 2001. *Debating the Past: Music, Memory, and Identity in the Andes.* Oxford: Oxford University Press.

Schade-Poulsen, Marc. 1999. *Men and Popular Music in Algeria: The Social Significance of Raï.* Austin: University of Texas Press.

Schechter, John Mendell. 1992. *The Indispensable Harp: Historical Development, Modern Roles, and Configurations in Ecuador and Latin America.* Kent, OH: Kent State University Press.

Seeger, Anthony. 1987. *Why Suyá Sing: A Musical Anthropology of an Amazonian People.* Cambridge: Cambridge University Press.

Shelemay, Kay Kaufman. 1997. "The Ethnomusicologist, Ethnographic Method, and the Transmission of Tradition." In Gregory F. Barz and Timothy J. Cooley, eds., *Shadows in the Field: New Perspectives for Fieldwork in Ethnomusicology.* New York and Oxford: Oxford University Press, pp. 189–204.

———. 1998. *Let Jasmine Rain Down: Song and Remembrance among Syrian Jews.* Chicago: University of Chicago Press.

Simonett, Helena. 2001. *Banda: Mexican Musical Life Across Borders.* Middletown, CT: Wesleyan University Press.

Slobin, Mark. 1976. *Music in the Culture of Northern Afghanistan* (Viking Fund Publication in Anthropology No. 54). Tucson: University of Arizona Press.

———. 1989. *Chosen Voices: The Story of the American Cantorate*. Urbana and Chicago: University of Illinois Press.

———. 1993. *Subcultural Sounds: Micromusics of the West*. Hanover, NH: University Press of New England.

Stock, Jonathan P. J. 1996. *Musical Creativity in Twentieth-Century China: Abing, His Music, and Its Changing Meanings*. Rochester, NY: University of Rochester Press.

———. 2001. "Toward an Ethnomusicology of the Individual, or Biographical Writing in Ethnomusicology. *The World of Music* 43(1): 5–19.

Sugarman, Jane C. 1997. *Engendering Song: Singing and Subjectivity at Prespa Albanian Weddings*. Chicago: University of Chicago Press.

Titon, Jeff Todd. 1980. "The Life Story." *Journal of American Folklore* 93(369): 276–292.

———, ed. 1984. *Worlds of Music: An Introduction to the Music of the World's Peoples*. New York: Schirmer Books.

———. 1988. *Powerhouse for God: Speech, Chant, and Song in an Appalachian Baptist Church*. Austin: University of Texas Press.

Turino, Thomas. 2000. *Nationalists, Cosmopolitans, and Popular Music in Zimbabwe*. Chicago: University of Chicago Press.

Tyler, Stephen A. 1986. "Post-Modern Ethnography: From Document of the Occult to Occult Document." In James Clifford and George E. Marcus, eds., *Writing Culture: The Poetics and Politics of Ethnography*. Berkeley: University of California Press, pp. 122–140.

Vander, Judith. 1988. *Songprints: The Musical Experience of Five Shoshone Women*. Urbana: University of Illinois Press.

Vélez, Maria Teresa. 2000. *Drumming for the Gods: The Life and Times of Felipe Garcia Villamil*. Philadelphia: Temple University Press.

Walser, Robert. 1993. *Running with the Devil: Power, Gender, and Madness in Heavy Metal Music*. Hanover, NH: Wesleyan University Press.

Weisethaunet, Hans. 1998. *The Performance of Everyday Life: The Gäine of Nepal*. Oslo: Scandinavian University Press.

## LIST OF MUSICAL ETHNOGRAPHIES, 1976–2002

Agawu, Kofi. 1995. *African Rhythm: A Northern Ewe Perspective*. Cambridge: Cambridge University Press.

Askew, Kelly. 2002. *Performing the Nation: Swahili Music and Cultural Politics in Tanzania*. Chicago: University of Chicago Press.

Austerlitz, Paul. 1997. *Merengue: Dominican Music and Dominican Identity*. Philadelphia: Temple University Press.

Averill, Gage. 1997. *A Day for the Hunter, a Day for the Prey: Popular Music and Power in Haiti*. Chicago: University of Chicago Press.

Baily, John. 1988. *Music of Afghanistan: Professional Musicians in the City of Herat*. Cambridge and New York: Cambridge University Press.

Bakan, Michael B. 1999. *Music of Death and New Creation: Experiences in the World of Balinese Gamelan Beleganjur*. Chicago: University of Chicago Press.

Becker, Judith. 1980. *Traditional Music in Modern Java: Gamelan in a Changing Society*. Honolulu: University of Hawaii Press.

Berger, Harris M. 1999. *Metal, Rock, and Jazz: Perception and the Phenomenology of Musical Experience.* Middletown, CT: Wesleyan University Press.

Berliner, Paul F. 1978. *The Soul of Mbira: Music and Traditions of the Shona People of Zimbabwe.* Berkeley: University of California Press.

———. 1994. *Thinking in Jazz: The Infinite Art of Improvisation.* Chicago: University of Chicago Press.

Besmer, Fremont. 1983. *Horses, Musicians, and Gods: The Hausa Cult of Possession-Trance.* South Hadley, MA: Bergin and Garvey.

Blau, Dick, Charles Keil, Angeliki Keil, and Steven Feld. 2002. *Bright Balkan Morning: Romani Lives and the Power of Music in Greek Macedonia.* Middletown, CT: Wesleyan University Press.

Bohlman, Philip V. 1989. *Land Where Two Streams Flow: Music in the German-Jewish Community of Israel.* Chicago: University of Illinois Press.

Brinner, Benjamin. 1995. *Knowing Music, Making Music: Javanese Gamelan and the Theory of Musical Competence and Interaction.* Chicago: University of Chicago Press.

Browner, Tara. 2002. *Heartbeat of the People: Music and Dance of the Northern Pow-Wow.* Urbana: University of Illinois Press.

Capwell, Charles. 1986. *The Music of the Bauls of Bengal.* Kent, OH: Kent State University Press.

Charry, Eric. 2000. *Mande Music: Traditional and Modern Music of the Maninka and Mandinka of Western Africa.* Chicago: University of Chicago Press.

Chenoweth, Vida. 1979. *The Usarufas and Their Music.* Dallas: SIL Museum of Anthropology.

Chernoff, John Miller. 1979. *African Rhythm and African Sensibility: Aesthetics and Social Action in African Musical Idioms.* Chicago: University of Chicago Press.

Cooke, Peter. 1986. *The Fiddle Tradition of the Shetland Isles.* Cambridge: Cambridge University Press.

Coplan, David B. 1994. *In the Time of Cannibals: The Word Music of South Africa's Basotho Migrants.* Chicago: University of Chicago Press.

Danielson, Virginia. 1997. *"The Voice of Egypt": Umm Kulthūm, Arabic Song, and Egyptian Society in the Twentieth Century.* Chicago: University of Chicago Press.

Diehl, Keila. 2002. *Echoes from Dharamsala: Music in the Life of a Tibetan Refugee Community.* Berkeley: University of California Press.

Ellis, Catherine J. 1985. *Aboriginal Music, Education for Living: Cross-Cultural Experiences from South Australia.* St. Lucia: University of Queensland Press.

Emoff, Ron. 2002. *Recollecting from the Past: Musical Practice and Spirit Possession on the East Coast of Madagascar.* Middletown, CT: Wesleyan University Press.

Erlmann, Veit. 1996. *Nightsong: Performance, Power, and Practice in South Africa.* Chicago: University of Chicago Press.

Feld, Steven. 1982. *Sound and Sentiment: Birds, Weeping, Poetics and Song in Kaluli Expression.* Philadelphia: University of Pennsylvania Press.

Fikentscher, Kai. 2000. *"You Better Work!": Underground Dance Music in New York City.* Middletown, CT: Wesleyan University Press.

Florine, Jane L. 2001. *Cuarteto Music and Dancing from Argentina: In Search of the Tunga-Tunga in Córdoba.* Gainesville: University Press of Florida.

Friedson, Steven M. 1996. *Dancing Prophets: Musical Experience in Tumbuka Healing.* Chicago: University of Chicago Press.

Goertzen, Chris. 1997. *Fiddling for Norway: Revival and Identity.* Chicago: University of Chicago Press.

Groemer, Gerald. 1999. *The Spirit of Tsugaru: Blind Musicians, Tsugaru-jamisen, and the Folk Music of North Japan.* With the Autobiography of Takahashi Chikuzan. Warren, MI: Harmonie Park Press.

Guilbault, Jocelyne. 1993. *Zouk: World Music in the West Indies.* Chicago and London: University of Chicago Press.

Hagedorn, Katherine J. 2001. *Divine Utterance: The Performance of Afro-Cuban Santería.* Washington, DC: Smithsonian Institution Press.

Hamilton, James Sadler. 1989. *Sitar Music in Calcutta: An Ethnomusicological Study.* Calgary: University of Calgary Press.

Hayward, Philip. 1998. *Music at the Borders: Not Drowning, Waving and Their Engagement with Papua New Guinean Culture (1986–96).* Sydney: J. Libbey.

Herbst, Edward. 1997. *Voices in Bali: Energies and Perceptions in Vocal Music and Dance Theatre.* Middletown, CT: Wesleyan University Press.

Hernandez, Deborah Pacini. 1995. *Bachata: A Social History of Dominican Popular Music.* Philadelphia: Temple University Press.

Hopkins, Pandora. 1986. *Aural Thinking in Norway: Performance and Communication with the Hardingfele.* New York: Human Sciences Press.

Howard, James H., Victoria Lindsay Levine, and Bruno Nettl. 1997. *Choctaw Music and Dance.* Norman: University of Oklahoma Press.

Keeling, Richard. 1992. *Cry for Luck: Sacred Song and Speech among the Yurok, Hupa, and Karok Indians of Northwestern California.* Berkeley: University of California Press.

Keil, Charles. 1979. *Tiv Song: The Sociology of Art in a Classless Society.* Chicago: University of Chicago Press.

Keyes, Cheryl L. 2002. *Rap Music and Street Consciousness.* Urbana: University of Illinois Press.

Kingsbury, Henry. 1988. *Music, Talent, and Performance: A Conservatory Cultural System.* Philadelphia: Temple University Press.

Kippen, James. 1988. *The Tabla of Lucknow: A Cultural Analysis of a Musical Tradition.* Cambridge: Cambridge University Press.

Kisliuk, Michelle. 1998. *Seize the Dance: BaAka Musical Life and the Ethnography of Performance.* New York and Oxford: Oxford University Press.

Koskoff, Ellen. 2000. *Music in Lubavitcher Life.* Urbana: University of Illinois Press.

Lassiter, Luke E. 1998. *The Power of Kiowa Song: A Collaborative Ethnography.* Tucson: University of Arizona Press.

Levin, Theodore. 1996. *The Hundred Thousand Fools of God: Musical Travels in Central Asia (and Queens, New York).* Bloomington: Indiana University Press.

Lewis, J. Lowell. 1992. *Ring of Liberation: Deceptive Discourse in Brazilian Capoeira.* Chicago: University of Chicago Press.

Lortat-Jacob, Bernard. 1995. *Sardinian Chronicles.* Chicago: University of Chicago Press.

Loza, Steven. 1993. *Barrio Rhythm: Mexican American Music in Los Angeles.* Urbana and Chicago: University of Illinois Press.

———. 1999. *Tito Puente and the Making of Latin Music.* Urbana: University of Illinois Press.

MacKinnon, Niall. 1993. *The British Folk Scene: Musical Performance and Social Identity.* Buckingham: Open University Press.

MacLeod, Bruce A. 1993. *Club Date Musicians: Playing the New York Party Circuit.* Urbana: University of Illinois Press.

Manuel, Peter. 1993. *Cassette Culture: Popular Music and Technology in North India.* Chicago: University of Chicago Press.

———. 2000. *East Indian Music in the West Indies: Tan-Singing, Chutney, and the Making of Indo-Caribbean Culture.* Philadelphia: Temple University Press.

McLean, Mervyn. 1996. *Maori Music.* Auckland: Auckland University Press.

Mitchell, Frank. 1978. *Blessingway Singer: The Autobiography of Frank Mitchell, 1881–1967*, edited by Charlotte Frisbie and David McAllester. Tucson: University of Arizona Press.

Moisala, Pirkko. 1991. *Cultural Cognition in Music: Continuity and Change in the Gurung Music of Nepal.* Jyväskylä, Finland: Gummerus Kirjapaino Oy.

Monson, Ingrid T. 1996. *Saying Something: Jazz Improvisation and Interaction.* Chicago: University of Chicago Press.

Moyle, Richard M. 1979. *Songs of the Pintupi: Musical Life in a Central Australian Society.* Canberra: Australian Institute of Aboriginal Studies.

———. 1986. *Alyawarra Music: Songs and Society in a Central Australian Community.* Canberra: Australian Institute of Aboriginal Studies.

Muller, Carol Ann. 1999. *Rituals of Fertility and the Sacrifice of Desire: Nazarite Women's Performance in South Africa.* Chicago: University of Chicago Press.

Myers, Helen. 1998. *Music of Hindu Trinidad: Songs from the Indian Diaspora.* Chicago and London: University of Chicago Press.

Nelson, Kristina. 1985. *The Art of Reciting the Qur'an.* Austin: University of Texas Press.

Nettl, Bruno. 1995. *Heartland Excursions: Ethnomusicological Reflections on Schools of Music.* Urbana: University of Illinois Press.

Neuman, Daniel M. 1990 [1980]. *The Life of Music in North India: The Organization of an Artistic Tradition.* Chicago: University of Chicago Press.

Olsen, Dale A. 1996. *Music of the Warao of Venezuela: Song People of the Rain Forest.* Gainesville: University Press of Florida.

Pegg, Carole. 2001. *Mongolian Music, Dance, & Oral Narrative: Performing Diverse Identities.* Seattle: University of Washington Press.

Pejcheva, Lozanka, and Ventsislav Dimov. 2002. *The Zurna Tradition of Southwest Bulgaria.* Sofia: Bulgarian Musicology Researches.

Peña, Manuel H. 1985. *The Texas-Mexican Conjunto: History of a Working-Class Music.* Austin: University of Texas Press.

———. 1999. *The Mexican American Orquesta: Music, Culture, and the Dialectic of Conflict.* Austin: University of Texas Press.

Porter, James. 1995. *Jeannie Robertson: Emergent Singer, Transformative Voice.* Knoxville: University of Tennessee Press.

Quigley, Colin. 1995. *Music from the Heart: Compositions of a Folk Fiddler.* Athens: University of Georgia Press.

Qureshi, Regula Burckhardt. 1986. *Sufi Music of India and Pakistan: Sound, Context, and Meaning in Qawwali*. Chicago: University of Chicago Press.

Rees, Helen. 2000. *Echoes of History: Naxi Music in Modern China*. New York and Oxford: Oxford University Press.

Reily, Suzel. 2002. *Voices of the Magi: Enchanted Journeys in Southeast Brazil*. Chicago: University of Chicago Press.

Reyes, Adelaida. 1999. *Songs of the Caged, Songs of the Free: Music and the Vietnamese Refugee Experience*. Philadelphia: Temple University Press.

Rice, Timothy. 1994. *May It Fill Your Soul: Experiencing Bulgarian Music*. Chicago: University of Chicago Press.

Romero, Raúl R. 2001. *Debating the Past: Music, Memory, and Identity in the Andes*. Oxford: Oxford University Press

Roseman, Marina. 1991. *Healing Sounds from the Malaysian Rain Forest: Temiar Music and Medicine*. Berkeley: University of California Press.

Sakata, Hiromi Lorraine. 1983. *Music in the Mind: The Concepts of Music and Musician in Afghanistan*. Kent, OH: Kent State University Press.

Sarkissian, Margaret. 2000. *D'Albuquerque's Children: Performing Tradition in Malaysia's Portuguese Settlement*. Chicago: University of Chicago Press.

Schade-Poulsen, Marc. 1999. *Men and Popular Music in Algeria: The Social Significance of Raï*. Austin: University of Texas Press.

Schechter, John Mendell. 1992. *The Indispensable Harp: Historical Development, Modern Roles, and Configurations in Ecuador and Latin America*. Kent, OH: Kent State University Press.

Seeger, Anthony. 1987. *Why Suyá Sing: A Musical Anthropology of an Amazonian People*. Cambridge: Cambridge University Press.

Shelemay, Kay Kaufman. 1998. *Let Jasmine Rain Down: Song and Remembrance among Syrian Jews*. Chicago: University of Chicago Press

Simonett, Helena. 2001. *Banda: Mexican Musical Life Across Borders*. Middletown, CT: Wesleyan University Press.

Slobin, Mark. 1976. *Music in the Culture of Northern Afghanistan* (Viking Fund Publication in Anthropology No. 54). Tucson: University of Arizona Press.

———. 1989. *Chosen Voices: The Story of the American Cantorate*. Urbana and Chicago: University of Illinois Press.

———. 2000. *Fiddler on the Move Exploring the Klezmer World*. New York and Oxford: Oxford University Press.

Stock, Jonathan P. J. 1996. *Musical Creativity in Twentieth-century China: Abing, His Music, and Its Changing Meaning*. Rochester, NY: University of Rochester Press.

Stokes, Martin. 1992. *The Arabesk Debate: Music and Musicians in Modern Turkey*. Oxford: Clarendon Press.

Stone, Ruth M. 1982. *Let the Inside Be Sweet: The Interpretation of Music Event Among the Kpelle People of Liberia*. Bloomington: Indiana University Press.

Sugarman, Jane C. 1997. *Engendering Song: Singing and Subjectivity at Prespa Albanian Weddings*. Chicago: University of Chicago Press.

Summit, Jeffrey A. 2000. *The Lord's Song in a Strange Land: Music and Identity in Contemporary Jewish Worship*. Oxford and New York: Oxford University Press.

Sutton, R. Anderson. 1991. *Traditions of Gamelan Music in Java: Musical Pluralism and Regional Identity.* Cambridge: Cambridge University Press.

———. 2002. *Calling Back the Spirit: Music, Dance, and Cultural Politics in Lowland South Sulawesi.* Oxford: Oxford University Press.

Tenzer, Michael. 2000. *Gamelan Gong Kebyar: The Art of Twentieth-Century Balinese Music.* Chicago: University of Chicago Press.

Titon, Jeff Todd. 1988. *Powerhouse for God: Speech, Chant, and Song in an Appalachian Baptist Church.* Austin: University of Texas Press.

Turino, Thomas. 1993. *Moving Away from Silence: Music of the Peruvian Altiplano and the Experience of Urban Migration.* Chicago: University of Chicago Press.

———. 2000. *Nationalist, Cosmopolitans, and Popular Music in Zimbabwe.* Chicago: University of Chicago Press.

Vander, Judith. 1988. *Songprints: The Musical Experience of Five Shoshone Women.* Urbana: University of Illinois Press.

———. 1997. *Shoshone Ghost Dance Religion: Poetry Songs and Great Basin Context.* Urbana: University of Illinois Press.

Vélez, Maria Teresa. 2000. *Drumming for the Gods: The Life and Times of Felipe Garcia Villamil.* Philadelphia: Temple University Press.

Wade, Peter. 2000. *Music, Race, and Nation: Música Tropical in Colombia.* Chicago: University of Chicago Press.

Walser, Robert. 1993. *Running with the Devil: Power, Gender, and Madness in Heavy Metal Music.* Hanover, NH: Wesleyan University Press.

Waterman, Christopher Alan. 1990. *Jùjú: A Social History and Ethnography of an African Popular Music.* Chicago: University of Chicago Press.

Waxer, Lise. 2002. *The City of Musical Memory: Salsa, Record Groove and Popular Culture in Cali, Columbia.* Middletown, CT: Wesleyan University Press.

Weisethaunet, Hans. 1998. *The Performance of Everyday Life: The Gäine of Nepal.* Oslo: Scandinavian University Press.

Williams, Sean. 2001. *The Sound of the Ancestral Ship: Highland Music of West Java.* Oxford: Oxford University Press.

Witzleben, J. Lawrence. 1995. *Silk and Bamboo Music in Shanghai: The Jiangnan Sizhu Ensemble Tradition.* Kent, OH: Kent State University Press.

Wong, Deborah. 2000. *Sounding the Center: History and Aesthetics in Thai Buddhist Performance.* Chicago: University of Chicago Press.

Yung, Bell. 1989. *Cantonese Opera: Performance as a Creative Process.* Cambridge: Cambridge University Press.

Zanten, Wim van. 1989. *Sundanese Music in the Cianjuran Style: Anthropological and Musicological Aspects of Tembang Sunda.* Providence, RI: Foris Publications.

# Ethnomusicology
# in Times of Trouble

I am not quite sure when the world fell apart. When I began my study of ethnomusicology in 1968, there was a great deal of excitement and optimism about this relatively new field of study, even though the United States was in the middle of a horrible war in Vietnam. It seemed that, as we say in English, "the world was our oyster." We could apparently go anywhere (with the possible exception of Vietnam) and study any music that struck our fancy. Since then, however, not only has this naïve optimism and energy been subjected to a withering postcolonial critique but, especially since the end of the Cold War in 1991, the situation for many people in the world seems only to be getting worse and worse, making the prospect of doing fieldwork in a growing number of places in the world nearly unimaginable. For a few people, our personal worlds have probably improved during this period, but what of the rest of the world, including the poor and unfortunate in our own countries? The United Nations today lists more than sixty countries in which there is open, armed conflict between groups or between resistance groups and the government. The HIV/AIDS pandemic has wracked some parts of the world, most notably Africa. All reports indicate that the gap between rich and poor is growing, both in developed, capitalist countries and between rich and poor regions of the world. Climate change seems to be posing an ever more obvious threat to life on our planet, and rising ocean water levels are causing some people in the Pacific to plan for a future far from their native atolls. Where can we go to work ethnomusicologically today, and what kind of work should we be doing there?[1]

---

1. This chapter is a revision of a paper presented at the 2013 World Conference of the International Council for Traditional Music (ICTM) in a panel on "new research." I began with

It is my contention in this chapter that only in the last fifteen years or so have ethnomusicologists fully embraced a new set of themes concerning the relationship of music to the social, political, economic, and ecological crises facing so many people in today's world, a set of themes that constitutes a new form of ethnomusicology in times (and places) of trouble.[2] These new themes represent a major break, it seems to me, from the way ethnomusicology was conducted for the first half century of its history beginning in 1950.

More than twenty years ago, by the early 1990s, anthropologists already had a long history of reporting on the very real world of traditional societies beset by modernization and globalization in various forms: disease, exploitation of formerly pristine forests and lands, missionization, the impact of oppressive government regimes and policies, the shock of war, and on and on. Twenty years ago I could not find much evidence that ethnomusicologists had, in fact, begun such work. Back then I wondered when we in ethnomusicology would start conducting such studies, and why we had not already begun.[3] It is clear now that only recently have ethnomusicologists begun to engage in a sustained way with music's role in solving or worsening contemporary social, economic, political, and ecological problems, and it is this work that I am reviewing in this chapter.

this brief introduction: "The 'new research' that I want to talk about today is most emphatically not my own new research. It is new research being done by members of ICTM, many of whom are in the audience today. The new research that I am singling out for attention concerns the study of music in places and times of trouble, and I intend my comments to honour their pioneering work."

2. Ethnomusicologists, in their attempt to understand the relationship between music and the cultural, social, economic, and political processes it reflects and influences, typically organize their work around one or more particular themes or issues. Alan Merriam, in his 1964 book *The Anthropology of Music,* provided probably the first extended list of such themes, twelve in number, for the nascent field: (1) shared cultural concepts about music, (2) the relationship between aural and other modes of perception (synesthesia), (3) physical and verbal behavior in relation to music, (4) musicians as a social group, (5) the teaching and learning of music, (6) the process of composition, (7) the study of song texts, (8) the uses and functions of music, (9) music as symbolic behavior (the meaning of music), (10) aesthetics and the interrelationship of the arts, (11) music and culture history, and (12) music and cultural dynamics. Ethnomusicologists have added significantly to this list in the half century since Merriam published his seminal view of the field.

3. David McDonald asked a related question a few years ago: "Why haven't ethnomusicologists sought to understand the histories of death, displacement, and dispossession effecting and affecting the societies within which they work?" (2009: 59). John Morgan O'Connell wrote, "The study of music in war and music for peace has received surprisingly little attention in ethnomusicology" (2011: 112), and Margaret Kartomi, before a helpful review of war- and peace-related studies in ethnomusicology, claimed that "ethnomusicology has neglected war and peace studies" (2010a: 453).

Why has it taken so long for ethnomusicologists, and only a few of them at that, to come to grips with an ethnomusicology of troubled times and places? I think there are five principal reasons for this delay. First, ethnomusicologists often, but not always, conduct their research on music that they love. That is, many of us are moved, first of all, by the sensual and aesthetic pleasure that music provides and only later come to the intellectual and social themes and questions that an anthropology of music investigates. Second, music is associated, in the anglophone imagination, with good things; "that's music to my ears" goes the common expression when hearing felicitous news (cf. Nettl 2005: 18). So the possibility that music can be associated with the worst aspects of human existence is neither attractive nor intuitive. Third, ethnomusicological paradigms suggest that music is produced principally in stable social settings where an entire society, an effective government, or a few wealthy patrons support music making. When societies fall apart under the pressure of war, violence, widespread illness, unrest among minority groups, or ecological devastation, it may surpass our imagination that music will be produced in such settings. A fourth reason, perhaps, is that in the early days of ethnomusicology, scholars concerned themselves primarily with what the International Council for Traditional Music (ICTM) labels "traditional music" performed in traditional settings. This predisposition may have led us to ignore the new genres and styles of music necessary to deal psychologically, emotionally, and socially with contemporary real-world problems. Fifth, it is hard to imagine working in unstable and dangerous environments that lack the infrastructure to support safe research conditions and that harbor distracted populations unable to engage productively with music researchers. All of these reasons seem to have combined to make ethnomusicologists slow, compared to their colleagues in anthropology, to deal with the severe problems facing people around the world, and to consider how music is being used to ameliorate or to exacerbate those problems.

A brief review of the literature reveals that concern for the study of music in times and places of trouble began relatively recently. Some of the earliest studies originated in the countries that emerged from the fire of war in the former Yugoslavia. Perhaps predictably, the first ethnomusicologists to deal with the impact of war on music were those living amidst its terrors and consequences, not those with the freedom and the money to travel abroad to study music in a "foreign" culture—ethnomusicologists like me, in other words. These studies from the countries of the former Yugoslavia first appeared in English in 1998 when Croatian scholars who had lived through the horrible, ethnic-cleansing wars attending the break-up of Yugoslavia in the 1990s published a heart-felt collection of essays called *Music, Politics, and War: Views from Croatia*, edited by Svanibor Pettan (1998a). A year later, American ethnomusicologist Adelaida

Reyes (1999) wrote a book-length study of the music of refugees from Vietnam. These were among the earliest harbingers of a move in this new direction in ethnomusicological study. A review of the major journals in our field since the late 1990s reveals surprisingly few studies that continue this line, but about a decade later a number of edited collections of essays on these themes appeared, including *Music in the Post–9/11 World*, edited by Jonathan Ritter and J. Martin Daughtry (2007); *The Oxford Handbook of Medical Ethnomusicology*, edited by Benjamin D. Koen (2008); *Music and Conflict*, edited by John Morgan O'Connell and Salwa El-Shawan Castelo-Branco (2010); *Applied Ethnomusicology: Historical and Contemporary Approaches*, edited by Klisala Harrison et al. (2010); and *The Culture of AIDS in Africa: Hope and Healing in Music and the Arts*, edited by Gregory Barz and Judah M. Cohen (2011).

As ethnomusicologists absorb studies of these new themes, at least three questions ought to be asked about them, questions that place this research in the larger context of the history of the field of ethnomusicology. First, will an ethnomusicology of times and places of trouble change our theories and methods in any way? Second, can our understanding of the nature of music, built up in countless studies conducted in relatively peaceful, stable settings, prove helpful in ameliorating cases of conflict, violence, disease, and social disruption? Third, how will the study of music in times and places of trouble affect our understanding of the nature of human music making? I provide preliminary answers to these three questions by examining six themes that constitute what I am calling an ethnomusicology in times of trouble: (1) music, war, and conflict; (2) music, forced migration, and minority studies; (3) music, disease, and healing; (4) music in particular tragedies; (5) music, violence, and poverty; and (6) music, climate change, and the environment.

Before I begin, here are two caveats.

First, although many of the studies I cite have an applied aspect to them, this chapter is not about applied ethnomusicology per se. The subfield of applied ethnomusicology may be traced to a set of influential articles on the topic by Jeff Todd Titon, Daniel Sheehy, Bess Lomax Hawes, Anthony Seeger, and Martha Ellen Davis in a special issue of *Ethnomusicology* in 1992 devoted to "music and the public interest" (Titon 1992).[4] Many of these articles focus on sustainability and preservation of traditions, particularly in the Americas. Beginning

---

4. Applied ethnomusicology, by other names, has a history that goes back at least into the early twentieth century. It includes the work of Charles Seeger and John and Alan Lomax, in the United States, and the work of musical folklorists in Europe intent on finding ways, often through arrangements, choreographies, amateur and professional performance ensembles, and festivals, to keep rural, village traditions alive both for their own sake and in the interest of national identity.

in the late 1990s, applied ethnomusicologists from central and southeastern Europe extended applied projects to "life-challenging" problems in troubled places in their backyards (Pettan 2008). The literature in applied ethnomusicology has many strains: from those who suggest all of our work is applied in some ways to those who restrict it to engagement with systemic social change; from those who view it as serving a "higher purpose" than academic work to those who are leery of making a sharp distinction between pure and applied research; from those who view it as an alternate career to those who regard it as a cherished aspect of their scholarly and pedagogical persona; from those helping to preserve traditions threatened principally by modernization to those working in areas threatened by war, violence, disease, and climate change; and from those who regard applied ethnomusicologists as selfless and theoretical ethnomusicologists as selfish to those who worry that applied ethnomusicologists are caught in the same webs of self-interest as supposedly pure researchers. Harrison sums up the variety in the field, writing that "applied ethnomusicology currently consists of a series of applied ethnomusicologies" (2012: 525).[5]

Second, for the poor, dispossessed, and oppressed in this world, every day is a time of trouble. Such troubles have their roots in time immemorial and are hardly the product of the last twenty years or so. Ethnomusicologists, since the beginning, have studied musical traditions that flourish in environments of relative poverty and want. Rather than focus on the below-standard material and spiritual conditions of the music makers, however, we have a long history of celebrating the richness of the music created under these conditions and its presumed psychological, cultural, and social benefits. In the United States, the musical traditions of African Americans are perhaps the *locus classicus* of these kinds of studies. The musical richness of communities in most of the cases of poverty familiar to ethnomusicologists is so great that even insiders, who are relatively poor in economic terms, do not view themselves as impoverished in cultural terms (Dirksen 2013; Titon 2013a). What may be different in today's times of trouble is that more people live in "absolute poverty" than ever before, while the "relative poverty" of others is sinking lower and lower (see Harrison 2013b for the distinction between absolute and relative poverty). It may be that

---

5. Useful recent histories, overviews, and definitions of applied ethnomusicology include Pettan (2008), Harrison and Pettan (2010), Hofman (2010), Van Buren (2010), Harrison (2012), and Dirksen (2012b), as well as the websites of the Society for Ethnomusicology (SEM) Applied Ethnomusicology Section, founded in 1998, and the ICTM Study Group on Applied Ethnomusicology, founded in 2007. For the ethical and applied implications of "pure" research, see Hellier-Tinoco (2003), Seeger (2008), and Berger (2014). Other recent publications related to this field include special issues of *Folklore Forum* (Fenn 2003); *Muzikološki Zbornik/Musicological Annual* 44(1) (Pettan 2008); and the *Yearbook for Traditional Music* devoted to music and poverty (Harrison 2013a).

a third category of psychological or cultural poverty, including the denial of human rights, upward social mobility, occupational choice, freedom to construct one's own identity, and access to cultural expressions such as music, is worsening in these times of trouble as well.

## MUSIC, WAR, AND CONFLICT

Working in war zones, post–war zones, and other places of violence, conflict, and profound loss has led many ethnomusicologists to design or participate in practical projects to ameliorate the conflict, heal the wounds of loss and separation, and, as John M. O'Connell puts it, "promot[e] a functional harmony . . . where groups in conflict achieve inter-communal understanding through sonic expression" (2011: 116). He believes that ethnomusicology is the ideal discipline for creating projects that "offer[] parity of esteem to the musical traditions of communities in conflict" (p. viii). On the other hand, one of the sobering realizations brought to the fore in these studies is that groups in conflict often use music to shut out, antagonize, exacerbate differences from, terrorize, and even torture "others," while ethnomusicologists, and those favoring peace, generally believe that music is an ideal expressive form for conflict resolution, intercultural understanding, and healing.[6] As O'Connell puts it, music is "a double-edged sword used both as a poison to excite hostility and as a potion to foster friendship" (2011: 117).

In Northern Ireland, during the "Troubles" between Catholic Republicans and Protestant Unionists from the 1960s to the 1990s, Protestant extremists used loud fife-and-drum bands to mark places as their own on certain holidays, throwing music in the faces (ears) of those they opposed and terrorizing them with their loud iconic threats of military-style violence. The 1998 peace accords that brought an end to the violence did not end the use of music as a marker of ethnic difference. They also put in place mechanisms for supporting and funding cultural distinctions in music created during the Troubles. This is worrisome since, as David Cooper reports, "the danger inherent in [their] long-term use is the maintenance of a silo mentality and the establishment of a further site of conflict, in which our 'Ulster-Scots' music is placed in opposition to their 'Irish' music" (2010: 103).[7]

6. On the US government's use of music as torture in its wars in Afghanistan and Iran, see Cusick (2006).

7. See also O'Connell (2011) for the use of nationalist discourses on traditional music in the Republic of Ireland to create a symbolically violent and personally troubling distinction between an Irish us and an English other.

In a study of Palestinian people's everyday experience of violence, David McDonald (2009) argues that the study of musical performance can extend and contribute to theories of the political and economic causes and effects of violence being developed in other disciplines. Viewing violent behavior and mimetic performances of violence as part of a coherent system "laden with cultural meaning" (p. 59), he argues that ethnomusicologists, with their theoretical understanding of the effects of musical performance on identities and subjectivities, can contribute to "theorizing the performative capacities of violence and . . . the meanings violent performances carry for victims, perpetrators, and witnesses alike" (cf. Loza et al. 1994). He explores the intricate way that stone-throwing violence, musical performances as "a form of cultural violence," and other expressive genres like film, dance, graffiti, posters, funerals, and literature are symbolically coherent (McDonald 2009: 60). A Palestinian musician corroborated McDonald's reading of music "as direct (violent) encounters with occupation forces," stating, "I know exactly what my music can do. . . . Music is resistance . . . What I do on stage and what martyrs do on the streets are one and the same, just with different instruments" (pp. 58, 61).

Some ethnomusicologists have reported on the devastating effects of war on traditional musical practices. In Afghanistan, for example, the Taliban banned most music making, and Islamists transformed romantic songs into laments and tales of heroism. Even after the end of Taliban rule, music teachers were hard to find, since so many musicians had emigrated. Veronica Doubleday concludes that "the constant, destructive presence of armed conflict needs to end if Afghanistan's remarkable musical culture is to regenerate fully and flower again" (2007: 309). In a similar vein, Margaret Kartomi (2010a, 2010b) reports that the long civil strife in the province of Aceh, Indonesia, between Muslim separatists and the government, especially between 1989 and 2004, caused most local musical activities, such as music for weddings, circumcisions, and other festivals, to come to a complete halt because people felt insecure. The government censored the performance of songs supporting the separatists, as well as religiously based songs and rituals, and only a few government-sponsored events were held. The dearth of performance opportunities led to a significant decline in the quality of performances. At the theoretical level she suggests that "to understand the effects of war on the performing arts in society it is necessary to analyse the cause(s) of the conflict, the type(s) of military personnel engaged, and the waxing and waning intensity of the war" (Kartomi 2010a: 474). After listing a number of wars and post–war zones that are in need of study, Kartomi concludes that

the collective research task is enormous, given the fact that wars show no sign of reducing in number and intensity across the globe. Concerned ethnomusicologists arguably need to step up their studies of this area of human engagement, at least until humankind finds a way of substantially reducing, and even abolishing, war altogether. (p. 478)

Studying music in places and times of trouble has also led some ethnomusicologists to broaden their studies beyond musical sound to the study of sound in general. J. Martin Daughtry (2012), for example, has studied the sound world of soldiers in Iraq and Afghanistan. He describes how they are trained to discern the specific nature of the threat to their lives by distinguishing between the sounds of incoming fire. How far is it away from them? Is it celebratory fire or hostile fire? Is it small-arms fire or artillery fire? These are life-or-death sonic distinctions of greater importance than learning to distinguish between the major and the minor modes. The soldiers then adapt this training to their musical experiences, teaching themselves how to listen simultaneously to music on headsets, often to pump themselves up for battle, and still discern external threats by listening to the sonic environment beyond their headsets. It seems inevitable that our studies of music in times and places of violence and war will lead us to broaden the scope of our studies to the sonic environment in which musical life occurs.

## MUSIC, FORCED MIGRATION, AND MINORITY STUDIES

Wars and other forms of conflict, as well as economic deprivation, often force people to migrate from their homelands to other parts of the world, where they not infrequently become unwelcome minorities within nation-states defined by nationalist ideology as coterminous with the majority nationality. In one strain of research on such people, they form culturally productive diaspora communities and maintain relationships with homelands, a process that protects them, spiritually at least, from the predations of unfriendly local actors or the sense of loss they endure. Much research in this domain celebrates the dynamic musical lives that diaspora communities are able to create, often in societies that define themselves as multicultural rather than mononational (Levin 1996; Sugarman 1997; Shelemay 1998). A second strain of research has been dealing with the relatively recent times of trouble in Europe, where the wars in the 1990s in the former Yugoslavia and economic opportunity in the European Union have attracted migrants from eastern and southeastern Europe, the Middle East, and Africa. The problems these immigrants encounter are so stark and pervasive that the ICTM created a study group on the music of minorities. One of the important legacies of this research problem is the strong strain of "applied" research that it has engendered. Two examples indicate the general direction of this research.

In the wake of the wars attending the break-up of the former Yugoslavia, Svanibor Pettan (1998b, 2010) produced CDs, films, and other publications aimed principally at policymakers to educate them about the plight of Roma (Gypsy) musicians displaced by the war between Serbs and Albanians in Kosovo. In another project designed to deal with the feelings of loss and separation felt by those forced to leave Bosnia because of the war, he worked in Norway to create musical bridges between Bosnian immigrants and Norwegians through shared musical performances of Bosnian repertoire. His goals included "strengthening Bosnian cultural identity" in their new home and "enlightening majority groups" about the plight of immigrant minorities in their midst. Pettan, acting on what he calls "an ethnomusicology of conscience," employed an ethnomusicological understanding, developed in myriad studies of traditional music, of one of the ways music functions for human groups: to communicate across social and ontological boundaries. He believes that carefully defined musical projects can ameliorate the problems faced by those displaced by war.[8]

In Austria, Ursula Hemetek (2006, 2010) has devoted much of her career to championing the plight of non-German minorities, some of them autochthonous and some recent migrants from southeastern Europe and Turkey. Her many projects, in collaboration with other Austrian ethnomusicologists and civic and governmental organizations, include collecting and publishing Styrian Slovene songs to prove that these people have their own language and culture and are thus worthy of being recognized as a *Volksgruppe* under Austrian law and of enjoying the rights associated with that status; presenting concerts of Turkish musicians in Vienna to help overcome negative stereotypes in the wake of 9/11; and helping new Roma immigrants from southeastern Europe establish their identity as a *Volksgruppe*.

In the postcommunist era, the Roma of eastern and southeastern Europe have had to endure debilitating poverty and racial discrimination in employment. No longer guaranteed jobs and safety as they were under communist governments, many have left their home countries in search of money and a better life in the European Union. Now there, the problems they faced at home have not faded; rather, the Roma are typically viewed as a criminal group without a culture of their own. As Hemetek (2006: 36) points out, the problem for minorities is domination by and subordination to dominant groups. She and others took on the project of helping them enact their self-identity and demonstrate their culture to an Austrian audience and government to secure the privileges of recognized "ethnic groups" in Austria. The process began in 1989 after a Roma youth was denied entry to a disco because of his race. The first

8. See Sweers (2010) for a similar intervention by an ethnomusicologist working in Germany.

Romani political organization in Austria was founded shortly after the incident, with the goal of achieving recognition as a *"Volksgruppe,* a political category in Austria granting certain rights to ethnic minority groups" (p. 43), including government funds to preserve their culture and the inclusion of their language in elementary schools where they live. The organization understood that they would have to make public in-group markers of ethnicity such as language and music and that ethnomusicologists could help them to do so. In 1990, scholars and community organizers developed what Daniel Sheehy calls "new 'frames' for musical performance" for non-Roma listeners at folk festivals and in schools (1992: 330). These and other efforts, such as making recordings, were a success in the sense that Roma were accorded the status of a *Volksgruppe* in 1993, and "to a certain extent Romani culture has become part of Austrian national consciousness" (Hemetek 2006: 48). Unfortunately, this has not prevented discrimination and violence against the Roma; in 1995, a right-wing terrorist bomb killed four Roma. One of the theoretical implications of Hemetek's work with Roma immigrants to Austria is connected to her observation that many young Roma do not value what some scholars might call traditional music. Instead, they seek to make their music "as modern as possible." So one of the first cultural reactions to the bomb attack was "a rap in German as a political statement against racism" (p. 51). In her conclusion she writes, "Researchers should no longer expect 'difference' or the 'exotic' as the starting point; rather, strategies have to change according to political realities" (p. 53).

## MUSIC, DISEASE, AND HEALING

Ethnomusicologists have long been interested in the relationship between music, illness, and healing. However, only recently have they finally turned their attention to what role music might play in dealing with diseases and health issues that help to constitute times of trouble, in particular the global HIV/AIDS pandemic. In the case of HIV/AIDS, many local eastern and southern African musicians, community groups, and health organizations are using music, dance, and theater to educate people about the clinical reality of the disease in a context where public policy and cultural ideologies combine to obfuscate the causes of the disease and deceive people into ignoring safe sexual practices.[9]

Gregory Barz (2011) describes how songs have been utilized in Uganda to deal with HIV/AIDS through health education, biomedical interventions, and

---

9. See Barz (2006) and Van Buren (2010) for reports on their efforts to help locals in Africa and in England caught in the grip of this disease.

promotion of communication about disease, and as a way of linking children to their history. Barz is optimistic about music's efficacy in this case, arguing that musical interventions, in conjunction with governmental and medical programs, can be part of the solution. Partly as a consequence of musical interventions in this context, the incidence of HIV/AIDS has dropped significantly in Uganda over the last two decades. On the other hand, Ric Alviso (2011), working in Zimbabwe, described a very different situation. The government there, preoccupied with other issues and perhaps inclined to see HIV/AIDS as another plague that colonialism has visited on them, has largely ignored the problem. Talk about it has been veiled in an embarrassed silence. One musical artist, the so-called "queen of the *mbira*," performed a song with her band about HIV/AIDS hoping to educate people about condom use and other safe-sex practices. Sadly and ironically, all the members of her band died of AIDS, and Alviso concludes that music alone was not an agent of change in this cultural context. In comparing the case in Uganda with the one in Zimbabwe, we can perhaps conclude that in the former case music participated in the construction of a new "cultural system" of safe sexual practices. In Zimbabwe, on the other hand, there was not a culture of change, and musical performance seems to have been ineffective on its own in provoking or "constructing" new cultural attitudes and practices. Here is a real-world challenge to ethnomusicologists' claims about the potential for music to model new and perhaps yet unimagined modes of cultural and social behavior. Such instances might cause us to modify this claim about the nature of music in light of this and other apparently negative instances that may come to light in the future as we accumulate more case studies of music in times of trouble.

## MUSIC IN PARTICULAR TRAGEDIES

It would be difficult to claim that there has been a rise in the number of environmental tragedies that people have had to deal with, but in the last decade or so three of them have received worldwide and ethnomusicological attention: (1) Hurricane Katrina's ruin of New Orleans in 2004 (Spitzer 2006), (2) the Indian Ocean tsunami of 2004 (Kartomi 2010a, 2010b), and (3) the earthquake in Haiti in 2010 (Dirksen 2012a, 2013). Dirksen's studies document remarkable instances, both before and after the earthquake in Haiti, where "several groups engaged in the rawest form of grassroots organizing" by "band[ing] together to tackle neighborhood problems" and engaging in both music making and community service (Dirksen 2012a). Such organizations include a classical music school in Cité Soleil that offers students music lessons and the chance to participate in a symphonic band as an alternative to gang involvement and drug use, a professional music theater troupe that has run intensive performance training for youth in tent cities, a hip-hop collective that has assisted US deportees with integrating into Haitian society, and a rap Kreyòl group that launched a long-term project to remove trash from the streets while simultaneously releasing singles highlighting Haiti's environmental degradation. These groups use cultural action to address on a small scale the needs of the population that elsewhere might be met by a state with solid infrastructure. Thus, in certain contexts, cultural production provides a modest means to press for change and community development and may in fact involve efforts directed toward the reduction of violence and poverty (Dirksen 2012a).

The "hip-hop collective," for example, took on the job of educating the public about the hazards of uncollected rubbish in the streets of Port-au-Prince both in their songs about the degraded urban environment and through practical action: they collected trash and cleaned the streets twice a day in the year before the earthquake. After the earthquake, "the constant battle with daily survival interfered with the best of plans" (Dirksen 2013: 52), but they did not give up on social action. Some of them turned their attention to an even more pressing problem than garbage: access to potable water in their neighborhood. The impulse of some musicians to critique existing political, economic, and social conditions led in this case to social action quite unrelated to music making itself. Dirksen observed that this sort of "cultural action" has a long history in Haiti and thus resonated with a broad range of musical artists. Is Haitian culture unique in this respect, or is cultural action an inherent, if largely unexplored, potential of group music making everywhere? If the latter, then what are the conditions that might stimulate such a move from musical to social or political action? These are theoretical questions that an ethnomusicology in times of trouble invites us to ask.

While no amount of bravery, resilience, and initiative can mask the human toll of tragedies such as the Haitian earthquake, silver linings occasionally lift the clouds that attend them. Margaret Kartomi (2010a, 2010b), for example, tells the fascinating story of the restoration of artistic traditions in Aceh, Indonesia, in the wake of the 2004 tsunami, which killed an estimated 200,000 people. The death and havoc the tsunami caused helped to end the separatist conflict in Aceh that had been going on for decades. The tsunami had the effect of leading to a peace accord between the antagonists so that both sides could take up the task of post-tsunami recovery. Kartomi describes the various efforts to restore the musical traditions of the region, including building new musical instruments and establishing schools for teaching children, all motivated by the belief that musical performances are therapeutic and thus would help people recover from the trauma, suffering, and damage of the war and tsunami. Here, local people acted out both their own and an ethnomusicological theory about the healing capacity of musical performance.

## MUSIC, VIOLENCE, AND POVERTY

Yet another aspect of our troubled times is the violence facing many people around the globe who live in neighborhoods and regions wracked by poverty, unemployment, and drug trafficking. What might the ethnomusicology of such lives suffused with violence look like, and what implications might such studies have for our understanding of ethnomusicology? Brazilian scholar Samuel Araújo and his colleagues and students at the Ethnomusicology Laboratory of the Federal University of Rio de Janeiro provide one answer (Araújo et al. 2006). They argue that, in addition to the dangers of real physical violence, residents of a poor neighborhood of Rio de Janeiro called Maré are subjected to debilitating symbolic violence as well. This symbolic violence is perpetrated on the residents of Maré by governmental policy; police actions; the interpretations of social scientists operating from privileged positions outside and "above" local, lived experience; and the suppression in the broadcast and recorded media of a genre of music produced by the residents of Maré to narrate their own experiences in this neighborhood. The genre goes by the colorful names "prohibited funk" (*funk prohibidão*) or "evil funk" (*funk do mal*).

The research group's principal methodological move was to try to eliminate the structural inequality between university-based researchers and their subjects, the poor people disconnected from sources of power. If the standard modus operandi of ethnomusicology is to write interpretations of the musical life of the poor for the benefit of the powerful within a kind of vertical power structure, these researchers tried to create a horizontal relationship in which the university researchers worked with local, community-based groups as equals. They argued that, in the Brazilian case, this imagined conversation between equals was virtually impossible, but they force us to wonder whether we should all be trying harder to construct real intellectual equality between "us" (the researchers) and "them" (the subjects of research). Araújo and Cambria argue against do-good efforts that assume that the population the researchers aim to serve is an aesthetic and musical *tabula rasa*, a "lethal" form of symbolic violence (2013: 38). They further argue that the theoretical potential of such horizontal, nonviolent interventions is quite high: "Once the 'culture of silence' that oppressed people are caught in is broken, apparently simple questions usually answered with common-sense 'truths' (such as 'what is samba?,' 'what does funk music represent?,' 'what is good music?,' and even, 'what is music?') began to acquire new meanings and answers" (p. 39; see also Araújo 2008).

The Haitian case that Dirksen documents contains an interesting mix of top-down and bottom-up projects. While Araújo and others decry the colonialist symbolic violence of the former, imagining that such projects do not reach some of the most needy and participate in a larger system of real and symbolic violence perpetrated by the powerful on the poor, there is some evidence that top-down projects aimed at helping the poor can be effective. Harrison, for example, reports on the positive effects of music and performing arts programs in a neighborhood of Vancouver known as "Canada's poorest postal code" (2013b: 59). As in the Haitian case, many types of music and performing arts programs are offered to poor residents in the neighborhood, and she offers substantial anecdotal evidence that participation in these programs raises the self-esteem and economic status of participants. Harrison goes on to argue that since economic and social status are directly correlated to longer and healthier lives, these kinds of interventions may have effects on well-being and mortality that go well beyond their aesthetic, psychological, and economic benefits. Long-term studies of such cases seem to have enormous potential to verify and extend ethnomusicological theories of the health benefits of musical performance (cf. Koen 2009).

## MUSIC, CLIMATE CHANGE, AND THE ENVIRONMENT

Musicians from every culture respond in one way or another to the animal and natural sounds of their environment. Bird songs have been a widespread and obvious choice, whether the "cucu" of the European medieval canon "Sumer is icumen in"; Vivaldi's "Spring" concerto from the *Four Seasons*; Haydn's "Bird" Quartet, Op. 33, No. 3; the nightingales and partridges of Prespa Albanians; or the Bosavi *muni* bird. Natural and built sonic environments have also inspired Kaluli "lift-up-over sounding," George Antheil's *Ballet Méchanique,* and, presumably, Eddie Van Halen's "Eruption," to name just a few. These "celebratory," culturally coherent, iconic approaches to animal and natural sounds have become more "anxious" in the last forty years as composers and musicians react negatively to urban noise pollution (Schafer 1977) and more recently to the threat of climate change and global warming.[10]

Tina Ramnarine (2009), for example, describes the acoustemology—a term Feld (1996) coined to describe the way people know their world through sound—of the Sámi of northern Europe, famous as reindeer herders. Sámi use a genre, *joik,* to vocalize people, landscapes, and animals into existence, in the process placing themselves discursively in the environment

---

10. The distinction between "anxious" and "celebratory" is borrowed from Steven Feld's characterization of narratives "about the world, and the music, of 'world music'" (2000: 179).

rather than in relationship to it—a way of talking about the human–nature relationship rather different from European-derived ones. Ramnarine pays close attention to the "symphonies" of Sámi composers who place *joiks* within a recorded soundscape of birdsong, water sounds, and reindeer bells to express the unity of man and nature and to call attention to indigenous concerns about the degradation of the polar environment due to climate change, nuclear-waste dumping, and forest logging. In some recordings, Sámi composers have placed *joiks* in a sound environment that includes snowmobiles and other motorized equipment as a way of engaging critically with their emerging soundscape as experienced, not with a mythical, idealized, "natural" past. These new Sámi compositions are in harmony with the newly noisy polar soundscape and challenge, according to Ramnarine, "the notion that sound mediates between humans and their environments, inviting us instead to consider human musical creativity situated within sonic ecosystems and across species-boundaries" (p. 205). Studying music and sound in this way opens up the possibility for what Ramnarine calls "environmental ethnomusicology" (p. 205) or what Nancy Guy (2009), in her study of popular songs about environmental degradation in Taiwan, calls "ecomusicology." Her vision of ecomusicology leads her to ask an important question that implies both a critical stance not typical of ethnomusicology to date and a new function for music: does music contribute to our survival, or is it indifferent to our possible extinction?

This greening of academic music studies is not restricted to ethnomusicology; scholars of popular music and European classical music have also taken it up. In the domain of popular music, the anthropologist Mark Pedelty begins his book *Ecomusicology: Rock, Folk, and the Environment* with the provocative line, "U2 hates the planet" (2012: 1). He goes on to complain about the enormous carbon footprint of their massive touring stage shows, even as they sing about the poisoned environment in songs like "Where the Streets Have No Name." While more local music making might begin to address the problem, this unsustainable music is what most people love and listen to. Since only a relatively few will drop out of that scene in favor of local community music, this solution will probably do little to sustain the environment globally.

Jeff Todd Titon (2009, 2013b), Thomas Turino (2009), Huib Schippers (2010), and others interested in musical sustainability might respond that "you have to start somewhere" to provide alternative models to, and defend endangered musical traditions from, the commercial popular music scene. One of the few ways acting locally makes sense ecologically is if local action becomes a metaphorical domino that, when tipped over, starts a chain reaction that eventually leads people everywhere to change their approach to music consumption so that wasteful acts of production are disincentivized. Pedelty, on the other hand, refuses to "glorify local music or suggest that it holds all the answers to environmental engagement, community building, or social change" (2012: 8). "Ecomusicology must grapple with the most widespread and popular of global musics" (p. 20). In a review of efforts by some rock bands to mitigate the environmental impact of their tours and their fans' travel to concerts even as they fail to sing songs about the environment, he concludes that "judging from the sounds surrounding us today, popular music is more likely to form a soundtrack for excessive consumption than to inspire more sustainable orientations" (p. 38).

A group of five historical musicologists, in a "colloquy" published in the *Journal of the American Musicological Society* in 2011, took up environmental issues under the rubrics "ecomusicology" and "ecocritical musicology" (see also Ingram 2013). Two of them attend to music in the present time of trouble. Aaron Allen argues that Western classical string players' demand for bows made from Brazilian *pernambuco* is "ecologically destructive" because the wood is nearly extinct "due to many ecological pressures" (2011: 419). He implies that musicians (and musicologists) in this "elite" tradition should be alert to the effects of their choices, which are "felt well beyond the ephemeral space of the concert hall." Alexander Rehding makes an interesting theoretical suggestion, dividing concerns for the environment, including climate change, into two camps: (1) an "apocalyptic mode" accompanied by "a profound sense of acute crisis" and (2) "a sense of nostalgia" for a simpler, better time in the past (2011: 410). He suggests that music, with its "appeal to the power of memory," may be better suited to the latter. He argues that while "the attention-grabbing apocalyptic route ... raise[s] awareness by instilling a sense of acute crisis," ecomusicologists may find it more productive to "enlist the commemorative and community-building powers of music in the service of ecological" projects (pp. 412–414). Maintaining this distinction in practice may be difficult, as the Taiwanese and Sámi examples illustrate.

Finally, Jeff Titon (2009, 2013b) has written extensively on how to sustain threatened musical traditions, employing a metaphor that transfers concern for the natural environment, expressed in terms of sustainability, ecology, ecosystems, and opposition to economic growth and development, to concern for sustainability of any local musical tradition, whether threatened by environmental change and degradation or not. His application of the notion of ecosystem to musical cultures may be quite productive. Such a move implies, among other things, that ecomusicologists cannot in good conscience or good scholarship adhere to the disciplinary boundaries of music study. Maintaining such boundaries risks ignoring the global ecosystem of contemporary music in these times of trouble, whether they are local participatory musical get-togethers; huge stadium rock concerts; Western classical music concerts and touring soloists, orchestras, and conductors; or the music of people living in deserts and rainforests and on inundating atolls.

## CONCLUSIONS

I draw twelve conclusions from this brief overview of the six themes that I believe constitute an ethnomusicology in times of trouble—conclusions that begin to answer the three questions I raised at the beginning of the chapter.

On the question of whether an ethnomusicology of times and places of trouble will change our theories and methods in any way, I suggest the following:

1. Studying music in conditions of gross social and economic inequality can drive ethnomusicologists to rethink their methods and move them away from vertical knowledge structures to horizontal ones in which knowledge is created in equal partnerships with communities and community musicians.
2. Studies of music in times and places of trouble tend to engage ethnomusicologists in local, practical projects and, as a consequence, may have the effect of diminishing the conceptual distance between so-called theoretical and so-called applied work in our field (Sheehy 1992).
3. If we are not already there, an ecosystems approach to musical sustainability will require attention to all the music of the world, not simply to those genres that have, in the past, defined our discipline's boundaries.
4. As we engage with the political, social, economic, and ecological problems affecting today's world, our theories about the nature of music should contribute to research well beyond the boundaries of our discipline.

On the question of whether our understanding of the nature of music may prove helpful in ameliorating cases of conflict, violence, disease, and social disruption, I suggest the following:

5. Ethnomusicologists' understandings of the nature of music and its power to generate meaning in human culture and to function in human societies can provide the means to create helpful and effective social and educational programs and policies.
6. The impulse to act practically depends partly on the context and seems to be amplified when ethnomusicologists work at home rather than abroad.

7. There is more work to be done on how musical behavior in groups may be marshaled to generate social action, as in the Haitian case.
8. Music may only be effective in ameliorating severe cases of disruption when it is combined with other forms of social and cultural action.

On the question of whether the study of music in times and places of trouble will affect our understanding of the nature of human music making, I suggest the following:

9. People use music for good and for evil.
10. The study of music in places of trouble calls into question ethnomusicologists' claims that music can, of itself, change and construct new social orders and cultural understandings.
11. The study of music in times and places of trouble may push ethnomusicologists further in the direction of the study of sound as the field of practice within which the nature of music is conceived, to an "ethnosonicology" perhaps or, more likely, to "sound studies."
12. Finally, our studies of music in places and times of trouble may lead us to new theories about the nature of music, new theories "forged," as Anthony Seeger (2008) has put it, "in the crucible of action."

## REFERENCES

Allen, Aaron S. 2011 "Prospects and Problems for Ecomusicology in Confronting a Crisis of Culture." *Journal of the American Musicological Society* 64(2): 414–424.

Alviso, Ric. 2011. "Tears Run Dry: Coping with AIDS Through Music in Zimbabwe." In Gregory Barz and Judah M. Cohen, eds., *The Culture of AIDS in Africa: Hope and Healing in Music and the Arts*. New York: Oxford University Press, pp. 56–62.

Araújo, Samuel. 2008. "From Neutrality to Praxis: The Shifting Politics of Ethnomusicology in the Contemporary World." *Muzikološki Zbornik/Musicological Annual* 44(1): 12–29.

Araújo, Samuel, and members of the Grupo Musicultura. 2006. "Conflict and Violence as Theoretical Tools in Present-Day Ethnomusicology: Notes on a Dialogic Ethnography of Sound Practices in Rio de Janeiro." *Ethnomusicology* 50(2): 287–313.

Araújo, Samuel, and Vincenzo Cambria. 2013. "Sound Praxis, Poverty, and Social Participation: Perspectives from a Collaborative Study of Rio de Janeiro." *Yearbook for Traditional Music* 45: 28–42.

Barz, Gregory. 2006. *Singing for Life: HIV/AIDS and Music in Uganda*. New York: Routledge.

———. 2011. "Interlude: Singing for Life: Songs of Hope, Healing, and HIV/AIDS in Uganda." In Gregory Barz and Judah M. Cohen, eds., *The Culture of AIDS in*

*Africa: Hope and Healing in Music and the Arts.* New York: Oxford University Press, pp. 20–34.

Barz, Gregory, and Judah M. Cohen, eds. 2011. *The Culture of AIDS in Africa: Hope and Healing in Music and the Arts.* New York: Oxford University Press.

Berger, Harris M. 2014 "New Directions in Ethnomusicological Research into the Politics of Music and Culture: Issues, Projects, and Programs." *Ethnomusicology* 58(2): 315–320.

Cooper, David. 2010. "Fife and Fiddle: Protestants and Traditional Music in Northern Ireland." In John Morgan O'Connell and Salwa El-Shawan Castelo-Branco, eds., *Music and Conflict.* Urbana: University of Illinois Press, pp. 89–106.

Cusick, Suzanne. 2006. "Music as Torture/Music as Weapon." *TRANS: Transcultural Music Review* 10. Retrieved from http://www.sibetrans.com/trans/articulo/152/music-as-torture-music-as-weapon

Daughtry, J. Martin. 2012. "Belliphonic Sounds and Indoctrinated Ears: The Dynamics of Military Listening in Wartime Iraq." In Eric Weisbard, ed., *Pop When the World Falls Apart: Music and Troubled Times.* Durham, NC: Duke University Press, pp. 111–144.

Dirksen, Rebecca. 2012a. "Power and Potential in Contemporary Haitian Music: Mizik Angaje, Cultural Action and Community-led Development in Pre- and Post-Quake Port-au-Prince." PhD dissertation abstract, University of California, Los Angeles.

——. 2012b. "Reconsidering Theory and Practice in Ethnomusicology: Applying, Advocating, and Engaging beyond Academia." *Ethnomusicology Review* 17. Retrieved from http://ethnomusicologyreview.ucla.edu

——. 2013. "Surviving Poverty by Employing Cultural Wealth: Putting Music in the Service of Community in Haiti." *Yearbook for Traditional Music* 45: 43–57.

Doubleday, Veronica. 2007. "9/11 and the Politics of Music-Making in Afghanistan." In Jonathan Ritter and J. Martin Daughtry, eds., *Music in the Post–9/11 World.* New York: Routledge, pp. 277–314.

Feld, Steven. 1996. "Waterfalls of Song: An Acoustemology of Place Resounding in Bosavi, PapuaNewGuinea." In Steven Feld and Keith Basso, eds., *Senses of Place.* Santa Fe, NM: School of American Research Press, pp. 91–135.

——. 2000 "Sound Words." In Patricia Kruth and Henry Stobart, eds., *Sound.* Cambridge: Cambridge University Press, pp. 173–200.

Fenn, John, ed. 2003. "Applied Ethnomusicology" [Special issue]. *Folklore Forum* 34(1–2).

Guy, Nancy. 2009. "Flowing Down Taiwan's Tamsui River: Towards an Ecomusicology of the Environmental Imagination." *Ethnomusicology* 53(2): 218–248.

Harrison, Klisala. 2012. "Epistemologies of Applied Ethnomusicology." *Ethnomusicology* 56(3): 505–529.

——, ed. 2013a. "Music and Poverty" [Special half-issue]. *Yearbook for Traditional Music* 45.

——. 2013b. "Music, Health, and Socio-Economic Status: A Perspective on Urban Poverty in Canada." *Yearbook for Traditional Music* 45: 58–73.

Harrison, Klisala, Elizabeth Mackinlay, and Svanibor Pettan, eds. 2010. *Applied Ethnomusicology: Historical and Contemporary Approaches.* Newcastle upon Tyne: Cambridge Scholars.

Harrison, Klisala, and Svanibor Pettan. 2010. "Introduction." In Klisala Harrison, Elizabeth Mackinlay, and Svanibor Pettan, eds., *Applied Ethnomusicology: Historical and Contemporary Approaches.* Newcastle upon Tyne: Cambridge Scholars, pp. 1–20.

Hellier-Tinoco, Ruth. 2003. "Experiencing People: Relationships, Responsibility and Reciprocity." *British Journal of Ethnomusicology* 12(1): 19–34.

Hemetek, Ursula. 2006. "Applied Ethnomusicology in the Process of the Political Recognition of a Minority: A Case Study of the Austrian Roma." *Yearbook for Traditional Music* 38: 35–57.

———. 2010. "The Music of Minorities in Austria: Conflict and Intercultural Strategies." In Klisala Harrison, Elizabeth Mackinlay, and Svanibor Pettan, eds., *Applied Ethnomusicology: Historical and Contemporary Approaches.* Newcastle upon Tyne: Cambridge Scholars, pp. 182–199.

Hofman, Ana. 2010. "Maintaining the Distance, Othering the Subaltern: Rethinking Ethnomusicologists' Engagement in Advocacy and Social Justice." In Klisala Harrison, Elizabeth Mackinlay, and Svanibor Pettan, eds., *Applied Ethnomusicology: Historical and Contemporary Approaches.* Newcastle upon Tyne: Cambridge Scholars, pp. 22–35.

Ingram, David, ed. 2013. "Ecomusicology" [Special issue]. *Green Letters: Studies in Ecocriticism* 15(1).

Kartomi, Margaret. 2010a. "Toward a Methodology of War and Peace Studies in Ethnomusicology: The Case of Aceh, 1976–2009." *Ethnomusicology* 54(3): 452–443.

———. 2010b. "The Musical Arts in Aceh After the Tsunami and the Conflict." In Klisala Harrison, Elizabeth Mackinlay, and Svanibor Pettan, eds., *Applied Ethnomusicology: Historical and Contemporary Approaches.* Newcastle upon Tyne: Cambridge Scholars, pp. 200–213.

Koen, Benjamin D. 2009. *Beyond the Roof of the World: Music, Prayer, and Healing in the Pamir Mountains.* New York: Oxford University Press.

———, ed. 2008. *The Oxford Handbook of Medical Ethnomusicology.* New York: Oxford University Press.

Levin, Theodore. 1996. *The Hundred Thousand Fools of God: Musical Travels in Central Asia (and Queens, New York).* Bloomington: Indiana University Press.

Loza, Steven, Milo Alvarez, Josefina Santiago, and Charles Moore. 1994. "Los Angeles Gangsta Rap and the Aesthetics of Violence." *Selected Reports in Ethnomusicology* 10: 149–161.

McDonald, David A. 2009. "Poetics and the Performance of Violence in Israel/Palestine." *Ethnomusicology* 53(1): 58–85.

Merriam, Alan P. 1964. *The Anthropology of Music.* Evanston, IL: Northwestern University Press.

Nettl, Bruno. 2005. *The Study of Ethnomusicology: Thirty-One Issues and Concepts.* Urbana: University of Illinois Press.

O'Connell, John Morgan. 2011. "Music in War, Music for Peace: A Review Article." *Ethnomusicology* 55(1): 112–127.

O'Connell, John Morgan, and Salwa El-Shawan Castelo-Branco, eds. 2010. *Music and Conflict.* Urbana: University of Illinois Press.

Pedelty, Mark. 2012. *Ecomusicology: Rock, Folk, and the Environment.* Philadelphia: Temple University Press.

Pettan, Svanibor, ed. 1998a. *Music, Politics, and War: Views from Croatia*. Zagreb: Institute of Ethnology and Folklore Research.

———. 1998b. "Music, Politics, and War in Croatia in the 1990s: An Introduction." In Svanibor Pettan, ed., *Music, Politics, and War: Views from Croatia*. Zagreb: Institute of Ethnology and Folklore Research, pp. 9–27.

———. 2008. "Applied Ethnomusicology and Empowerment Strategies: View from across the Atlantic." *Muzikološki Zbornik/Musicological Annual* 44(1): 85–99.

———. 2010. "Music in War, Music for Peace: Experiences of Applied Ethnomusicology." In John Morgan O'Connell and Salwa El-Shawan Castelo-Branco, eds., *Music and Conflict*. Urbana: University of Illinois Press, pp. 177–92.

Ramnarine, Tina. 2009. "Acoustemology, Indigeneity, and Joik in Valkeapää's Symphonic Activism: Views from Europe's Arctic Fringes for Environmental Ethnomusicology." *Ethnomusicology* 53(2): 187–217.

Rehding, Alexander. 2011. "Ecomusicology between Apocalypse and Nostalgia." *Journal of the American Musicological Society* 64(2): 409–414.

Reyes, Adelaida. 1999. *Songs of the Caged, Songs of the Free: Music and the Vietnamese Refugee Experience*. Philadelphia: Temple University Press.

Ritter, Jonathan, and J. Martin Daughtry, eds. 2007. *Music in the Post–9/11 World*. New York: Routledge.

Schafer, R. Murray. 1977. *The Tuning of the World*. New York: Knopf.

Schippers, Huib. 2010. "Three Journeys, Five Recollections, Seven Voices: Operationalizing Sustainability in Music." In Klisala Harrison, Elizabeth Mackinlay, and Svanibor Pettan, eds., *Applied Ethnomusicology: Historical and Contemporary Approaches*. Newcastle upon Tyne: Cambridge Scholars, pp. 150–160.

Seeger, Anthony. 2008. "Theories Forged in the Crucible of Action: The Joys, Dangers, and Potentials of Advocacy and Fieldwork." In Gregory Barz and Timothy Cooley, eds., *Shadows in the Field: New Perspectives for Fieldwork in Ethnomusicology*, 2nd ed. New York: Oxford University Press, pp. 271–288.

Sheehy, Daniel. 1992. "A Few Notions about Philosophy and Strategy in Applied Ethnomusicology." *Ethnomusicology* 36(3): 323–336.

Shelemay, Kay Kaufman. 1998. *Let Jasmine Rain Down: Song and Remembrance Among Syrian Jews*. Chicago: University of Chicago Press.

Spitzer, Nick. 2006. "Rebuilding the 'Land of Dreams' with Music." In Eugenie Ladner Birch and Richard M. Wachter, eds., *Rebuilding Urban Places after Disaster: Lessons from Hurricane Katrina*. Philadelphia: University of Pennsylvania Press, pp. 305–328.

Sugarman, Jane C. 1997. *Engendering Song: Singing and Subjectivity at Prespa Albanian Weddings*. Chicago: University of Chicago Press.

Sweers, Britta. 2010. "Polyphony of Cultures: Conceptualization and Consequences of an Applied Media Project." In Klisala Harrison, Elizabeth Mackinlay, and Svanibor Pettan, eds., *Applied Ethnomusicology: Historical and Contemporary Approaches*. Newcastle upon Tyne: Cambridge Scholars, pp. 215–232.

Titon, Jeff Todd, ed. 1992. "Music and the Public Interest" [Special issue]. *Ethnomusicology* 36(3).

———. 2009. "Music and Sustainability: An Ecological Viewpoint." *The World of Music* 51(1): 109–137.

———. 2013a. "Music and the US War on Poverty." *Yearbook for Traditional Music* 45: 74–82.

———. 2013b. "The Nature of Ecomusicology." *Música e Cultura* 8(1): 8–18.

Turino, Thomas. 2009. "Four Fields of Music Making and Sustainable Living." *The World of Music* 51(1): 95–117.

Van Buren, Kathleen J. 2010. "Applied Ethnomusicology and HIV and AIDS: Responsibility, Ability, and Action." *Ethnomusicology* 54(2): 202–223.